Jerry Bauer

About the Author

ELEANOR HERMAN was born in Baltimore, Maryland. She studied journalism and German at Towson State University and languages in Europe. For eight years she was associate publisher for North America for NATO's *Nations and Partners for Peace* magazine. She is married and lives in McLean, Virginia, where she writes history from a woman's perspective.

Eleanor Herman

WILLIAM MORROW

An Imprint of HarperCollinsPublishers

sex

with KINGS

❋

FIVE HUNDRED YEARS OF YEARS OF ADULTERY, POWER, RIVALRY, AND REVENGE

This 2011 edition published by Barnes & Noble, Inc.,
by arrangement with HarperCollins Publishers.

Barnes & Noble, Inc.
122 Fifth Avenue
New York, NY 10011

First published in 2004 by William Morrow, an imprint of
HarperCollins.

HarperCollins books may be purchased for educational, business,
or sales promotional use. For information, please write: Special
Markets Department, HarperCollins Publishers Inc., 10 East 53rd
Street, New York, NY 10022.

ISBN: 978-1-4351-3212-2

Printed and bound in the United States of America.

11 12 13 14 ❖/RRD 10 9 8 7 6 5 4 3 2 1

To my mother, Louise, in Heaven

CONTENTS

ACKNOWLEDGMENTS

I am inexpressibly grateful to many individuals for their encouragement and assistance.

My late mother, the artist Louise Herman Donahue, nurtured me with creativity, encouraged my curiosity, and bequeathed to me unforgettable love and laughter. She gave me the priceless gift of dreaming, a gift that forever remains with me although she does not.

My father, journalist Walter Focke Herman, proud of his medieval royal ancestors, inspired me in my earliest years to love history. Sitting at his knee I first heard the screams of battle, smelled the smoke of burning castles, saw the pageantry of royal processions. To him I am also grateful for his hawkeyed editing of the manuscript.

My sister, Christine Merrill, an artist of rare talents successfully living her dream, prodded me constantly often to my great annoyance to live mine. I don t believe I would have completed this project without her stubborn but loving insistence that I do so.

Many thanks to Susanne Becerril, Karen Griswold, and Helena Hoogterp for their unceasing encouragement and support of this project and its author.

I am particularly grateful to my good friend Leslie Harris, proprietor and designer of Noblesse Oblige Renaissance costumes, for getting me into the spirit, and the corset, of a royal mistress. Wearing one of their gorgeous but restricting gowns has sharpened my understanding of their gorgeous but restricted lives.

I am astonished at the patience of my wonderful husband, Michael Dyment, who listens to my nonstop chatter of kings and queens, of mistresses and royal bastards, and tolerates my elaborate court costumes at countless events without showing a shred of embarrassment.

Clearly this book would not have been possible without the diaries, letters, dispatches, and memoirs of the past, nor indeed without the dozens of biographies and histories written by modern authors reporting and interpreting the original sources. To all writers past and present upon whose work I have heavily relied, and who are listed in the bibliography, I am deeply grateful.

And lastly, to make sense out of the chaotic events of the past, the historian must view them through a particular philosophical prism. For this I am immeasurably indebted to *A Course in Miracles,* a work of keen psychological insight and great spiritual power.

Sex

WITH KINGS

INTRODUCTION

When the destiny of a nation is in a woman's bedroom,
the best place for the historian is in the antechamber.

—CHARLES-AUGUSTIN SAINTE-BEUVE

❈

IF PROSTITUTION IS THE WORLD'S OLDEST PROFESSION, THEN
the finer art of being a mistress must be the second oldest.

When we imagine the finest mistress of all—she who is fit for a
king—we see a hazy, shimmering image of a woman whose hands
caress and mold history. She stands, for the most part, in the
shadows of a world where the spotlight shines solely on men
bludgeoning history into shape. Now and then we hear the
rustling of a silk skirt, or hear her musical laughter echoing
from behind the throne.

The rise of the royal mistress in European courts was sudden,
springing up from departing medieval mists. For a thousand
years after the fall of Rome, royal sin was hidden in the thick
hangings of a four-poster bed and then lamented in the stuffy

darkness of the confessional. The powerful Catholic Church cast a jaded eye on adultery, and the jezebels of the court were kept firmly in the background.

Sometimes a woman's first name was linked to a feudal monarch, a Maude or a Blanche, and nothing else is known. Numerous royal bastards, acknowledged by kings, seemed to sprout from thin air, and we can only assume they had mothers. This near-total lack of information of royal love affairs derived not only from church demands for discretion. Illiteracy reigned just as surely as the monarchs themselves, monarchs who were for the most part unable to sign their names.

It is only because of her avarice that we know anything about the English medieval mistress Alice Perrers. The courtesan of Edward III (1312–1377), greedy Alice used her position during the last decade of the old king's life to rape the treasury, becoming one of the largest landowners in England. Deftly exploiting Edward's senility, she convinced him to buy her the same jewels over and over again, each time pocketing the cash he gave her to procure them. As if this weren't enough, sitting at her royal lover's deathbed, Alice pried valuable rings from his stiffening fingers and ran off with them. A scandalized Parliament confiscated her estates in seventeen counties, her jewels (including 21,868 pearls), and other gifts from the king. Litigious Alice spent the rest of her life in court trying to get them back, as attested by treasury records, parliamentary decrees, and lawsuits.

Where the English were clumsy, the French were nimble. Some seventy years after the embarrassing Alice Perrers, the prototypical royal mistress rose in golden glory like a phoenix from the ashes of dark centuries. Ably wielding political influence over country and king, Agnes Sorel was—naturally—a Frenchwoman at the French court. Graceful Agnes succeeded in rousing Charles VII (1403–1461) from his debilitating apathy to rally his troops and drive English invaders from French soil. Charles, a sad clown-faced, knock-kneed little man lost in his thickly padded tunics, made a poor king before Agnes, and returned to being a poor king after her.

The earliest surviving portrait of a royal mistress is of Agnes, painted in 1449, a time when secular portraits were not yet common, and many of the rich and famous still bribed church artists to paint their faces on saints. Oddly enough, Agnes was painted as the Virgin Mary in a two-part church panel. In her panel, now in the Koninklijk Museum of Antwerp, Agnes, wearing a crown and an ermine cape, reveals a ripe plump breast to the baby Jesus, who seems completely uninterested and looks away. The other panel, however, now in the Staatliche Museum of Berlin, shows a good friend of hers, Etienne Chevalier, on his knees in worshipful devotion. This diptych of the king's mistress, mother of his illegitimate children, depicted as the Mother of God must have shocked the devout, their shock compounded by the vision of her friend worshiping her exposed breast.

It is probably no coincidence that shortly after the painting was completed, the powers of heaven sent the Grim Reaper to harvest Agnes. At the age of about forty, after fifteen years as the king's lover, friend, and counselor, Agnes lay dying in childbirth. Perhaps she was looking back from a grander place when she saw her vanquished body and said softly, "It is a little thing and soiled and smelling of our frailty."[1] She closed her eyes. The grief-stricken king made her a posthumous duchess and buried her in splendor.

Our knowledge of royal mistresses increases exponentially with the advent of the sixteenth century. The flowering of thought known as the Renaissance brought fresh air to a stultified Europe. Suddenly ships sailed the seven seas, bringing back undreamed-of riches. Monasteries were searched for moldering manuscripts bearing the wisdom of ancient pagan sages. Societies which had worshiped at the feet of a stone Virgin for a thousand years suddenly frolicked before a curvaceous statue of Venus. In this process the Vatican lost its key to the lockbox of all knowledge; its ironclad grip over morals and manners was substantially weakened—even in nations that remained Catholic after the Reformation.

The invention of the printing press triggered an explosion of literacy among the nobility. Letter writing became a favorite pastime for courtiers eager to indulge rustic relatives with juicy court gossip. From them we hear of the queen's tears, the mistress's temper tantrums, and the king's insatiable lust. Madame de Maintenon, the final favorite and morganatic wife of Louis XIV (1638–1715), wrote more than ninety thousand letters in her lifetime. Louis's sister-in-law Elizabeth Charlotte, duchesse d'Orléans, wrote sixty thousand letters about life at the court of Versailles over a fifty-year period. Madame de Sévigné, who knew Louis XIV's mistresses personally, wrote three times a week for twenty-five years to her beloved daughter tucked away in Provence. Some of the personal correspondence of kings and their mistresses themselves has survived fire, flood, worms, and deliberate destruction, and a portion of it deals with the romantic side of life.

Additionally, ambassadorial reports provide detailed views into court life. In an era when a king's whim meant peace or war, feast or famine, no royal detail was considered insignificant. Some official dispatches discussed the king's bowel movements. Louis XIV, knowing that the many mistresses of Charles II (1630–1685) had great influence over him, instructed his ambassadors to England to send "detailed reports of all that goes on in the Court of Great Britain and particularly *in the privy part.*"[2] Many of these titillating dispatches have survived.

Diaries became the fashion, giving eyewitness accounts of royal intrigues. One of the best-known diarists was Samuel Pepys, who worked in a high-level position in the English Naval Office in the 1660s and had a lascivious fascination with Charles II's mistresses. He reported seeing them in the park and at the theater, compared their beauty, described their clothing, and made love to them in his dreams. He gleefully wrote that he had kissed Nell Gwynn after her play, and that the sight of Lady Castlemaine's rich undergarments hanging on a clothesline proved very beneficial indeed.

Memoirs became popular, though they must be read with care and compared with other documents of the period. Written with an aim of publication, many memoirs had the dual purpose of self-vindication and finger-pointing. Shortly before her death in 1615, Queen Marguerite of France wrote her memoirs to provide herself with a virtue as crisply white as parchment, throwing in numerous stories of her husband's unseemly behavior with mistresses, though leaving out her own unseemly behavior with lovers. The vengeful duc de Saint-Simon, who left Versailles a disappointed courtier in 1722, stubbornly scratched his quill across forty volumes of memoirs, his ink mixed with hearty doses of venom.

Contemporary biographies started popping up, but even they must be scrutinized. Count Karl von Pöllnitz traveled the courts of Europe starting in 1710 and in 1740 became Frederick the Great's master of ceremonies. Fascinated by the amorous adventures of Augustus the Strong of Saxony (1670–1733), who reputedly fathered more than three hundred illegitimate children, Count von Pöllnitz published a biography in 1734, the year after the king's death. While the basic facts of the king's love affairs were true, we can imagine that the count polished up the conversations he reported, for comic effect.

Along with literacy came a new appreciation of women's valuable civilizing influence on society. The French court of the sixteenth century began accepting the idea that women were just as intelligent and capable as men, but infinitely more attractive. Almost overnight, royal mistresses became admired, imitated, and lauded.

In the sixteenth through the eighteenth centuries, the position of royal mistress was almost as official as that of prime minister. The mistress was expected to perform certain duties—sexual and otherwise—in return for titles, pensions, honors, and an influential place at court. She encouraged the arts—theater, literature, music, architecture, and philosophy. She wielded her charm as a weapon against foreign ambassadors. She calmed the king when he was angry, buoyed him up when he was despondent, encouraged him to greatness when he was weak. She attended religious services daily, gave alms to the poor, and turned in her jewels to the treasury in times of war.

François I of France (1494–1547) was the first king to give the title *maîtresse-en-titre*—official royal mistress—to his favorite. He enjoyed several mistresses in succession with great aplomb. By the second half of the sixteenth century, French mistresses wielded more power than any others in Europe would for nearly two hundred years. Diane de Poitiers, mistress of Henri II (1519–1559), became a member of the French council, an exclusive assembly convened for deliberating governmental matters. Diane made laws and imposed taxes, and she signed official decrees with the king in a joint signature, HenriDiane. Gabrielle d'Estrées, mistress of Henri IV (1553–1610), also joined the council, made laws, received ambassadors, and assisted greatly in ending the religious civil war.

Over in England, Henry VIII (1491–1547) made a muddle of things by insisting on marrying two women he lusted after and subsequently chopping off their heads. The following century Charles II lost no time mounting a mistress the very day he mounted the throne. On his coronation day in 1660 he bedded the auburn-haired Barbara Palmer, who nine months later gave him a daughter. As a reward he created her the countess of Castlemaine. Charles explained that "he was no atheist but he could not think God would make a man miserable for taking a little pleasure out of the way."[3]

Unburdened by fidelity—even to his mistress—Charles was one of the few monarchs who had several principal mistresses at his court at one time. He could never quite match the French for aplomb, and his harem closely resembled a squawking henhouse. The week of his death in 1685, the king was surrounded by all his hens, as described by the scandalized diarist John Evelyn, who lamented "the inexpressible luxury and profaneness, gaming and all dissoluteness" he witnessed. King Charles was "sitting and toying with his concubines Portsmouth, Cleveland, and Mazarin, etc., a French boy singing love songs in that glorious gallery, whilst about twenty of the great courtiers and other dissolute persons were at basset [a card game] round a large table, a bank of at least 2000 in gold before them."[4]

Charles's first cousin Louis XIV of France ornamented his court with a string of fragrant mistresses. Athénaïs de Montespan—who boasted a tenure of thirteen years—was in many ways a clone of her English counterpart Barbara, Lady Castlemaine, who held sway for a dozen years. Both were beautiful, grasping, hard, and glittering, though Athénaïs was to her contemporaries perhaps the more palatable, her rough edges smoothed over by a healthy smearing of French panache. Both added to the glory of their respective nations, all the while looting the treasury, and both were sorely missed when they were replaced by less colorful substitutes.

Even as French fashion, architecture, music, and art were replicated in paler versions throughout Europe, so was the French concept of the *maîtresse-en-titre*. By the late seventeenth century, the role of royal mistress at a great court was considered so indispensable that even the stuffy German kingdoms followed suit. Frederick III, elector of Brandenburg (1657–1713), an uxorious prince who despised infidelity, appointed a beautiful court lady as his official mistress and loaded her down with jewels, even though he never touched her—his wife would have killed him.

Augustus the Strong of Saxony was chosen king of Poland in 1697 and suddenly found himself ruling two nations. He had a mistress of nine years' standing in Saxony, and his minister advised him to choose a Polish woman for the same honor in Warsaw. According to Count von Pöllnitz, the king was advised as follows: "For, as your Majesty has two Courts, one in Saxony, and the other at Warsaw, you ought to be a complete monarch, and in justice, keep a mistress at each Court. This will conduce undoubtedly to the satisfaction of both nations. At present the Polanders except against your keeping a Saxon mistress. If you forsake her, to be enamored with a Polish lady, the Saxons will find equal reason to complain. Whereas by being amorous six months in Poland, and the other six months in Saxony, both nations will be satisfied."[5]

While the seventeenth-century kings of France, England, and Germany were kicking up their heels with well-rewarded mistresses, the royal court of Spain remained an oasis of suffocating medieval Catholicism. The land that spawned the Inquisition was more pious than the Vatican, where rollicking cardinals indulged in lively orgies. Genetically unsound, the desiccated Spanish kings ruled over a somber court where the mass burning of heretics constituted the favorite spectator sport.

The Spanish royal mistress had no recognized position, certainly no hope of acquiring power at court, and very little in the way of financial reward. Her life after dismissal was even more dismal—she was banished to a convent. The king being only one step away from God, no ordinary mortal could hope to touch a woman who had been sanctified by the monarch's embraces.

It was reported that Philip IV of Spain (1605–1665) chased a young woman through his palace and hurled himself at the door she had barred against him, commanding her to let him in. The sobbing girl cried, "No, no, Sire! I don't want to be a nun!"[6]

King John V of Portugal (1689–1750) didn't bother sending his dismissed mistresses to a convent; he found his mistresses among nuns, turning one Lisbon convent into his personal harem and child care center. The mother superior provided him with a son who grew up to be an archbishop.

But Iberian customs were not popular with the rest of Europe. Trying to imitate Charles II, when George, elector of Hanover (1660–1727), inherited the throne of Great Britain in 1714, he imported not one, but two royal mistresses into his new land. George's German mistresses failed to impress his British subjects, who were shocked—not at his moral laxity, but at his taste in women. One was tall and thin to the point of emaciation, the other short and fat enough to burst, the pair of them hopelessly *ugly*. For his part, the king was pleased when his English subjects ridiculed his mistresses, even when someone sent an old nag with a broken saddle through the streets of London bearing a sign that read, "Let nobody stop me—I am the King's Hanover equipage going to fetch His Majesty and his whore to England."[7] Such jokes reflected well on his masculinity, George concluded.

When George's son Prince George of Hanover, the future George II (1683–1760), took an English mistress, his elderly grandmother applauded it as an excellent means of improving his knowledge of the language. Some twenty years later, Lord

Hervey described King George II's relationship with the same woman, Mrs. Howard, as one of form more than passion. The king "seemed to look upon a mistress rather as a necessary appurtenance to his grandeur as a prince than an addition to his pleasures as a man, and thus only pretended to distinguish what it was evident he overlooked and affected to caress what it was manifest he did not love."[8] The king was heard to call his faithful mistress "an old, dull, deaf, peevish beast."[9]

Once again, things were handled with far greater style on the southern side of the English Channel. George's contemporary Louis XV (1710–1774) installed Madame de Pompadour as *maîtresse-en-titre* in 1745. Beautiful, gracious, brilliant, and kind, Madame de Pompadour practically ruled France for nineteen years. She encouraged artists and writers, produced plays in which she sang and danced, invested in French industry, designed châteaus, cut gems, made engravings, experimented in horticulture, and ran the army during the Seven Years' War.

But at the height of her power she warily eyed the approaching storm. "After us, the deluge," she said, though it was not Madame de Pompadour but her successor, Madame du Barry, whose pretty powdered head rolled onto the straw-covered scaffold.[10] In France palaces were ransacked and burned. The tombs of kings and courtiers were cracked open and plundered, the bones strewn about. With the sudden crashing force of a guillotine, the French Revolution severed the power of royal mistresses across Europe as its effects rippled like waves in all directions. The lavish self-indulgence of a civilization was indeed deluged, drowned in a sea of wine-dark blood. Gone with it was the glorification of a fallen woman bedecked in crown jewels.

In the wake of the Revolution, though customs had changed, the sexual needs of kings had not. Royal mistresses continued aplenty, but those doomed to live in the mediocrity of the nineteenth century expected far less than their more fortunate predecessors. They would not be created duchesses or countesses, given palaces and castles, eye-popping incomes, a seat on the council, and a magnificent suite of rooms at the palace. The nineteenth-century royal mistress hoped for a nice house in town, a few pieces of jewelry, a credit line at the most fashionable dressmaker, and the overwhelming aroma of power that got her invited to all the best parties.

Ludwig I of Bavaria (1786–1868) bucked this trend and paid dearly for it. In 1847 he forced his unwilling parliament to create his nasty mistress Lola Montez the countess of Landsfeld. Within months he had a revolution on his hands; Lola was chased out of town by an angry mob, and Ludwig abdicated. If Lola had tried her ploy seventy years earlier, she would likely have succeeded.

Before the French Revolution, newspapers were carefully censored, and no ungenerous reference to the king was permitted. Lampoons—verses tacked up on lampposts—flourished, and were ripped off and read in taverns by delighted citizens. Many lampoons ridiculed the king's mistress. But with the advent of the free press in the nineteenth century, newspaper headlines trumpeted the latest royal scandal. Ribald cartoons portrayed fat and aging monarchs in bed with their greedy mistresses. Royals became more circumspect with regards to illicit liaisons. Their behavior modification went only so far as appearances, however. Adulterous royal sex was as frequent as ever, just hidden under a colorless pall of respectable hypocrisy.

In 1900 the aging Belgian king Leopold II (1835–1909) often walked in public gardens with his sixteen-year-old mistress, Caroline Delacroix. But when a cabinet minister approached him, Caroline was expected to fall meekly behind and pretend to be a sister of one of the king's aides-de-camp.

Queen Victoria's eldest son, Edward VII (1841–1910), conducted his affairs so skillfully that many people were convinced the ladies were merely good friends and that any other speculation was slanderous. Edward visited his lady friends in the afternoon for tea, when their husbands were out on business—or visiting their own mistresses—and would never think of returning home inconveniently.

The sexual revolution of the twentieth century bypassed European royal families, who clung to Victorian traditions with one hand and gripped the scepter with the other. Those dynasties fortunate enough to withstand the rising tide of democracy kept their mistresses firmly in the background, with one major exception. Like his ancestor Henry VIII, King Edward VIII of Great Britain (1894–1972) bungled things by insisting on marrying his mistress, Wallis Warfield Simpson. Unlike Henry, Edward didn't cut off his wife's head—though in time perhaps he would have liked to—but it can be said he cut off his own. Public outrage, which had been muted by the gallows and the stake in Henry's time, resulted in Edward's abdication.

Prince Charles of Great Britain's love for his old flame Camilla Parker-Bowles ripped apart his marriage to Princess Diana and astonished the world. Traditionally, princes married ugly but suitable virgins and took beautiful mistresses. But when Charles deserted the preternatural radiance of Diana in favor of the fox-and-hounds plainness of Camilla, the public howled in ridicule.

From the dawn of time, power has been a mighty aphrodisiac. Royal mistresses, whether vaunted or concealed, have always existed, and will always exist. "Nothing has been more fatal to men, and to great men, than the letting themselves go to the forbidden love of women," lamented the aging James II of England (1633–1701). "Of all the vices it is the most bewitching and harder to be mastered if it be not crushed in the very bud."[11] But like James, most kings did not crush the forbidden love of women in the bud, only when it had withered on the stalk.

SEX WITH THE KING

When there's marriage without love,
there will be love without marriage.

—BENJAMIN FRANKLIN

❋

WE PICTURE THE ROYAL MISTRESS AS, FIRST AND FOREMOST, a sexual creature. She has a heaving bosom, a knowing smile, eyes sparkling with desire. Ready to fling her velvet skirts above her head at a moment's notice, she offers irresistible delights to a lecherous monarch. The entreaties of his anguished family, the bishop's admonitions, his own sense of royal sin and guilt, are useless against the mistress's enticements when compared to those of the woodenly chaste queen.

Indeed, the horrifying state of most royal marriages created the space for royal mistresses to thrive. A prince's marriage, celebrated with lavish ceremony, was usually nothing more than a personal catastrophe for the two victims kneeling at the altar. The purpose of a royal marriage was not the happiness of husband and wife, or good sex, or even basic compatibility. The production of princes was the sole purpose, and if the bride trailed treaties and riches in her wake, so much the better.

Napoleon, franker than most monarchs, stated, "I want to marry a womb."[1] And indeed most royal brides were considered to be nothing more than a walking uterus with a crown on top and skirts on the bottom.

DISASTER AT THE ALTAR

Princesses were brought up from birth to be chaste almost to the point of frigidity, thereby ensuring legitimate heirs. While virtue could be taught, beauty could not. Ambassadors, selling the goods sight unseen to a prospective royal husband, inflated the looks of the princess with hyperbolic praise, often bringing a flattering portrait as evidence.

In 1540 Henry VIII was duped by the portrait trick in his search for a fourth wife. He wanted to cement an alliance with France and wrote François I asking for suggestions. François graciously replied with the names and portraits of five noble ladies. But Henry was not satisfied. "By God," he said, studying the flat, unblinking faces on canvas, "I trust no one but myself. The thing touches me too near. I wish to see them and know them some time before deciding."[2] He wanted to hold a kind of royal beauty pageant at the English-owned town of Calais on the north coast of France where he would personally select the winner after close inspection.

The French ambassador replied acidly that perhaps Henry should sleep with all five in turn and marry the best performer. François sneeringly remarked, "It is not the custom in France to send damsels of that rank and of such noble and princely families to be passed in review as if they were hackneys [whores] for sale."[3]

Chastened, Henry returned to perusing portraits and decided on a Protestant alliance based on a lovely likeness of Anne of Cleves. But when the royal bridegroom met Anne he was shocked at how little resemblance there was between this hulking, pockmarked Valkyrie and the dainty, smooth-faced woman in the portrait. The king was "struck with consternation when he was shown the Queen" and had never been "so much dismayed in his life as to see a lady so far unlike what had been represented." He roared, "I see nothing in this woman as men report of her, and I marvel that wise men would make such report as they have done." He continued, "Whom shall men trust? I promise you I see no such thing as hath been shown me of her, by pictures and report. I am ashamed that men have praised her as they have done—and I love her not!"[4]

Try as he might, the king could not extricate himself from the marriage to his "Flanders mare," as he dubbed Anne. The duchy of Cleves would be offended if Henry returned the goods. Two days before the wedding, Henry grumbled, "If it were not that she had come so far into my realm, and the great preparations and state that my people have made for her, and for fear of making a ruffle in the world and of driving her brother into the arms of the Emperor and the French King, I would not now marry her. But now it is too far gone, wherefore I am sorry."[5]

Henry went to his wedding with less grace than many of his victims had gone to their executions. On the way to the chapel, he opined to his counselors, "My lords, if it were not to satisfy the world and my realm, I would not do what I must do this day for any earthly thing."[6]

The wedding night was a fiasco. The morning after, when Lord Thomas Cromwell, who had arranged the wedding, nervously asked Henry how he had enjoyed his bride, the king thundered, "Surely, my lord, I liked her before not well, but now I like her much worse! She is nothing fair, and have very evil smells about her. I took her to be no maid by reason of the looseness of her breasts and other tokens, which, when I felt them, strake me so to the heart, that I had neither will nor courage to prove the rest. I can have none appetite for displeasant airs. I have left her as good a maid as I found her." The rest of the day he told everyone who would listen that "he had found her body disordered and indisposed to excite and provoke any lust in him."[7]

True to the double standard of the time, no one asked Anne what she thought of the king's appearance. Her royal bridegroom boasted a fifty-seven-inch waist and a festering ulcer on his leg. Anne was quickly divorced and glad to depart with her head still on her shoulders. But Lord Cromwell felt the full force of Henry's wrath in the form of an ax cleaving his neck.

Through debacles like these, everyone soon learned that portraits lied. In 1680 Louis XIV ordered Bavarian princess Maria Anna Christina as a bride for his son and heir. The lovely portrait carted about the court was irrelevant compared to the marriage treaty. According to Madame de Sévigné, as the bride was approaching, "the King was so curious to know what she looked like that he sent Sanguin [his chief butler] whom he knows to be a truthful man and no flatterer. 'Sire,' that man told him, 'once you get over the first impression, you will be delighted.' "[8] The unhappy couple managed to catapult three children into the world before the neglected wife died.

Even less fortunate with his Bavarian princess was the future Joseph II of Austria (1741–1790). In 1765 Joseph found his bride Princess Josepha so loathsome he was unable to consummate the marriage. "Her figure is short," he reported bitterly, "thickset and without a vestige of charm. Her face is covered with spots and pimples. Her teeth are horrible."[9]

"They want me to have children," he lamented in another letter. "How can one have them? If I could put the tip of my finger on the tiniest part of her body which was not covered by pimples, I would try to have a child."[10] Joseph was not grieved when his young wife died of smallpox shortly after the wedding.

Not all princes agreed to be slaughtered on the altar of Hymen for the good of the state. In the 1670s the future James II of England found himself widowed with no son and cast about Europe for an attractive young wife. Louis XIV, hoping to seat a Frenchwoman on the English throne, evidently had difficulties finding a candidate both beautiful and virtuous at the court of Versailles. Finally, deciding that a wife's appearance could be of no great significance, Louis pushed forward a noble but repulsive French widow, Madame de Guise. The French minister

Louvois wrote to England hopefully, "If the Duke of York is desirous of a wife in order to have children, he cannot make a better choice than Madame de Guise, who has been pregnant three times in two years, and whose birth, wealth, and prospects of fecundity appear to me to atone for her want of beauty."[11]

James declined the offer, and the disappointed French ambassador wrote scoffingly to his king that the duke of York insisted on finding a *beautiful* wife. Madame de Guise and her fecundity were dropped. James married the loveliest princess in Europe, fifteen-year-old Mary of Modena, a tall, slender, ravishing brunette with whom he fell deeply in love.

The future George IV of Great Britain (1762–1830) had avoided putting his neck in the noose for years but finally, hamstrung by debts, was bribed to marry Princess Caroline of Brunswick by his royal father and Parliament. George, a dandy who spent hours tying his cravat, was poorly suited to the good-natured but ill-mannered princess, who had no regard for dress or personal hygiene.

When the prince was first introduced to his newly arrived bride, he was so thunderstruck with terror at her appearance that he wiped his brow, whispered, "I am not well," and called for brandy to quell a fit of faintness.[12] Neither was the bride well pleased with her groom. After George had stumbled away, Caroline said to her lady-in-waiting, "Is the Prince always like that? I find him very fat and not nearly so handsome as his portrait."[13]

George managed to rise to the occasion with his wife three times during the first two nights of marriage. He wrote to a friend, "She showed . . . such marks of filth both in the fore and *hind* part of her . . . that she turned my stomach and from that moment I made a vow never to touch her again."[14] Fortunately for George, he had already made Caroline pregnant during his halfhearted efforts. With the birth of an heir the pressure was off, and George never did touch her again. In 1821 the British people were treated to a rare sight—prizefighters hired by the new king barring the doors of Westminster Abbey as Caroline bellowed that she be allowed in and crowned alongside her estranged husband. The same year, when Napoleon expired, the king was informed that his "greatest enemy" was dead. George's face was suffused with joy as he exclaimed, "Is she, by God!"[15]

But the most mismatched couple of all was without a doubt Louis XIV's brother, Philippe, duc d'Orléans, called "Monsieur," a transvestite who much preferred male lovers to female, and Elizabeth Charlotte, daughter of the elector of the Palatinate. Many at the French court sneered at an alliance with the elector, a man so poor he had to have his shoes patched. But German princesses were renowned for their fertility. Moreover, since the groom's lover the chevalier de Lorraine was suspected of poisoning Monsieur's beautiful first wife Princess Henrietta of England in a fit of jealousy, Louis XIV decided that an ugly second wife would stand a better chance of survival.

In 1670 when the hopeful bride arrived in France to meet the husband she had already married by proxy, she found an effeminate fop wearing rouge, diamond earrings, cascading rows of lace and ruffles, dozens of clanking bracelets, beribboned pantaloons, and high-heeled shoes. His face was submerged in a frizzy black wig, and waves of his cologne almost suffocated her. When introduced, Monsieur swept into a bow, taking in at a glance his bride's broad, good-natured German face, freshly scrubbed from her journey, her broad German rear end, and clothing of such rustic simplicity that her new French ladies-in-waiting were appalled. The horrified groom whispered to his gentlemen, "Oh! how can I sleep with that?"[16]

Rising from her curtsy, the bride was so shocked at her new husband's appearance that she couldn't utter a word of her prepared speech. She finally managed to force a smile. We can hear her muttering to herself behind a painted fan, "Oh! How can I sleep with *that*?"

Elizabeth Charlotte endured a great deal during her thirty-year marriage that most royal brides were spared. Monsieur insisted on applying makeup to her face—perhaps in the hopes of rendering it more attractive—which she immediately scrubbed off. He often irked her by stealing her dresses and diamonds for himself and his male lovers. He enjoyed breaking wind—though perhaps that was the only thing they had in common. Elizabeth

Charlotte, not wanting to touch him as she slept, positioned herself so far to the edge of the bed that she often fell off, waking up with a start.

It is a testament to this couple's royal self-discipline that the marriage produced three children, though the clanking saints' medallions that Monsieur tied to his private parts may have had something to do with it. When he finally called a halt to unwelcome sexual relations, Elizabeth Charlotte was tempted to tell his lovers, "You are welcome to gobble the peas; I don't like them."[17]

SEX WITH THE KING

In contrast to a prince's forced performance with his wife, we can imagine his more enjoyable relations with his mistress—the tender foreplay, the artistic technique, the frenzied culmination, the drowsy contented aftermath. Imagine we must, for history has bequeathed us relatively few records of the sex lives of kings and their mistresses. Most sexually suggestive letters written by the enflamed pair were burned in the lifetime of their recipients—sometimes in the last moments of life—or shortly afterward by embarrassed relatives. A few such letters remain to titillate us, as well as numerous stories that shed light on the sexual relationships between kings and mistresses.

Barbara, Lady Castlemaine, described her royal lover Charles II as being magnificently endowed, prompting her friend Lord Rochester to write:

> *Nor are his high desires above his strength*
> *His scepter and his prick are of a length.*[18]

Hearing this couplet, Louis XIV's mistress the princesse de Monaco remarked that while Louis's power was great, his "scepter" was small compared to that of his royal cousin across the English Channel.

In the 1540s the future Henri II of France was so enthralled with his strawberry blonde mistress Diane de Poitiers that he had little appetite for his plain brown wife, the dauphine, Catherine de Medici. Studious Catherine was described by one ambassador as a fine woman when her face was veiled, and her face when unveiled resembled nothing so much as a plank of wood. She had been selected as Henri's bride only because of her close relationship with the pope and a rich dowry including several cities, jewels, horses, and furnishings. In 1542 after nine years of marriage Henri and Catherine had produced no children, not even a pregnancy.

Though eighteen years older than her royal lover, Diane kept immaculate care of herself and was far sexier than the dauphine. Slender and athletic, Diane began each day with a bracing ride on horseback for up to three hours. Ever mindful of her clear white skin, she always wore a black velvet mask outside, daily drank a mixture containing gold, and bathed in asses' milk and cold water. Terrified of wrinkles, Diane slept sitting up on pillows. Her beauty regimen worked. Henri made love to Diane almost every night and left his wife alone in her cold bed.

The penalty for a barren princess was often annulment, banishment, and life in a convent. Diane, while no great friend of Catherine's, was pleased that she was dull and plain and had absolutely no influence over her husband. Diane feared a new alliance, a beautiful foreign princess who would win Henri's heart away from her. Better, she resolved, to assist Catherine in bearing an heir.

On appointed nights, Diane would begin the lovemaking session getting Henri incredibly aroused, then send him upstairs to his wife's room to finish the job. Having done his dynastic duty, the prince would go back downstairs to fall asleep in Diane's arms. Soon after this practice began, Catherine became pregnant and bore a healthy son. Henri rewarded his mistress "for the good and commendable services" she had done for the dauphine.[19]

Intelligent Catherine did not understand what her husband saw in his aging mistress. Curious, she had an Italian carpenter drill two holes in her floor, directly above Diane's bedroom. She and her lady's maid would watch Henri and Diane make love in the flickering shadows of the fire, roll off the bed, and exhaust their passion on the floor. Catherine was astonished at the great gentleness Henri showed Diane and, weeping, told her lady-in-waiting that he had "never used her so well."[20]

The lovely hazel-eyed Madame de Pompadour, who became Louis XV's mistress in 1745, opined that she was used *too* well. For the poster child of royal mistresses had a disturbing secret— she was frigid. There is some evidence that indicates she suffered from a chronic vaginal infection with a foul white discharge, for which there was no cure at the time. "I have acquired a cold sea-bird," lamented Louis XV.[21] Sometimes he was so disappointed in her performance that he would leave her bed without the usual good-bye kiss.

Louis XV had a voracious sexual appetite and enjoyed love-making several times a day. But his mistress, always teetering somewhere between sickness and health, quickly became exhausted and had to pretend she was enjoying his exertions. We can picture her, a silken woman on satin sheets, her nakedness warmed by the candles' glow, waiting for the king to be finished.

Hoping to stimulate her libido, Madame de Pompadour began to experiment with a diet of celery, truffles, and vanilla that only succeeded in harming her health. One day when her friend the duchesse de Brancas expressed concern, the royal mistress burst into tears and said, "I'm terrified of not pleasing the King anymore and of losing him. You know, men attach a great deal of importance to certain things and I, unfortunately for me, am very cold by nature. I thought I might warm myself up if I went on a diet to heat the blood. . . . You don't know what happened last week, the King said it was too hot, an excuse to spend half the night on my sofa. He'll get tired of me and find somebody else."

The duchess sagely advised her friend, "But your diet won't stop him, and it will kill you. No, you must make yourself indispensable to the King by always being nice to him. Don't rebuff him, of course, at these other moments, but just let time do its work and in the end he'll be tied to you forever by force of habit."[22]

If Madame de Pompadour had lost her position when she stopped having sex with the king, she would have been out of a job by sometime in the early 1750s. As it was, she skillfully changed their love affair into a deep friendship, becoming an astute political adviser and one-woman entertainment committee.

It is ironic that Louis XV's principal mistress when he was a young man—Madame de Pompadour—was frigid, and his mistress when he was old—Madame du Barry—was one of the most talented prostitutes of her day. Or perhaps not. While still young, Louis relied on Madame de Pompadour's devotion, charm, and intelligence, and got his sexual relief elsewhere. As an aging monarch trembling before the gates of death, he had little need of intelligence. He wanted frequent athletic sex to convince him he was still alive. As he aged, he had difficulty finding women who aroused him, until he met the enthusiastic Parisian prostitute he made his final mistress.

Jeanne du Barry walked into Louis's life at the right time for both of them. If she had been a few years earlier, under the firm reign of Madame de Pompadour, she would have been a mere fling. As it was, her arrival some four years after Madame de Pompadour's premature death brought a melancholy monarch back to life and created for herself a career she had never dreamed of.

The duc de Richelieu, an aging roué, had enjoyed the beautiful blonde so much that he recommended her to the jaded king. After their first sexual encounter, the king told the duke, "I am delighted with your Jeanne. She is the only woman in France who has managed to make me forget that I am sixty."[23]

But instead of bedding her and sending her away, as he had all the others, he kept her around. Almost apologetically he said to his friend the duc d'Ayen that he had "discovered some pleasures entirely new to him." In reply, the duke sniffed, "That, Sire, is because you have never been to a brothel."[24]

The king had been led to believe that Jeanne was a respectable married woman who had enjoyed a few affairs with noblemen and bankers. His faithful valet and longtime procurer, Lebel—alarmed at the king's inclination for so inappropriate a woman—

finally told Louis during his morning toilette that Jeanne's sexual talents were the result of years of professional training, that she didn't even offer the respectable cover of being married. We can picture Louis, being powdered and perfumed, with a regal wave of the hand ordering Lebel to shut his mouth and find the woman a suitable husband. Reeling from the shock, Lebel—who had served the king for most of his life—died soon after.

Court physicians admonished Louis that his mistress was too young for him and suggested that an older woman might be better for his heart. But this was not a recommendation likely to win the king's agreement. Meanwhile, some courtiers said they had never seen Louis in better health—he seemed younger and more energetic than he had been in years.

But a few weeks before his death, the sixty-four-year-old monarch realized that even Jeanne was losing her ability to arouse him. He confided to his doctor, "I am growing old and it is time I reined in the horses." The doctor immediately responded, "Sire, it is not a question of reining them in. It would be better they were taken out of harness."[25]

The aging monarch, facing death and the divine judgment he knew could not be far off, sometimes suffered bitter pangs of remorse for his carnal sins and refused to see his mistress. But these twinges of conscience were soon replaced by other twinges, and Louis found himself once more in her shapely white arms. The king's hot-blooded Bourbon temperament lasted, literally, until the moment of death. Even as his putrefying body was riddled with smallpox, Louis stretched forth a pus-ravaged hand to fumble his mistress's enticing breasts.

Perhaps Louis XV got his relentless libido from his predecessor, Louis XIV, who burdened his mistresses not only with his ravenous sexual needs but, worse, with his infinite fertility. Louise de La Vallière gave birth to four children in seven years. Her successor, the brilliant Athénaïs de Montespan, bore seven children in nine years. Dour Madame de Maintenon was past menopause when she secretly married Louis, but at the age of seventy-five she complained to her priest that the king insisted on sex every day, sometimes several times. The priest replied that as God had appointed her to keep the king from sinning, she must simply endure it. It was believed that a too frequent indulgence in sex gave men "gout, constipation, bad breath and a red nose," all of which Louis suffered from, but not enough to curb his appetite.[26]

While sex between even the lustiest pair usually fizzled after a few years, Czar Alexander II (1818–1881) and his pretty brunette mistress Katia Dolguruky enjoyed a passionate sex life throughout a fifteen-year relationship that ended only with his death. Though profoundly stupid, Katia was thirty years younger than Alexander and adored lovemaking. In 1870 the czar wrote her, "What I felt within me you saw for yourself, just as I saw what was happening to you. That was why we clenched each other like hungry cats both in the morning and in the afternoon, and it was sweet to the verge of madness, so that even now I want to squeal for joy and I am still saturated in all my being."[27]

In 1876 the czar's health seemed to be failing. He was examined by the court physician who could find no illness and indicated diplomatically that the fifty-eight-year-old czar was suffering from exhaustion and "excesses in sexual relations."[28] But this medical opinion did not deter the czar. Soon after, he wrote Katia, "I enjoyed our love-making madly, and am still all steeped in it. You are so tempting, it is impossible to resist! There is no word for this delirium."[29]

The same year, as Katia prepared to deliver her third child, she lamented the fact that she would not be able to have sex for some time after the birth. "I feel so heavy," she wrote, "but I am not grumbling because it is my fault, and I confess I cannot be without your fountain, which I love so, and therefore after my six weeks are over I count on renewing my injections."[30]

The love affairs of Napoleon III (1808–1873) were not nearly as satisfying. The emperor's libido had forced him to marry the only woman who had refused to have sex with him, Eugénie de Montijo, the beautiful daughter of a petty Spanish grandee. One wit said that Napoleon III had become emperor by election, but Eugénie became empress by erection.

But when Napoleon discovered that his wife's virtue was, in

fact, frigidity, he roamed the court like a lion sniffing for prey, prowling the ballrooms on sexual hunting expeditions. In the 1860s, now in his fifties, the emperor was unable to sustain foreplay and dove into his pleasure with little concern for his partners.

The marquise de Taisey-Châtenoy endured one of these encounters after having made a rendezvous with the emperor during a ball at the Tuileries. After midnight, he arrived in her bedroom in mauve pajamas looking faintly ridiculous. She reported, "There follows a brief period of physical exertion, during which he breathes heavily and the wax on the ends of his mustaches melts, causing them to droop, and finally a hasty withdrawal, leaving the Marquise unimpressed and unsatisfied."[31]

A journalist and acquaintance of the imperial family Jules de Goncourt wrote, "When a woman is brought into the Tuileries, she is undressed in one room, then goes nude to another room where the Emperor, also nude, awaits her. [The chamberlain] who is in charge, gives her the following instruction: You may kiss His Majesty on any part of his person except the face."[32]

One woman, the wife of a court official, sought a private audience with the emperor to discuss her husband's career. She reported that she "did not even have time to make a token protest before he laid hold of me in an intimate place. . . . It all happens so quickly that even the staunchest principles are rendered powerless."[33]

Some of Napoleon's predatory expeditions were completely unsuccessful. One evening the lecherous emperor entered a dimly lit drawing room, sat down on a sofa next to a fetching creature in an ornate gown, slipped his hand beneath the skirt to find a shapely leg within a silk stocking, and pinched it. The bishop of Nancy stood up bellowing in protest.

The kinkiest sexual relationship on record between monarch and mistress was that of raven-haired Lola Montez and Ludwig I of Bavaria. Ludwig developed an obsession with the dancer's feet. In her exile, he wrote her, "I take your feet into my mouth, where I have never had any others, that would have been repugnant to me, but with you, it's just the opposite."[34] And another letter, "I want to take your feet in my mouth, at once, without giving you time to wash them after you've arrived from a trip."[35]

Their letters indicated that Lola performed oral sex on Ludwig, and at other times he masturbated as he sucked on her feet. It is likely that these practices occurred in lieu of sexual intercourse, which Lola had with the king on only a handful of occasions. Perhaps she had little sexual attraction for a man thirty-four years her senior with a knob growing in the middle of his forehead. She often excused herself from intercourse on the grounds of menstruation, poor health, or the danger of pregnancy.

In addition, during their fifteen-month relationship in Munich, Ludwig would ask her to wear pieces of flannel in two places next to her skin—we can only imagine which two places—and give them to him. Later, during her exile, he made the same request and she sent him the flannel she had worn. He particularly wanted to know which side of the flannel had been against her skin, as he would wear this side next to his. He insisted on knowing if she had worn the flannel in both places.

During Lola's exile, she sent Ludwig a letter with a little circle she had drawn to represent her mouth for him to kiss. Ludwig replied, "The drawing in your letter that is meant to represent your mouth (each time I give it a kiss), I took at first to represent your *cuño* [vagina], and my *jarajo* [penis] began to get erect. As much pleasure as your mouth has given me, your *cuño* would have pleased me greatly. I give kisses to one and to the other."[36]

By all accounts Lillie Langtry and the future Edward VII of Great Britain had a lusty sex life. Edward was stunned in 1877 when he first saw the long-legged, voluptuous redhead who walked "like a beautiful hound set upon its feet."[37] He quickly made her his first official mistress, and for three years they were almost inseparable. Lillie related that one day the prince said to her, "I've spent enough on you to buy a battleship." To which she tartly replied, "And you've spent enough in me to float one."[38]

_____

Fidelity in an Adulterous Relationship

Like biblical patriarchs, Turkish sultans, and Chinese emperors, European kings were usually involved in sexual relationships with several women at a time. While usually only one woman held the title of official mistress—*maîtresse-en-titre*—there were invariably lesser lights, some that were quickly extinguished, others that occupied a lower orbit but gleamed faintly for many years.

In accordance with the time-honored tradition of the sexual double standard, while the kings and princes were rolling around in bed with other women, their mistresses were supposed to wait quietly in their apartments, embroidering perhaps, or planning a gala dinner to entertain the unfaithful lover. Such was the case of Mademoiselle de Choin, the mistress of Louis, dauphin of France (1661–1711), heir to the throne of his father, Louis XIV. Louis's devotion to his mistress—he would secretly marry her after his wife's death—did not preclude his copulating with actresses he saw on the Paris stage or anyone else who came his way.

On one occasion the dauphin invited a pretty young actress to visit him in his rooms at Versailles. She arrived with an older, unattractive female companion. Informed that the actress had arrived, the dauphin opened the door to the antechamber, grabbed the woman closest to him—which happened to be the ugly older woman—and pulled her into his room. When his friend and procurer Monsieur Du Mont found the sexy actress waiting in the antechamber, highly amused at the mistake, he banged on the dauphin's door, crying, "That's not the one you want! You've taken the wrong one!" The door opened, and the dauphin shoved the ugly one out. "Wait, here she is!" said Du Mont, pushing the pretty one toward him. "No, the business is done," the dauphin said. "She will have to await another occasion."[39]

In contrast, most royal mistresses would not have dared risk love affairs with other men. A few who did were generously forgiven by their womanizing monarchs. But many would have expected a punishment similar to that of Madame d'Esterle, who became mistress of Augustus, king of Poland and elector of Saxony, in 1704. When the playboy king discovered that Madame d'Esterle had been having affairs with several gentlemen at court, he gave her twenty-four hours to pack her bags and leave the country. Worse was the vengeance of Peter the Great (1672–1725), who in 1703 discovered that his mistress of thirteen years, Anna Mons, had been sleeping with the Swedish ambassador. Peter, who throughout his relationship with Anna had routinely enjoyed drunken orgies, was so enraged at her infidelity that he threw her in prison along with thirty of her friends.

For a woman who publicly declared that whoredom was her profession, plucky Nell Gwynn proved remarkably faithful to Charles II, even after his death. Bereft of her royal lover, pretty Nell was courted by numerous suitors. She sadly informed one ardent admirer that she "would not lay a dog where the deer laid."[40]

Ironically, Charles's nobly born mistresses, the imperious duchesses, were not nearly as faithful as his spunky whore. Auburn-haired Barbara Palmer, whom Charles created the countess of Castlemaine and duchess of Cleveland, was the most notorious. Perhaps Charles tolerated her blatant infidelity because she was his dream sex partner. One childhood acquaintance of Barbara's described her as "a lecherous little girl . . . [who] used to rub her thing with her fingers."[41]

In 1667 Lady Castlemaine was enjoying an affair with the renowned court rake Harry Jermyn. One day when the king made an unexpected visit to his mistress, Harry had to dive under her bed. When she was pregnant the sixth time, the king knew very well the child was not his. He had not been certain about some of her prior five but had decided to claim paternity, since there was a good chance. This sixth child, however, he would not own.

Lady Castlemaine was furious that the king was making her look like a whore. "God damn me, but you shall own it!" she cried. "I will have it christened in the Chapel at Whitehall and owned as yours . . . or I will bring it into Whitehall Gallery and dash its brains out before your face." Charles maintained, "I did not get this child." "Whoever did get it, you shall own it," cried the shrew.[42] It was reported that in a few days the king begged forgiveness of his mistress, on his knees.

In 1671 the king was told that Lady Castlemaine was sleeping with playwright William Wycherley at the house of a female friend. Charles went to investigate for himself and ran into Wycherley on the landing, trying to disguise himself by wrapping his cloak about him. The king said nothing but went upstairs and found Lady Castlemaine in bed. He asked her to explain what she was doing there. "It is the beginning of Lent," she said, "and I retired hither to perform my devotions." The king snorted, "Very likely. And that was your confessor I met on the stairs."[43]

As Lady Castlemaine grew older she developed a keen desire for younger, brawny bucks of the lower classes. In the ultimate disrespect of class boundaries, she allowed her footman to make love to her in her bath and had sex with Jacob Hall, a rope dancer, in his booth at the county fair in full view of a fascinated public.

One court wit put her amorous adventures in verse:

> *Full forty men a day provided for this whore*
> *Yet like a bitch, she wags her tail for more.*[44]

Lady Castlemaine was always in love, and loved lustily. She was generous with her young lovers, tapping her pensions from the king to support them. John Churchill, the future duke of Marlborough, was in bed with Lady Castlemaine one day when her royal lover dropped by unannounced. Churchill dove out the window. Charles walked over to the window, looked down, and remarked dryly, "I forgive you, for you do it for your bread."[45]

When Churchill demanded five thousand pounds, Lady Castlemaine agreed to prostitute herself to seventy-something Sir Edward Hungerford, who had expressed the desire "to be where Charles had been before."[46] Lady Castlemaine told him her price was ten thousand pounds—she wanted to keep a little extra for herself—to which the wealthy lecher readily agreed. But she sent another woman to meet Sir Edward in a dark room and collect the payment. She then let Sir Edward know he had been tricked and offered to *really* prostitute herself to him for another ten thousand. Wisely, Sir Edward declined the offer.

A significant portion of Lady Castlemaine's income as royal mistress—an estimated one hundred thousand pounds—found its way into the greedy hands of John Churchill. Yet one evening when Lady Castlemaine asked to borrow a few guineas over cards, he indignantly refused. The royal mistress was so enraged that she got a nosebleed and burst her corset strings.

Lola Montez's unfaithfulness to her royal lover was on a scale equal to, or perhaps surpassing, that of Lady Castlemaine two centuries before her. Her blatant infidelity contrasted sadly with the steadfast loyalty of King Ludwig. Shortly after she was forced out of Munich, Ludwig wrote her a letter he never sent, begging her to remain faithful to him. As for his fidelity to her, he wrote, "Much beloved, think of the past 16 months, how your Luis has conducted himself in this time we have known each other. You will never find a heart like mine."[47]

But Lola had already enjoyed numerous lovers during her tenure as royal mistress in Munich and would continue her dissipations in exile. In Munich she entertained numerous lovers in her hotel suite and afterward in the house Ludwig had bought and refurbished for her. Lola rarely ventured outside without a group of young men dancing attendance under the guise of bodyguards, and her student fan club from the University of Munich.

Reports constantly streamed in to the king about Lola's affairs. He refused to believe them, concluding that Lola was being slandered. Once Lola was exiled and Ludwig abdicated, he had plenty of time to consider coolly the numerous reports that came filtering in of her blatant philandering as she traversed Europe. Even as Lola begged Ludwig to send her money and promised him eternal loyalty, her lifestyle was so shocking that her two female companions, whose purpose was to lend her an air of respectability, packed up and left.

The retired monarch would have other mistresses to warm his

lonely heart, but he would never completely heal from his relationship with Lola. The loss of his throne did not bother him as much as the realization that his beloved Lolita was a faithless liar. Until his death twenty years later, the toppled king wandered around his estates writing bad poetry about his broken heart.

François I was more fortunate than most kings in wreaking his revenge on the lover of his faithless mistress—although he didn't know it at the time. In 1518 his *maîtresse-en-titre*, the twenty-three-year-old Françoise de Foix, dame de Châteaubriant, was unfaithful. One night her lover, Admiral Bonnivet, hearing the king coming, jumped out of his mistress's bed and hid himself in her large fireplace. Luckily, it was summer and the hearth was filled with scented pine branches behind which Bonnivet concealed himself. Unluckily, the hearth also served as a latrine, and before making love to his mistress the king unknowingly urinated on poor Bonnivet hiding behind the boughs, soaking him to the skin.

TWO

BEYOND THE BED—
THE ART OF
PLEASING A KING

'Tis not a lip or eye we beauty call,
but the joint force and full result of all.

—ALEXANDER POPE

❊

SEXUAL TALENTS ALONE WOULD NOT RAISE A WOMAN TO THE position of *maîtresse-en-titre*. The king could lift the skirts of almost anyone in his realm as few or as many times as he wanted without giving her the official title and its corresponding emoluments. The king's servants, knowing their master's taste, often scrubbed up cheerful prostitutes and dumped them in the royal bed. These women gratefully accepted a piece of gold on their way out the door. Chambermaids cleaning the king's rooms were sometimes subjected to the sudden and irrepressible lust of their monarch. Smoothing down their rumpled petticoats, they took their brooms and buckets and discreetly went on to clean the next chamber.

With court ladies the king had dalliances—which included

private suppers followed by lovemaking and gifts of expensive jewelry. These noblewomen, unlike the prostitutes and chambermaids, were eligible to become the official mistress if the monarch chose to bestow the honor upon her. But in most cases, he did not. What qualities made a woman a serious candidate for royal mistress?

We are tempted to choose beauty as the most important quality. We see the king's mistress as a Baroque Aphrodite gleaming in silks, dripping with lace, glittering in jewels. Sweeping into a ball, she demolishes the king with a single glance, prompting him, weak-kneed, to utter those fateful words, "Who is she?"

She has translucent skin, shining ringlets, a face and figure of astonishing beauty. Beneath her elegant veneer lurks an animal passion that men can sense across the room. Her voice is low and throaty, her smile devastating. She pins thunderstruck men to the spot with a glance from her luminous eyes. Laughing, she leaves us, her train rustling behind her, and we detect the heady notes of her perfume clinging to the air. Well do we understand why the king has selected her.

But if we chose beauty as the single most important quality of the royal mistress, we would be flat-out wrong. The woman who wore all her assets on her skin, and offered none from within, simply did not last. Good looks without intelligence and kindness resulted in a few frenzied interludes of dropped breeches and rumpled petticoats, rarely in an offer of the position of *maîtresse-en-titre*. Many monarchs sampled the charms of the most beautiful women in their courts and found them absolutely *boring*.

Many a plain woman, on the other hand, captivated her king, but not with a grand entrance at a ball. She would require frequent contact with the monarch to reveal her inner beauty, her good nature, keen intellect, and clever wit. He would begin to look forward to their conversations, the comfort he felt in her presence, the laughter she provoked in him. And soon the court would snicker that the king had taken an ugly mistress.

With or without beauty, with or without sexual talents, the successful royal mistress made herself irreplaceable, catering to each of the king's five senses. She was ready to converse gaily with him when she was tired, make love until all hours when she was ill, cater to his every whim, serve his favorite foods, sympathize when he was cranky, massage his feet, decorate his homes, and raise his illegitimate children—sometimes sired with women other than herself. And all of this must be done *cheerfully*.

Only a few monarchs enjoyed passionate foot-stomping battles with their mistresses. Typically, the royal mistress did not scold, browbeat, or throw jealous tantrums. Sitting on her perch of dignified serenity, she selected her battles carefully, only rarely flapping down with talons bared.

In the king's presence his mistress was never to be tired, ill, complaining, or grief-stricken. She wore a mask of beaming delight over any and all discomforts. When Louis XIV bestowed upon his mistresses and their friends the honor of traveling in his carriage from one palace to the other, it was in actuality a great torment. The duc de Saint-Simon reported, "The expedition would not have covered a quarter of a league before the King would be asking the ladies in his carriage whether they did not care to eat something. . . . Then they were all obliged to say how hungry they were, put on an air of jollity, and set to with good appetite and willingness, otherwise the King became displeased and would show his resentment openly. . . . The King liked fresh air and insisted on having all the windows lowered; he would have been extremely displeased had any lady had the temerity to draw one of the curtains to keep out the sun, the wind or the cold. There was no alternative but to pretend not to notice that, nor any other kind of discomfort. . . . To feel sick was an unforgivable crime."[1]

Perhaps worst of all, the ladies were not permitted to mention the needs of nature. During one six-hour ride from Versailles to Fontainebleau, the duchesse de Chevreuse was in such dire need of a chamber pot that she almost collapsed. Fixing a smile upon her face, she never mentioned her agony to the king. Upon reaching Fontainebleau, she raced into the nearest room—which happened to be the chapel—and relieved herself there in the first vessel she found—which happened to be a holy chalice.

But the royal mistress's discomforts did not end there. She was forced to participate in the king's hobbies whether she liked them or not. Smiling broadly, she rode with him through the cold woods on the hunt and nodded her approval as he cornered and killed screaming animals, then dismembered their bloody carcasses. Laughing gaily, she spent hours in wet fields watching the royal hawks devour little birds. Chuckling merrily, she pretended to relish boring card games until the wee hours of the morning. And then, moaning in feigned ecstasy, she endured unwelcome sex.

We rarely hear of a queen exerting herself to exhaustion to please the king. While the mistress sang, and hunted, and recited poetry, and brought in jugglers, and made love all night, and ate when not hungry, and denied the needs of her bladder and bowels, the queen glided through her marriage with solemn lethargy. Why did the mistress have to work so hard, while the queen did not? Quite simply, because the mistress could be dismissed at any moment, while the queen was a permanent fixture in the palace—like the marble floors or stone columns—until her death. No matter what a queen's behavior—short of blatant adultery—she would retain her marriage and her position. The mistress, on the other hand, could lose all she possessed with a snap of the royal fingers.

THE ART OF PLEASING

The quintessential royal mistress was Jeanne-Antoinette d'Etioles, marquise de Pompadour, who reigned for nineteen years over Louis XV and France. This twenty-four-year-old from the middle class crashed the forbidding gates of Versailles in 1745, survived countless plots and counterplots by jealous nobles to unseat her, and left court only as a corpse on a stretcher. What silken cords bound the king to her?

Initially she entranced handsome Louis with her beauty and charm. Comte Dufort de Cheverny wrote, "Not a man alive but would have had her for his mistress if he could. Tall, though not too tall; beautiful figure; round face with regular features; wonderful complexion, hands and arms; eyes not so big, but the brightest, wittiest, and most sparkling I ever saw. Everything about her was rounded, including all her gestures. She absolutely extinguished all the other women at Court, although some were very beautiful."[2]

But Madame de Pompadour's beauty was like that of a hothouse flower that soon began to wither in the poisonous atmosphere of Versailles. In her twenties she boasted a fresh, ethereal beauty, with perfect skin, silken chestnut hair, and dark hazel eyes. She set off the purity of her look by simple costumes of rose, pink, or blue silk and satin, trimmed with the requisite lace. But as the rigors of court life sapped her natural beauty, she increased the magnificence of her gowns and jewels to distract the observer from her face—richer lace, larger gems, heavy brocades and velvets embroidered with gold and silver and pearls. One evening she appeared in a dress trimmed with lace worth 22,500 livres, the cost of an estate.

Frigidity is, of course, a great disadvantage to a mistress. To compensate for her poor performance at night, during the day Madame de Pompadour devoted every moment to amusing a monarch who quickly grew bored. Louis escaped the stiff etiquette of Versailles by fleeing to her apartments and barring the door. There he found an entire world created for his personal comfort. His mistress decorated her rooms in colors and fabrics that he found relaxing. She filled them with sweetly scented flowers from the palace greenhouses, even in winter. She ordered dishes and wines that pleased the royal palate.

Madame de Pompadour became an avid student of the king's moods, his every facial expression, the cadence of his words. She knew when he was hiding boredom, anger, or frustration behind his mask of royal calmness. The twitch of an eyelid, the lilt of a syllable, would tell her the behavior necessary to please him. Did he want a comfortable silence? Should she recount an amusing story, play a somber tune on the harpsichord, stand up and perform a monologue?

Louis must have climbed the secret spiral staircase leading from his apartments to hers with great anticipation. What would she discuss with him that evening? Building, perhaps. Madame de Pompadour had a mania for building palaces and asked the king's advice on architecture, improvements, and decorations. Perhaps she would have architectural plans laid out for his approval. Or maybe the subject would be botany. His mistress created a botanical garden at the Trianon Palace on the grounds of Versailles where she conducted experiments and grew the first strawberries in France especially for her royal lover. She also had a greenhouse built so that Louis could have fresh oranges and lemons at any time of year.

Perhaps she would report on the progress of the farmyard she had created for him on the palace grounds, complete with a dairy and milk cows. Or maybe she would discuss the art of gem cutting she had taken up, or her plans for a porcelain factory.

One of Louis's favorite diversions was to listen to Madame de Pompadour read from the private letters of his courtiers. All letters both into and out of court were opened, read for treacherous intent, and carefully resealed. Madame de Pompadour obtained from the palace police copies of the most amusing missives—which contained the most intimate details—to read to the king. After a hard day's work Louis roared with laughter as she read him these excerpts in a lively and entertaining manner.

To divert the royal boredom, Madame de Pompadour created a tiny theater, holding only a handful of guests, where she performed the lead roles, and the king was invariably the guest of honor. She was a talented actress; after her first performance, Louis came up to her and said with throaty sincerity, "You are the most charming woman in France."[3] Her theater was so successful that she performed comedy on Mondays and sang opera on Wednesdays—in between her other exhausting duties. Courtiers clawed each other out of the way to obtain invitations.

Perhaps her best role was that of royal listener. The king had the unfortunate habit of recounting the same stories innumerable times, of discussing the same themes—hunting, illness, and death. And his mistress, who hated talk of hunting, illness, and death, concealed her yawns behind a smile, nodded her head encouragingly, and hoped that her eyes sparkled with sufficient interest as she heard the same old stories, the boring, macabre old stories, yet again.

Madame de Pompadour's relentless devotion to amusing the king caused her untold hardship. She rose early for Mass and endured late dinners followed by unwanted lovemaking. Rich food, great quantities of wine, and unending correspondence and court duties exhausted her. Nor could she leave her apartments for exercise or a change of scene lest the king suddenly appear wanting food, conversation, or sex. Despite the daunting challenges of her schedule, she never permitted herself to show fatigue, boredom, or illness, never expressed frustration, anger, or crankiness.

In her early years as royal mistress, Madame de Pompadour was often required to accompany Louis on his frequent hunts, either on horseback or in a carriage, in all kinds of weather. Despite the fact that these excursions often gave her pneumonia, she put on her riding habit and her omnipresent smile and went off to join the king. As she grew older, and sicker, this was the one duty she gave up.

Madame de Pompadour turned to thick white lead powder to hide the dark circles under her eyes and the sallow color of her skin. Blemishes caused by the lead powder were covered by more lead powder or fashionable black patches. And to create the illusion of blooming good health, she rubbed heavy rouge on her cheeks. The layers of rouge, patches, and powder served as a complaisant mask behind which she could hide exhaustion, pain, and anger.

One evening Madame de Pompadour, suffering from one of her horrendous migraines, sent word to the king that she was ill and unable to attend dinner. Louis frowned and asked her messenger if she was feverish. The messenger replied that she was not. "Very well, then, let her come down!"[4] commanded the king. And his violently ill mistress was forced to rise from her sickbed, lace herself into her ball gown, hang diamonds from her ears and throat, powder and rouge her face, and most important, paint a smile on her pained mouth.

In 1754 Madame de Pompadour's only child, ten-year-old

Alexandrine, died suddenly in her convent school. Days later Madame de Pompadour's father, heartbroken over the loss of his only grandchild, also died. Overcome with grief, the royal mistress knew that however much the king liked talking about death and illness, he grew bored in their presence. Having lost a beloved father and darling daughter within a fortnight, she once again dried her tears and put on her diamonds. The prince de Croy, who visited her shortly afterward, reported, "I saw the Marquise for the first time since the loss of her daughter, a dreadful blow that I thought had completely crushed her. But because too much pain might have harmed her appearance and possibly her position, I found her neither changed nor downcast." Though the prince saw her chatting cheerfully with the king, he thought that she "was in all likelihood just as unhappy inside as she seemed happy on the outside."[5] Indeed, for many years Madame de Pompadour would confess to friends, "For me happiness has died with my daughter."[6] She was just not permitted to show her pain.

Madame de Pompadour, who truly loved Louis, wrote to a friend, "Except for the happiness of being loved by the one you love, which is the best of all conditions, a solitary and less brilliant life is much to be preferred."[7] Her lady's maid, Madame du Hausset, who well understood the stresses of Madame de Pompadour's life, said, "I pity you sincerely, Madame, while everybody else envies you."[8]

In Madame de Pompadour the king enjoyed a charming companion constantly at his beck and call. Having lost his parents at the age of three, living apart from the rest of humanity as a kind of demigod, Louis was inexorably lonely by nature. In her low apartments under the eaves of Versailles, she offered him the warm and loving home he had never had with parents or siblings, and certainly never with his ill-suited wife. At great cost to herself, she diminished for him the pain of living, the loneliness in a crowd that only a monarch can suffer.

Devastated by Madame de Pompadour's early death—which was no doubt hastened by her nineteen exhausting years as his mistress—Louis waited four years before choosing another *maîtresse-en-titre,* the Parisian prostitute Madame du Barry, in 1768.

Madame du Barry lacked her predecessor's intelligence but boasted greater beauty. One young officer went to petition the new favorite and was so overwhelmed by her loveliness that he nearly forgot what he had come for. "I can still see her carelessly seated or rather reclining in a large easy chair," he recalled, "wearing a white dress with wreaths of roses. She was one of the prettiest women at a Court which boasted so many, and the very perfection of her loveliness made her the most fascinating. Her hair, which she often left unpowdered, was of a beautiful golden color and she had so much that she scarcely knew what to do with it all. Her wide blue eyes looked at one with an engaging frankness. She had a straight little nose and a complexion of a dazzling purity. In a word, I like everyone else fell immediately under her charm."[9]

Madame du Barry's "dazzling" complexion was indeed a rarity in an age when most women's skin was marred by smallpox scars. And while many young women were missing teeth—sometimes *all* their teeth—Madame du Barry had a wide white grin.

Her meticulous grooming habits were highly unusual for the eighteenth century. Most courtiers covered the crusty filth and overpowering stench of their bodies with velvets, laces, and a hearty dose of cologne. Women inserted head scratchers into their elaborate coiffures to ease the itch of flea bites on greasy scalps. But there would be no filth, stench, or head fleas for Madame du Barry, who simmered in rose-scented bathwater several times a week.

Madame du Barry augmented her substantial natural beauty with stunning clothes. Some of her gowns were deceiving in their simplicity—the cost of a diaphanous white robe, tied carelessly with a few exquisite ribbons, would have allowed a Paris family to live in comfort for a year. Other gowns were grander—of gold or silver tissue, embroidered with gold and silver thread and thousands of seed pearls. Her sleeves, skirts, and petticoats were flounced with the finest lace.

At the wedding of the king's grandson in 1773, Madame du

Barry appeared "shining like the sun in a dress of cloth of gold covered in jewels worth over five million *livres*," according to one eyewitness.[10] She owned one bodice encrusted with thousands of fine diamonds sewn in the shape of interlacing bows, costing millions of dollars in today's money. Each of her gowns had a matching pair of slippers with jeweled buckles—diamonds, amethysts, or sapphires.

But Madame du Barry had far more to offer Louis than her radiant beauty. Her sexual talents bound him to her, and her gaiety plucked him out of his frequent depressions. She was all women to him—a delightful child, a talented whore, a comforting mother. And, like Madame de Pompadour, she was always willing to forgive the malicious courtiers who made trouble for her.

Taking the example of her predecessor, Madame du Barry made herself the king's entertainment committee. She decorated her apartments to please Louis and stuffed them with his favorite flowers. Her mother had been a cook in many noble kitchens, and while haughty courtiers ridiculed this, Madame du Barry tempted the jaded royal palate with countless tasty dishes recommended by her mother. In addition, she brought in jugglers and clowns and had operettas and farces performed for the king's amusement.

While it was challenging enough to amuse the king in a palace, in the 1590s beautiful Gabrielle d'Estrées had the task of making Henri IV's surroundings comfortable on the field of battle. For several years at the outset of their relationship, Henri was campaigning with his army against rebel forces throughout France. Golden Gabrielle, even when heavily pregnant, insisted on staying by his side, living in cold, drafty tents. She saw to it that he had a good dinner after a day's battle, and she herself kept his clothes as clean as possible—often pounding them with rocks when she ran out of soap. While Henri was fighting on the field, Gabrielle remained in their tent writing his political and diplomatic dispatches. In the evening, they would discuss the events of the day.

Gabrielle was tall with a delicious figure and graceful walk.

Blessed with exquisite coloring—pale blonde hair and large blue eyes—she had a broad forehead, high cheekbones, and a nose just a bit too long for perfection. Her contemporaries—even enemies who hated Gabrielle for her Catholicism, her involvement in politics, and her warming the king's bed—waxed poetic when describing her beauty.

In addition to providing her royal lover with shining beauty and comfortable surroundings, Gabrielle offered him fierce political loyalty. During a ball in Paris, a messenger arrived informing the king that the Spanish had launched a surprise attack and captured the town of Amiens. Henri decided to march immediately. Gabrielle calmly went to her strong boxes in the Louvre, emptied them of fifty thousand pieces of gold, and gave Henri every penny to pay the initial costs of troops and provisions. While Henri mustered his troops, Gabrielle got in her carriage and visited the homes of the nobility to ask for donations, collecting an additional 250,000 ecus.

Still not satisfied, Gabrielle took her extraordinary jewels to the richest banker in Paris and pawned them. Still in her ball gown and dancing slippers, Gabrielle set out for the front, where she insisted on taking care of her royal lover despite real danger. Henri wrote, "Last evening I found three bullet holes burned into the fabric of my mistress' tent, and begged her to go to her house in Paris, where her life would not be endangered, but she laughed and was deaf to my pleas. . . . She replied that only in my presence is she pleased. I entertain no fears for myself, but daily tremble for her."[11]

One day, during a particularly fierce battle, a column of Austrian soldiers appeared, causing the French troops to flee in disorder. Oblivious of the cannonballs crashing around her, Gabrielle cried at the top of her voice for the French troops to stay and fight. The Austrians came within five hundred paces of the king's mistress as she continued exhorting her countrymen to bravery. Alarmed, Henri rode to her side and ordered her to be slung over a horse and taken to the rear of the camp. Out of fifty-six known mistresses in his lifetime, Henri was faithful only to Gabrielle. So smitten was the king with his brave and beautiful mistress that he vowed to marry Gabrielle and make her queen of France.

In the sixteenth through the eighteenth centuries, the king raised his mistress to his lofty level and ensconced her in apartments at the palace. Most likely she did not complain about the bitter cold that froze the ink in her inkwell and coated the wash water in her basin with a crust of ice. She understood that the distance of outhouses from the palace required bowls overflowing with human waste in almost every room, concealed behind elegant cabinets of inlaid rosewood until they could be removed. She did not expect her food to be warm; the distance of the palace kitchens from the royal suites precluded that. She knew that behind its thin wash of gilding, the court was a "tissue of malice," as Madame de Pompadour said, a place of vicious backbiting and petulant self-aggrandizement.[12]

By the nineteenth century, the monarch, instead of raising his mistress to his exalted if uncomfortable level, gratefully descended to hers. He escaped his golden prison by fleeing to her tidy bourgeois home, which offered the warmth, comfort, and privacy his court could not.

Austro-Hungarian emperor Franz Josef (1830–1916), a sad, weary little man bowed down by the weight of a crumbling empire, found joy over coffee and croissants with his mistress Katharina Schratt. A thirty-three-year-old comic actress at the Imperial Theater when their love affair began in 1886, Katharina was the only woman ever reported to make the emperor laugh out loud. Over a period of thirty years, Franz Josef found in her quaint home an oasis of entertainment and relaxation, far from the cold etiquette of the palace. Katharina did not weary him with politics but told him jokes and pleasant chatty gossip.

Katharina was one of those women whose aura of beauty quickly disintegrates when one analyzes her features. She had a face like a potato dumpling, a stubborn chin, thick, quizzical black eyebrows framing laughing eyes, a pointed little nose, and thin lips struggling to suppress a smile. Her curvaceous figure ran to plumpness in middle age. It was the joy she embodied, her warmth and kindness, that made her seem truly beautiful.

In 1895, the German ambassador Count Eulenberg described the forty-two-year-old actress as "ravishingly pretty with extraordinary youthful looks, marvelous coloring, shining golden hair and great blue eyes with the sweetest expression, a really good soul who never says an unkind word and is always pleasant and gay and ready to help whom she can. Apart from which she is delightful company and has a very original way of relating little anecdotes."[13]

The emperor loved his beautiful wife, Empress Elizabeth, who was always balancing precariously on the brink of insanity. But the anguished empress was in no position to amuse and comfort her husband, and she spent most of her time trekking across Europe in a fruitless effort to cast out her inner demons. In fact it was she who had chosen Katharina to be her husband's mistress to relieve her own guilt at deserting him. The empress kept throwing the two together—they were a bit slow to understand—until an affair began. It was a wise choice. Franz Josef wrote Katharina that his visits to her cheerful home were "the only rays of light in my otherwise dreary life."[14]

With his children married and his wife away, the lonely emperor often roamed the endless corridors of the royal palace alone, with no one to see to his personal comfort. He had dozens of servants to snap to his commands, but not one would have dared to see what he was lacking and make suggestions. Katharina filled this role, giving him a painted screen to protect him from the draft, a thick wool smoking jacket, a cozy little rug. His favorite gift was a hand mirror with the words in French "portrait of him whom I love."[15]

Untamed Shrews

While the vast majority of royal mistresses presented an unfailingly cheerful face to the king, there were some notable exceptions. Two of the worst harpies reigned in the 1660s and 1670s. Louis XIV's Athénaïs de Montespan and his cousin Charles II's Barbara, Lady Castlemaine, were both cunning, hotheaded, vengeful, and rapacious.

When she first became Louis XIV's mistress, Athénaïs de Montespan was the most beautiful woman at the French court. She had thick tawny hair, large, heavily lidded blue eyes, a straight nose, good teeth, and the cherubic lips so cherished at court. Her neck was long and shapely, her large bosom and white shoulders well suited to the daring off-the-shoulder gowns of the 1660s. As one courtier reported, "Her greatest charm was a grace, a spirit, a certain manner making a witticism."[16]

Unlike her predecessor Louise de La Vallière, whose beauty had lasted just about as long as the violets she had been compared to, Madame de Montespan kept her looks almost until the age of forty, but with the utmost exertion. She marinated herself daily in creams, oils, and flower essences to keep her complexion fresh. She spent lavishly on cosmetics, dabbing on the ivories, roses, and peaches of her complexion as if nature had not fully complied with her exacting requirements.

Daily attending royal dinners with highly fattening food—which the king insisted she eat—and with the limited exercise available to upper-class women at the time, Madame de Montespan often grew plumper than was fashionable. The Italian fortune-teller to the nobility, Primi Visconti, noted gleefully, "While she was descending from her carriage one day, I had a glimpse of one of her legs, and I swear it was almost as broad as my whole body."[17] To counter this tendency toward stoutness, Madame de Montespan had herself rubbed down with pomade two hours at a time, several times a week, as she lay naked on her bed. Periodically she disappeared to a health spa, where she starved herself back into shape.

In 1676 she returned from several weeks at the spa in Bourbon. When Madame de Sévigné visited court, she found the royal mistress "quite flat again in the rear end . . . her beauty is breathtaking. . . . While losing weight, she has lost none of her radiance . . . her skin, her eyes, her lips all aglow. . . . Her costume was a mass of French lace, her hair dressed in a thousand ringlets, the two at her temples quite long, falling against her cheek, her coiffure topped with black velvet ribbons and jeweled pins, her famous pearl necklace . . . caught up with superb diamond clips and buckles. In short, a triumphant beauty to show off, to parade before all the Ambassadors."[18]

Athénaïs de Montespan was like a golden lioness, a majestic feline beauty, purring contentedly, who at a moment's notice bares claws and fangs, ready to rip and tear. Her temper tantrums were notorious. When courtiers heard her shrill, angry voice wafting down the hall they avoided her wing of the palace rather than "passing through heavy fire."[19]

One day, while getting into a carriage with his queen and his mistress, Louis got a whiff of Madame de Montespan's strong perfume and angrily remarked that he had repeatedly requested her to wear less, as the scent made him ill. His mistress replied that she was forced to wear perfume because the king never bathed in his life and, frankly, stank. A shouting match ensued as the king and his mistress entered the carriage, the hapless queen following. Courtiers made bets on how long the mistress would last.

Oddly, Madame de Montespan's reign lasted thirteen years. The king must have enjoyed sparring with his imperious mistress. And she sometimes showed the good sportsmanship that most royal mistresses possessed. For instance, in the winter of 1678 she insisted on joining Louis on a tour of his frontiers although she was five months pregnant. She suffered repeated fevers but refused to return to Versailles, bumping over muddy roads with the king, sleeping with him in farmhouses, and never complaining. It was this behavior that bound the king to her, in between her temper tantrums.

Louis's cousin Charles II put up with his beautiful virago, Barbara, Lady Castlemaine, for nearly a dozen years. Barbara had dark auburn hair, a shapely figure, porcelain skin, an oval face, and flashing dark almond-shaped eyes under beautifully arched black brows. There was something delicate about her classical nose and ripe pouting lips, ironically evincing a hint of vulnerability.

Lady Castlemaine badgered, threatened, and intimidated Charles into submission with her unending stream of demands for money, titles, and honors for herself and her children and sometimes, in a burst of selflessness, for her friends. Her outrageous behavior knew no bounds. In 1666 the Great Fire of London destroyed the medieval St. Paul's Cathedral and damaged many of the tombs. The mummified corpse of the fourteenth-century bishop of London—"all tough and dry like a spongified leather"—was found intact and exhibited to visitors of the ruins.[20] Lady Castlemaine instructed the keeper to leave her alone with the body for a few moments. When he returned he found that the corpse's penis had been torn off and suspected that the lady had done so with her mouth.

But even the shrewish Lady Castlemaine knew it was her duty to provide the king with a good dinner. Her London house was situated on the banks of the Thames. One evening, when her cook complained that she could not prepare the beef because the river had risen and flooded the kitchen, Lady Castlemaine shrieked, "Zounds, you must set the house on fire but it must be roasted."[21]

Nearly two centuries after the twin termagants battled their royal lovers on either side of the English Channel, Lola Montez pounced with outstretched claws on Bavaria, combining the worst qualities of both. As greedy as Lady Castlemaine, as arrogant as Madame de Montespan, raven-haired Lola quickly wrapped the aging Ludwig I of Bavaria around her little finger. It was her passion that inflamed him. His long-suffering wife and former court mistresses seemed as dull as sheep compared to Lola's flash and fire. Azure eyes glinting, nostrils flaring, Lola would stamp her foot and threaten violence to herself when things didn't go her way. Lola kept knives and pistols secreted about her person for protection. She got in trouble with the law on several occasions for horsewhipping gentlemen who she felt had insulted her. Poor enslaved Ludwig would likely have kept Lola for years if his own subjects had not thrown her out of Bavaria after only sixteen months as royal mistress.

These three untamed shrews were, however, the exception rather than the rule. Most kings were like Louis XV, demanding cheerful amusement. When his usually complacent Madame du

Barry began throwing jealous scenes about his proposed marriage to a foreign princess, the king stopped coming to visit her. Only when she regained her composure did he return.

BORING BEAUTY

In the first decade of the eighteenth century, Augustus the Strong, elector of Saxony and king of Poland, fell in love at first sight with a certain Mademoiselle Dieskau for her platinum hair, large blue eyes, and "neck of dazzling whiteness." According to the elector's biographer, Mademoiselle Dieskau "was, her mind excepted, the most accomplished creature nature ever formed."[22]

But, he continues, "how beautiful soever Mademoiselle Dieskau really was, she could be called no better than a lump of snow. No vivacity could be found in her, she made no other answers than yes and no. The King was charmed with the great beauty of her person, he spoke to her . . . but was in despair when he found so little life in her."[23]

But the desires of his body soon overcame the needs of his mind, and Augustus found himself in Mademoiselle Dieskau's arms, having paid a large sum to her mother for the girl's virginity. His physical urges assuaged, he left Mademoiselle Dieskau soon after in search of a woman of greater intelligence.

Likewise, in 1680 Louis XIV was captivated by a new face at court, one Mademoiselle de Fontanges. Courtiers raved about her beauty. One ambassador described her as "an extraordinary blonde beauty, the like of which has not been seen at Versailles in many a year. A form, a daring, an air to astonish and charm even that gallant and sophisticated Court."[24]

But after the initial wave of enthusiasm over Mademoiselle de Fontanges's beauty died down, the next tide of gossip revolved around her shocking stupidity. The moment the girl opened her mouth, many tender fantasies inspired by her looks were immediately dispelled.

Madame de Caylus wrote, "The King, in truth, was attracted solely by her face. He was actually embarrassed by her foolish chatter . . . One grows accustomed to beauty, but not to stupidity."[25] One courtier called the new mistress "beautiful as an angel and stupid as a basket."[26] Louis quickly tired of his stupid basket.

The most bombastic empty-headed beauty was, without a doubt, nineteen-year-old Virginie di Castiglione, who in 1856 was sent by Italian prime minister Camillo Cavour to seduce Emperor Napoleon III of France, a mission she accomplished with lightning speed. Unburdened by modesty, Virginie called herself the most beautiful woman in the world and later expanded that to "the most beautiful woman of the century."[27]

Many agreed with Virginie's assessment of her beauty. Princess Metternich described Virginie's face as "a delicious oval, her eyes dark green and velvety, surmounted by brows that could have been traced by a miniaturist's pencil, her small nose . . . obstinate, yet absolutely regular, her teeth like pearls."[28]

The courtier Viel Castel recorded in his diary that Virginie "bore the burden of her beauty with insolence, and displayed it with effrontery."[29] He, like so many at court, was delighted by the "truly admirable" size of her bosom, and confessed that he tried hard to look under the sheer gauze covering to discern its shape. Virginie refused to wear a corset, that most requisite piece of nineteenth-century female attire, which turned the soft curves of the breasts into an impregnable fortress. She allowed her breasts to dangle freely. Viel Castel remarked that those breasts "seemed to throw out a challenge to all women."[30]

But what Virginie boasted in the bosom she lacked between the ears. While successful royal mistresses were absorbed in their men, Virginie was absorbed only in herself. Most of her conversation revolved around her own glorious beauty. Napoleon himself confided to his cousin Mathilde that while Virginie was "very beautiful, she bores me to death."[31]

Virginie's looks could not, in the long run, make up for her stone cold selfishness. She lasted only a year. "I have hardly commenced my life and my role is already finished," she lamented bitterly.[32]

ENCHANTING UGLINESS

When George I left Hanover to claim the British throne in 1714, he brought as his mistresses two of the ugliest women his new subjects had ever seen. The tall, skinny one bore a weighty name—Ermengarda Melusina, countess of Schulenberg. She had lost her hair to smallpox and wore unattractive wigs and dumpy dresses. Her plainness was offset by kindness and loyalty but not by scintillating conversation. Lady Mary Wortley Montagu wrote that while many found King George a dull man, Ermengarda was "duller than himself, and consequently did not find him so."[33]

The short, fat mistress was Sophia Charlotte Kielmansegge. Though ridiculed for her girth, she had a sparkling personality and a thorough education, and loved sex. As her mother had been mistress to George I's father, there was some speculation that George was having sex with his half sister. While the skeletal countess of Schulenberg was nicknamed "the Hop Pole," the stout Madame Kielmansegge was tagged "Elephant and Castle." Horace Walpole described her as having "two fierce black eyes, large and rolling, beneath two lofty arched eyebrows, two acres of cheeks spread with crimson, an ocean of neck that overflowed and was not distinguished from the lower part of her body, and no part restrained by stays."[34]

Philip Dormer Stanhope, the future Lord Chesterfield, described both mistresses as "two considerable specimens of the King's bad taste and strong stomach."[35] Referring to Madame Kielmansegge he added, "The standard of His Majesty's taste as exemplified in his mistresses, makes all ladies who aspire to his favor, and who are near the suitable age, strain and swell themselves, like the frogs in the fable, to rival the bulk and dignity of the ox. Some succeed, others burst."[36]

Charles II of England once said that his brother, the future

James II, was given his mistresses by his priests as a penance. In a century that worshiped the soft flesh of breasts and hips and rounded arms, James liked extremely slim women. His mistress Arabella Churchill was a "tall creature, pale-faced, and nothing but skin and bone."[37] Courtiers cackled at her appearance until she fell off her horse in front of a crowd, displaying her magnificent legs. One awestruck witness marveled that "limbs of such exquisite beauty could belong to Miss Churchill's face."[38] Though forced by the fashions of the time to conceal her most comely attributes inside yards of heavy skirts, Arabella often displayed the quick wit and lively intelligence which bound James to her through ten years and four children.

James's next mistress, sixteen-year-old Catherine Sedley, was equally skinny and pale but nearsighted and squint-eyed to boot. Though feisty and intelligent, she was clearly bewildered at having been chosen by James. "It cannot be my beauty for he must see I have none," she remarked incredulously. "And it cannot be my wit, for he has not enough to know that I have any."[39]

Louis, dauphin of France, the heir of Louis XIV, enjoyed a shockingly plain mistress for several years until his death. Ungainly, with a thick neck, heavy lips, and a ski-slope nose, Emilie de Choin was described as having the deportment of a barrel. At a court known for its graceful, witty women, Mademoiselle de Choin looked like a pug and seemed to have the brains of one.

Louis XIV's sister-in-law Elizabeth Charlotte wrote that Mademoiselle de Choin had black rotten teeth that stank so much that one could smell them at the other end of the room. But, she added, "She had the hugest bosom I ever saw; those enormous charms of hers were the Dauphin's delight."[40] To her horror, Elizabeth Charlotte witnessed the dauphin playing tunes with his fingers on Emilie's breasts as if they were kettledrums.

But good-natured Emilie made a pleasant home life for her royal lover, who had been unhappily married to two foreign princesses. Shrugging off his notorious tightfistedness, uncomplaining Emilie lived on a pension little better than that of a servant. Sometimes Louis would buy his mistress a small gift and then agonize for days over whether to give it to her or return it and get his money back. Yet rather than face the sacrificial altar a third time, Louis secretly married Emilie, the ugliest girl at court, and enjoyed playing her kettledrums until the day he died.

Perhaps the ruler best known for choosing ugly mistresses was Philippe, duc d'Orléans, who became regent of France in 1715. Philippe was the nephew of Louis XIV and son of the formidable Elizabeth Charlotte, who was scandalized by his taste in women. Casting about a court with the most beautiful women in the world, Philippe would always select the ugliest to pleasure him in bed. His mother huffed, "He is not difficult in this regard; as long as they are good-humored, impertinent and have a hearty appetite for food and drink, he does not worry about their looks."[41]

Never one to mince words, she once told her son that he visited his mistresses as he would his chamber pot and loudly reproached him for their ugliness.

"Bah! *Maman*," Philippe quipped, "in the night all cats are gray."[42]

THREE

RIVALS FOR A KING'S LOVE—THE MISTRESS AND THE QUEEN

Never has a woman who loves her husband liked his whore.

—QUEEN CATHERINE DE MEDICI

❄

IN 1726 QUEEN SOPHIA DOROTHEA OF PRUSSIA, ADVISING HER daughter Wilhelmina on a possible marriage to Prince Frederick William of England, remarked that the young man was "a good-natured prince, kind-hearted but very foolish. If you will have sense enough to tolerate his mistresses, you will be able to do what you like with him."[1]

A princess, trained from birth for the lofty role she would play as queen, understood the likelihood of her future husband's keeping a mistress. She had only to look about her own court to see the mistresses of her father, uncles, and brothers.

And yet the blushing royal bride invariably hoped *her* husband would be the exception; *her* husband would disport himself only in the sacred bower of Hymen, never returning to the sullied bed of Jezebel. Almost as invariably, she was disappointed.

Raised as a hothouse flower, a princess was rudely plucked from her native soil and tossed into a cold foreign land where she would, over time, wilt. Blinded by tears, she boarded the gaily bedecked vessel to take her to her new country, knowing she would probably never see her parents, sisters, brothers, or friends again. Heart pounding with fear, she would disembark in a country where she could barely understand the language. To the jubilant ringing of church bells and the hearty crackling of bonfires, she would be taken to a court with alien customs, fashions, and politics.

Initially, the princess bride, the new queen, was the blazing star of the court. Courtiers bowed and scraped before her, gave her expensive gifts, made pretty compliments, scurried behind her. But when the drum roll of the wedding festivities died down, the church bells were silenced, and the bonfires turned to ash, scheming courtiers usually grouped themselves around the king's dashing mistress rather than his dull foreign queen.

For all her vaunted position, the queen was at the mercy of her husband's whims as much as any woman in the kingdom. The king alone decided whether his wife would enjoy spacious royal apartments at the heart of the palace or cramped cold rooms in a distant wing. The king chose as her ladies-in-waiting either the young and radiant or the old and withered. The king determined whether she would live in luxurious splendor or pinch-fisted penury. The king instructed her either to attend royal events—balls, feasts, garden parties, theatrical performances—or to remain sequestered in her rooms.

Courtiers aped the king's treatment of the queen. If he treated her with respect, so did they. If he ignored and insulted her, so did they. If the queen was to remain a significant presence at court, she required her husband's staunch support.

The king's support for his wife, however, was often conditional, depending on how well the queen treated his mistress.

"It is easier to make peace in Europe than between two women," lamented Louis XIV in the 1670s.[2] History, before and after the Sun King, proved him correct.

Legend has it that in 1176 fifty-four-year-old Queen Eleanor of Aquitaine poisoned the beautiful young mistress of her husband, Henry II of England. Or stabbed her. Or drowned her in her bath. No one is certain, though the legend probably arose from the obvious hatred Eleanor bore Rosamund de Clifford, who was no mere sex partner, but the queen's rival at court. What is certain is that prickly Eleanor, bristling at her husband's flagrant adulteries, plotted to overthrow Henry. Dressed as a man to escape her husband's wrath, Eleanor was captured fleeing on horseback and spent the last sixteen years of Henry's life in prison.

Life was easier for the queen who could meekly accept her husband's philandering. In the 1440s Queen Marie of France remained on good terms with Agnes Sorel, the mistress of her husband, Charles VII. A Flemish visitor to the court pitied the plain queen, ferret-faced with large, frightened eyes and a long, inquisitive nose. Marie, who had never been close to pretty even at the peak of her youth, endured the golden loveliness of her husband's mistress at her side most of the time. The queen, the visitor wrote, was forced "to see her rival walk beside her and remain near her every day, to have her household in the King's palace, to enjoy the company and all the gatherings of the lords and the nobility, to appear before her, to possess more beautiful bedclothes, better rings and jewels, enjoy a better table and better everything. And with all this she must not only put up, but rather make it seem a pleasure."[3]

While pious Queen Marie always wore black after four of her fourteen children died, Agnes led the fashions at court. The courtier Jean Juvenal des Ursins was perturbed by what he considered indecency and sniffed that the king should not allow necklines so low that nipples and breasts were exposed. But apparently the king liked this fashion, as he made no move to ban it.

Marie, uncomplaining, devoted herself to her household, her religious duties, and her offspring. "He is my lord, he has authority over all my actions and I over none," the devoted wife repeated dutifully.[4] It would be a useful motto for queens in the centuries to come.

"THE CONTEMPT OF THE WORLD"

On a gentle May morning in 1662, the ship carrying twenty-three-year-old Catherine Braganza, princess of Portugal, entered Portsmouth harbor. Though no great beauty and a Catholic to boot, Catherine had been chosen as the wife of King Charles II for the rich dowry she trailed in her wake—the cession of Bombay and Tangier, which would open up India to England.

Standing on the ship's deck, tiny brunette Catherine was all hope and eagerness and fear. Hope that she would be a good queen, a beloved wife, a happy mother. Eagerness to meet her husband—handsome, swarthy Charles. Fear of finding herself cast adrift on foreign shores without her family.

But in addition to hope, eagerness, and fear, Catherine came to England armed with steely resolve. She had promised her mother, Portugal's fierce queen regent, that she would never, *ever* tolerate Charles's infamous mistress, Barbara, Lady Castlemaine, at her court. Her mother had lectured Catherine about this auburn-haired hussy who brazenly betrayed a good husband, raped the treasury, had given the king one royal bastard nine months after their liaison began, and was already pregnant again.

Sir John Reresby, who officially welcomed the princess in Portsmouth, announced with some misgivings that Catherine "had nothing visible about her capable to make the King forget his inclinations to the Countess of Castlemaine, the finest woman of her age."[5] And indeed, as church bells rang in London to announce the bride's arrival on English soil, Charles remained in London dining with his stunning and very pregnant mistress. As his bride waited in Portsmouth and bonfires were lit across the country, Charles spent every spare moment with Lady Castlemaine for six days straight.

By the time Charles finally bestirred himself to ride to Portsmouth, poor Catherine, humiliated with waiting, was ill of a fever. When Charles was introduced to his bride, he was shocked less at her buckteeth than at her hairdo, dressed in the Iberian style of corkscrews projecting horizontally from either side of her head and then hanging like sausages down to her shoulders. "At first sight," Charles told a friend, "I thought they had brought me a bat instead of a woman."[6]

The king gave her a quick kiss, then went to his own chamber and sank into bed relieved. He was tired from his journey and wrote his sister that he was glad he would not be expected to make love to Catherine that night. Trying to remain optimistic about his bride, the next day Charles told his chancellor, "Her face is not so exact as to be called a beauty, though her eyes are excellent good, and not anything in her face that in the least degree can shock one."[7]

The day of the royal wedding, in protest Lady Castlemaine ordered her underclothes to be washed and hung out to dry on the palace grounds for all the world to see. The diarist Samuel Pepys, walking in the Privy Garden, "saw the finest smocks and linen petticoats of my Lady Castlemaine's, laced with rich lace at the bottoms that I ever saw, and did me good to look upon them."[8]

Catherine had immediately fallen deeply in love with her tall, darkly swashbuckling husband, and Charles insisted a bit too often that he, too, was delighted. A sexual athlete, Charles likely found in Catherine a tightly furled bud, a bud that would never unfurl further. We can picture her, shy and chaste, a dutiful wife in bed, while Lady Castlemaine reveled with him in sexual abandon.

Beneath the smile Charles wore when beginning his married life simmered a secret which he knew would devastate his bride. To pacify Lady Castlemaine's wrath at his marriage, he had promised her the honor of becoming a lady of the queen's bedchamber. Not only would she live at court, but as a lady of the bedchamber Lady Castlemaine would be concerned with the most intimate details of the queen's life, including sexual relations with her husband, bodily functions, menstruation, and pregnancy. The position offered great status, as it was one of the few that could officially be given to a woman directly. It would cement Lady Castlemaine's standing in an envious, backbiting court.

Two months after the king's wedding, the royal mistress gave birth to their second child, and Charles glumly decided it was time to fulfill his promise to her, even at the risk of alienating his bride. He invited Lady Castlemaine to Hampton Court and, taking her by the arm, walked up to the queen to present her. Admiring the beautiful visitor, Catherine stood up smiling and extended her hand as her husband introduced Lady Castlemaine. Upon hearing the name, Catherine's reaction was gut-wrenching. She blanched and sank down visibly upset. Tears fell fast and heavy down her cheeks. Suddenly, blood dripped from her nose and she passed out on the floor. She was carried into an adjoining room, but Charles did not follow. He interpreted his wife's illness as defiance; wrath clouded his dark face as he took his mistress back to her coach.

When he reproached the queen for her insolent behavior, she was intransigent rather than contrite. Charles retaliated by sending home Catherine's retinue of Portuguese ladies and monks—many of them her childhood friends. Charles further isolated his wife by ignoring her completely. He caroused through the night with friends as the queen lay sleepless in her cold bed.

Charles's faithful lord chancellor, Edward Clarendon, begged him to give up Lady Castlemaine and restore his marriage. This would also quiet any dissent among his people, some of whom had already lost respect for the king's personal life. But Charles indignantly defended Lady Castlemaine. "I have undone this lady," he said, "and ruined her reputation, which was fair and untainted till her friendship with me, and I am obliged in conscience and honor to repair her to the utmost of my power."[9]

Charles was uneasy about becoming "ridiculous to the world" if he did not win this very public debate with his new wife.[10] He forced poor Lord Clarendon, who despised Lady Castlemaine, to persuade the queen to accept her as a lady of the bedchamber. To this request the queen replied, "The King's insistence upon that particular can proceed from no other ground but his hatred of my person. He wishes to expose me to the contempt of the world. And the world will think me deserving of such an affront if I submitted to it. Before I do that I will put myself on board any little vessel and so be transported to Lisbon."[11]

Charles stubbornly presented his wife with a list of ladies to be approved for bedchamber positions. At the top of the list was the name of Barbara, Lady Castlemaine. Equally stubborn, Catherine crossed out the name and again threatened to get on the next boat home.

The king moved his mistress to luxurious apartments in Hampton Court, above his own, their suites connected by a secret stair. He sat next to Lady Castlemaine at meals, laughing and talking gaily with her, while the queen sat in mute dejection. No one wanted to be seen talking to the queen, as it might awaken the prejudice of the king and Lady Castlemaine. As soon as Catherine retired, courtiers made insulting jokes about her.

By the end of summer, Catherine broke. Lonely, far from home, she simply couldn't stand the isolation anymore. She apologized to Charles and welcomed his mistress into her inner circle as a friend. The queen and Lady Castlemaine were often crammed into a coach with the king between them. Grateful Charles became an attentive husband. His respect for Catherine became friendship and eventually a kind of love. When Lady Castlemaine demanded that she be the first to ride with the king in a revolutionary new open carriage—and threatened to have a miscarriage on the spot if she was not—Charles selected Catherine for the honor. As the king held the hand of his beaming wife, his mistress was forced to join the procession that followed on horseback, and dejectedly kept her distance from the boisterous courtiers.

While bending her husband to her will by cheerful obedience, Catherine sometimes found herself in a position to exact revenge. Two days after Lady Castlemaine gave birth to her third royal bastard in September 1663, the queen—pretending to know nothing of royal bastards—insisted that Lady Castlemaine ride on horseback with her to Oxford or lose her position as lady of the bedchamber. The new mother, still sore and bleeding, clambered on top of the horse and rode uncomplaining, but gritting her teeth.

It is ironic that when Queen Catherine became seriously ill in 1663, no one in England was more interested in her recovery than the king's mistress. Lady Castlemaine knew that if Catherine died, Charles would marry the beautiful sixteen-year-old noblewoman Frances Stuart, who had aroused his lust but refused to assuage it. Lifted from the depths of bereavement into the heights of passion, Charles would have no need of his rancorous mistress. Barbara prayed heartily for the life of her royal lover's wife.

Similarly, in 1670 Charles's mistresses—he now had a harem—rallied around Queen Catherine when Lord Buckingham presented Parliament with a bill enabling the king to divorce his stonily barren wife and remarry. Clucking and cackling, the royal mistresses insisted that the barren, powerless queen stay exactly where she was. A nubile new queen would certainly sink their ships with all their cargo. And heaven forbid the new queen would bear a passel of royal children. Certainly Charles would neglect his numerous royal bastards.

But Charles, in an act of conscience, stopped the bill, stating, "It was a wicked thing to make a poor lady miserable only because she was his wife and had no children by him, which was no fault of hers."[12]

"AN OLD, DULL, DEAF, PEEVISH BEAST"
In contrast to the glory of England's merry monarch Charles II a half century earlier, beginning in 1714 "the Hanoverian dynasty

seem[ed] to have brought in . . . a sort of triumph of pudding, turnips, and muddy ale, over the lace, maypoles, champagne and burgundy of the preceding period," according to the courtier Brimley Johnson.[13]

Blonde, large-boned Queen Caroline of England certainly followed the pudding-and-turnip trend. Rather than nobly suffering her husband's infidelities as a crown of thorns on the head of a martyred queen, Caroline once told a courtier that, as regards her husband's mistresses, "She was sorry for the scandal it gave others, but for herself she minded it no more than his going to the close stool [toilet]."[14]

While still prince of Hanover, Caroline's husband, the future George II of England, took as his first mistress thirty-year-old Henrietta Howard, pretty, pleasant, and discreet. One courtier described Henrietta as "civil to everybody, friendly to many, and unjust to none."[15] Caroline was relieved at George's choice. While the typical wife bore the greatest malice toward her husband's first mistress, sensible Caroline knew that Henrietta would not plunder the treasury, snub her when she became queen, angle for political power, or sow disruptive intrigues at court.

As Queen Caroline's friend Lord Hervey described it, "The Queen, knowing the vanity of her husband's temper, and that he must have some woman for the world to believe he lay with, wisely suffered one to remain in that situation whom she despised and had got the better of, for fear of making room for a successor whom he might really love, and that might get the better of her."[16]

Like most other royal mistresses, Henrietta became a lady-in-waiting to the queen. Unlike others, however, Henrietta's position was not especially envied. Plump, red-faced George, renowned for tearing off his wig and kicking it across the floor when angry, bucked the trend by loving his wife and tolerating his mistress. Although he believed Caroline to be the most beautiful, intelligent, and charming woman in the world, he also considered a mistress to be an indispensable accessory of a monarch, along with the crown and scepter. George pointedly visited Henrietta every evening for several hours and locked the door. Courtiers speculated crudely about their sex life—one wit compared George to a mill horse plodding around its unending track—and most agreed that they usually spent the time playing cards.

By 1722, in her early forties, Henrietta was growing prematurely deaf. As she had primarily pleased George by being a good audience, he now began to grow impatient with her disability. For Henrietta, however, her deafness may have been a blessing, relieving the daily monotony of listening to George.

George became so irritated with his mistress that on one occasion, as Henrietta tied a kerchief around Caroline's neck, George snatched it off. "Because you have an ugly neck yourself you love to hide the Queen's," he raged.[17]

But George, a man of habit, did not dismiss his mistress. Then in 1729 Henrietta's husband, having been estranged from his wife for fifteen years, decided he could no longer live with his humiliation and ordered her back to her conjugal duties. He obtained a warrant from the lord chief justice permitting him to seize her wherever and whenever she should be found. Hearing this, Henrietta hid in the palace day and night. The queen, alarmed that the king no longer wanted Henrietta and Henrietta's husband did, intrigued to keep her in the palace. If Henrietta should go, George would feel required to select another official mistress, and the next one might not be so tractable.

When the brutish Mr. Howard—often angry, rarely sober—accosted the queen's carriage and threatened to pluck out his wife, Caroline knew something must be done. One suggestion was to bribe Howard with twelve hundred pounds a year to leave his wife in peace, to which the queen remarked she found it a bit hard to not only keep her husband's "trulls under my roof, but pay them, too."[18]

George gallantly stepped in and paid the twelve hundred pounds a year, which was undoubtedly what Mr. Howard had hoped for in making such a fuss. As Lord Hervey reported, Mr. Howard was required to sign a document for Henrietta swearing that "for the future to give her as little trouble in the capacity of husband as he had ever given her pleasure. And so this affair ended, the King paying 1200 pounds a year for the possession of what he did not want to enjoy, and Mr. Howard receiving them, for relinquishing what he would have been sorry to keep."[19]

By 1734, George was snubbing Henrietta for her friendships with several prominent men, including the poet Alexander Pope, whose sarcastic political verses were critical of the king. When Caroline spoke to George about his rude treatment of Henrietta, he angrily replied, "What the devil did you mean by trying to make an old, dull, deaf, peevish beast stay and plague me when I had so good an opportunity of getting rid of her!"[20]

And so ended a relationship of twenty years. The old, dull, deaf, and peevish beast suddenly found herself a widow and soon remarried. When the queen informed him of the marriage, George laughed that "my old mistress has married that old rake George Berkeley, and I am very glad of it. I would not make such a gift to my friends, and when my enemies rob me, please God it will always be in this manner."[21] Not a very gallant way to bid farewell to a lover of such long standing, but Henrietta was well rid of him and had the last laugh. She enjoyed a very happy marriage with that old rake George Berkeley, who was, in fact, a dozen years younger than his blushing bride. Henrietta survived her second husband by twenty years, living in comfort in the country.

As Caroline had feared, Henrietta was replaced by younger, prettier, more manipulating mistresses. Dying from an umbilical rupture in 1737, wrapped in towels as her intestines spilled out, the queen, sensible to the end, suggested that George remarry. But the king, heartbroken, hovering near her bed in her last agonizing moments, swore he would have only mistresses and never remarry.

"Oh, my God!" the dying queen said in French, with characteristic practicality, "that won't make any difference!"[22]

"THAT WHORE WILL BE THE DEATH OF ME"

Louis XIV, the most powerful man in Europe, suffered his own share of disputes between his wife and his mistresses. In 1660 at the age of twenty-two the handsome young king married the infanta Marie-Thérèse of Spain, a short, dwarflike product of generations of inbreeding. Fortunately for the queen, she did not suffer the insanity and physical handicaps of her relatives Juana the Mad, John the Imbecile, and Isabella the Insane. Her only debility was a childlike simplicity—though even this was cruelly ridiculed in the sophisticated world of Versailles.

Marie-Thérèse never learned to speak French well, and her new subjects found her coarse Spanish accent irritating. She had no idea of politics, literature, or witty conversation and preferred to spend hours playing cards. Courtiers patiently waited for a seat at the queen's card table, which almost amounted to winning the lottery, as she would invariably bet high and play poorly. Primi Visconti reported that "the Queen's losses provide the poor Princess d'Elbeuf with her sole means of support."[23]

Louis was faithful to his devoted wife for a full year before he began flirting with his brother's wife, Princess Henrietta of England. To distract him from such an unfortunate choice, Louis's mother, the dowager queen Anne, planted a trio of fresh young things in his path. These three graces wore special heron plumes in their hair and were placed prominently near him at banquets.

The ruse worked better than his mother had hoped. The king fell head over heels in love with one of them, Louise de La Vallière, the seventeen-year-old daughter of a petty nobleman. She had ash-blonde hair, dazzling white skin, and large blue eyes. One leg was a bit shorter than the other, so she wore specially made heels. Most attractive to the young king was her genuine mantle of innocence and kindness, of piety and modesty.

The queen was devastated to learn that her husband had taken a mistress. "That young girl with the diamond earrings," Marie-Thérèse said acidly one day in Spanish to a court lady, "is the one the King's in love with."[24]

Compared to other royal mistresses, sweet Louise de La Vallière did not deserve to become the target of the queen's venom-spitting rage. Ashamed before God for her adultery, humiliated before the queen for tender stolen moments with her husband,

Louise treated Marie-Thérèse with humility and respect. But the queen pointedly snubbed her at every opportunity.

Though realizing her husband had a mistress, Marie-Thérèse remained extremely naïve. The king's cousin Anne-Marie de Montpensier wrote, "One day at table she told me that the King had not come to bed until four o'clock in the morning. In answer to her questions, he had told her that he had been busy till then reading letters and writing his replies. When the Queen asked him whether he could not find another hour for that work, he turned his head away from her, lest she see him laugh. Lest she see me doing likewise, I kept my eyes down, fastened on my plate."[25]

Marie-Thérèse was always the last to know that her husband had taken a new mistress. She had thought Louis was still in love with his sister-in-law Henrietta when he had, in fact, become involved with Louise de La Vallière. Now, seven years later, still spewing her poison at Louise, the queen did not notice that the tornado had changed course and was heading in an entirely different direction. For Louis, now a dashing thirty, no longer wanted a sweet and modest mistress. He was ready for the hard, glittering Athénaïs de Montespan, Louise's best friend and the queen's lady-in-waiting.

Madame de Montespan had frequently raged to the queen against the effrontery of Louise de La Vallière, swearing she would rather die than play such a role. Suddenly it was Madame de Montespan who was the king's new favorite, while Louise retained an uncomfortable place on the sidelines, neither in nor out of the game. The queen's ignorance of this momentous shift became a court joke, but someone eventually informed her of it.

Madame de Caylus wrote, "She had loved Madame de Montespan because she had believed her to be a respectable woman, loyal to her duties and her husband. Thus Her Majesty's surprise equaled her sorrow when she later found her to be unlike what she had imagined. The Queen's distress was made no easier by Madame de Montespan's lack of consideration. . . . Of all the King's mistresses, Madame de Montespan is the one who caused

Her Majesty the greatest anguish; not only because that particular passion between Madame de Montespan and the King raged for so long, not only because she took such few pains to spare pain to the Queen but, above all, because it was pain inflicted by a woman whom the Queen had trusted and vouchsafed a special friendship."[26]

While Louise de La Vallière had always treated the queen with deference, Madame de Montespan tried to upstage and insult her at every turn. As lady-in-waiting to the queen, instead of meekly assisting her, the king's mistress often chastised her for taking too long getting dressed. Marie-Thérèse, rarely complaining to her husband, often lamented to her friends, "That whore will be the death of me!"[27] and "That slut will kill me yet!"[28]

In 1670 the king, anxious to take Madame de Montespan on a military campaign, needed to drag both the queen along as chaperone to avoid scandal and Louise to confuse the public about his relationship with Madame de Montespan. As the duc de Saint-Simon reported, "He paraded the two of them in the carriage with the Queen, along the frontier, at the encampments. . . . Crowds came running everywhere along the route, pointing at the carriage and naively calling to one another to come and see the three Queens!"[29]

In 1671 the poor queen found herself on another journey stuffed into a carriage with her husband and his two mistresses. One night, seven exalted travelers found themselves obliged to stay in the same room with one bed. Marie-Thérèse was given the bed, while the other six—the king, his brother and sister-in-law, his cousin Anne-Marie, Louise de La Vallière, and Athénaïs de Montespan, slept on mattresses on the floor. The flabbergasted queen cried out in her throaty Spanish accent, "What? All of us here together?" To which her husband retorted, "If you leave your bed curtains open, you can keep an eye on us all!"[30]

Marie-Thérèse often waited up quite late for her husband, who, out of courtesy to her, never failed to come to her bed, even if the sun was rising. When he finally did come, still warm from his mistress's embrace, his wife greeted him with a smile. She was grateful that the king showed the court his respect for her so clearly. As one courtier remarked, "The King renders her the full honors of her position. He eats and sleeps with her . . . converses with her as gallantly as if there were no mistresses in his life . . . and fulfills his connubial duties. . . . He usually has commerce with her about twice a month."[31]

At some point the queen stopped resisting the tide of beautiful nubile women rushing toward her husband. Perhaps time healed the first, ragged wounds into thick, strong scars. She even took to wearing Madame de Montespan's signature hairstyle—curls on the brow and each side of the head to just below the ear, and a braid coiled on the back of the head, entwined with ribbons and pearls. One day, noticing they were both wearing the same coiffeur, the queen explained, "I've cut my hair like this because the King likes it, not to steal your hair style."[32]

"BETTER SHE THAN ANOTHER"

In 1725 fifteen-year-old Louis XV married a dowdy twenty-two-year-old Polish princess for her family's proven fertility. Boring, religious, and intellectually limited, Marie Leczinska was called one of the two dullest queens in Europe by her own father, the other dull queen being his wife. Marie preferred to pray away her mornings in church, and wile away her afternoons in needlework and cards. Like all eighteenth-century ladies, she had studied music and painting. But her paintings never rose above the level of childish cartoons, and nothing horrified her ladies-in-waiting more than the queen's announcement that she would play the piano for them.

Marie was adrift in the dazzling French court, which boasted the most attractive, witty, and sophisticated men and women in Europe. She did, however, fulfill her promise of fecundity, launching no fewer than ten royal children into the world in as many years. Her frequent lament was, "What, always in bed, always pregnant, always giving birth!"[33]

For eight years, Louis was a royal anomaly in terms of his

punctilious fidelity to his wife. The promising lad grew into an extremely handsome man, with a well-formed physique, strong jaw, high cheekbones, and aquiline nose. Marie must have been pleased that despite her dullness and Louis's brilliance, Louis rarely looked at other women. She was devastated when Louis took one of her ladies-in-waiting, Madame de Mailly, as his mistress. Madame de Mailly was plain, kind, and content to walk around Versailles in torn petticoats rather than ask her royal lover for money. The king's next two mistresses—both sisters of his first—were not so generous. Insolent and grasping, they went out of their way to insult the queen publicly, to flaunt their beauty against her plainness, their wit against her dullness. His third mistress, Madame de Châteauroux, even had holes bored into the walls of the queen's apartments so that her friends could spy for her. When the king chose a new mistress, a Parisian bourgeoise rather than a haughty noblewoman, Marie must have hoped for better treatment.

To take up the position of *maîtresse-en-titre* and live at Versailles, Louis's mistress had to be given a title and officially presented at court. The title was easy—the king granted twenty-four-year-old Jeanne-Antoinette d'Etioles the marquessate of Pompadour. But the presentation was nerve-racking. The freshly minted marchioness had to be presented to the king and queen in two separate chambers before the eyes of the entire court. The candidate could not afford to make the least mistake. Her presentation involved walking forward in an enormous skirt extending three feet on either side and weighing more than forty pounds. She would curtsy to the monarchs, listening to the few words they deigned to say, then walk backward, curtsying, all the while kicking her long train out of her way. The entire procedure needed to appear effortless. Tripping over the train or, heaven forbid, falling, would ensure a lifetime of ridicule at court.

When Madame de Pompadour was presented to him, the king was stiffly nervous and muttered only a few words to his mistress. His presentation room had only a moderate attendance, as most of the courtiers had crammed themselves into the next room, eager to see the more interesting face-off between the mistress and the wife. It was an evening presentation, and the plump middle-aged queen, loaded down with ribbons, bows, laces, and sequins, stood silently in the flickering candles' glow as the fresh-faced young woman approached her. Perhaps she felt Madame de Pompadour's palpable terror so carefully hidden beneath her impregnable poise and exquisite gown. The worst thing the queen could say—indicating complete disdain of the person presented—was a little remark on the outfit the person was wearing. Breathless, the spectators leaned forward.

Queen Marie smiled and asked after a mutual acquaintance. The mistress, no doubt greatly relieved at the queen's very public gesture of kindness, whispered, "I have a profound desire to please you, Madame."[34] The two spoke an astonishing twelve sentences—courtiers counted—which ensured Madame de Pompadour's welcome at court. It was a kindness that would never be forgotten, and one that would serve the queen well for years to come.

Within a few weeks the king suffered a brief attack of jaundice, and Marie requested permission to visit him at his château of Choisy. Louis—who ordinarily would have rebuffed her—replied with unusual enthusiasm. When Marie arrived, he personally showed her the new decorations. At dinner, attended by both the queen and Madame de Pompadour, Louis treated his wife with great respect, and she "showed no desire to leave, but spoke graciously to Madame de Pompadour, who was respectful and not at all forward."[35]

The queen knew her husband was kinder to her at the instigation of Madame de Pompadour. The prince de Croy remarked that the mistress was "on good terms with the Queen, having persuaded the King to be nicer to her."[36]

Natural kindness aside, Madame de Pompadour knew that the queen's friendship would be helpful in the snake pit of Versailles. Her respectful consideration of the queen won her the approbation of fair-minded courtiers. The mistress routinely sent Marie bouquets of her favorite flowers, and convinced Louis that he should pay his wife's debts—most of which were to charities. More astounding, while the court was at Fontainebleau, artists were busy redecorating the queen's apartments at Versailles. When Marie returned, she found that her dusty old rooms had been transformed into the latest style, replete with regilded mirrors and walls, furniture upholstered in white satin, and a new bed with rich red damask hangings. Even more to the queen's liking, the walls had been hung with tapestries illustrating biblical scenes. Marie recognized Madame de Pompadour's exquisite taste behind the new decorations.

The queen was further shocked to receive an expensive New Year's gift from her husband—the first in years. It was a magnificent snuffbox of enamel and gold, with a small watch mounted on the lid. Fortunately, the queen did not know that Louis had originally ordered the gift for Madame de Pompadour's mother—who had just died.

But all wives are hurt when their husbands take mistresses. The queen would still have preferred to have Louis all to herself. Sighing, she often said, "Since there has to be one, better she than another."[37]

"IN TEARS AND LAMENTATIONS"

Like many kings, Henri IV of France believed a queen's duty was to oblige her husband in all things, follow his every command, and never complain. This duty included accepting his mistresses, even welcoming them. Henri had the misfortune to marry two women who were less than delighted at such a request.

In the early years of his marriage with Princess Marguerite, Henri, then only king of Navarre, fell in and out of love with a variety of ladies-in-waiting. Ravishing dark-haired Marguerite—who had numerous lovers herself—averted her eyes. She had never wanted to marry Henri, a bandy-legged petty prince with a nose larger than his kingdom, as wits said, and such an aversion to bathing that he smelled like a goat. And then her husband fell in love with Françoise de Montmorency, daughter of the baron de Fosseuse, and known as Fosseuse herself. As Marguerite wrote in her memoirs, "He was fond of the society of ladies, and, moreover, was at that time greatly enamoured with Fosseuse. . . . Fosseuse did me no ill offices, so that the King my husband and I continued to live on very good terms, especially as he perceived me unwilling to oppose his inclinations."[38]

But in 1581 the fifteen-year-old Fosseuse became pregnant and bruited about that Henri had promised to divorce Marguerite and marry her if she gave him a son. Marguerite, who remained childless, felt threatened. She tried to send the girl from court, but Henri, furious, insisted she remain. Henri became "cold and indifferent" to his wife, Marguerite wrote.[39] As the girl's belly expanded, both Fosseuse and the king swore to Marguerite that she was not pregnant.

One morning the royal physician entered the bedchamber and announced to an embarrassed Henri that Fosseuse was in labor. Marguerite awoke to find her shame-faced husband poking his long nose between her bed curtains. "My dear," he said, peering at her uneasily, ". . . will you oblige me so far as to rise and go to Fosseuse, who is taken very ill? . . . You know how dearly I love her, and I hope you will comply with my request."[40]

To which the complacent wife replied "that I had too great a respect for him to be offended at anything he should do, and that I would go to her immediately, and do as much for her as if she were a child of my own."[41]

Marguerite advised Henri to go hunting, drawing away a large part of the court with him, while she took the girl to a distant part of the palace where no one would hear her cries. When the king returned that evening, he learned that his mistress had produced a stillborn daughter. Crushed at the news, he asked his wife to return to his mistress and console her in her grief. But Marguerite's wifely patience ended here. She remembered how in previous months Fosseuse had flaunted the king's attentions, boasting that he would dump Marguerite and marry her if she gave him a son. Exhausted from the day's exertions, Marguerite flatly refused Henri's request, pointing out that she had been with the girl throughout her travails and could do no more. Henri was furious at her refusal. "He seemed to be greatly displeased at what I said," Marguerite wrote, "which vexed me the more as I thought I did not deserve such treatment after what I had done at his request in the morning."[42]

The marriage continued to deteriorate. After Marguerite tried to raise a rebellion against her husband, he exiled her to a remote castle. When Marguerite's brother Henri III died with no sons, Henri of Navarre, a cousin, became king of France, and he eventually divorced Marguerite, who had taken to strong drink, gluttonous eating, and sex with gardeners and stable boys.

After the death in 1599 of his mistress Gabrielle d'Estrées, whom he had planned to marry, the forty-six-year-old king started casting about for a suitable princess bride. His choice fell on Marie de Medici, niece of the grand duke of Tuscany. The lucky bride was selected more for her rivals' unsavoriness than for her own recommendations. The Spanish infanta was a repulsive antiquity, the German princesses were fat and awkward, and the attractive princess de Guise had been raised in the scorpions' nest of the king's most implacable enemies. Plus, Henri had borrowed heavily from Marie's uncle and hoped that the debt would be forgiven if he made her queen of France.

During his marriage negotiations, the king fell in love with the twenty-two-year-old noblewoman Henriette-Catherine de Balzac d'Entragues. The ultimate courtesan, Henriette offered the king far more than beauty—she possessed a grace, a charm, a cutting wit, and demanding and impetuous passions that excited him. She was lithe, supple, sinuous, the cold cogs of her mind grasping quickly any word or action that could feed her insatiable ambition. And her one ambition was to become queen of France.

Before Henriette had sex with the king, she demanded the outrageous sum of one hundred thousand crowns, to which the love-starved monarch readily assented. His minister the duc de Sully, who called Henriette "that malignant wasp," was compelled to fork over the money from the treasury.[43] In protest the duke had the sum brought in silver pieces rather than gold, and spread them out far and wide across the floor of the king's cabinet room to show Henri how much money he was wasting on the foolish girl. *"Ventre saint-gris!"* cried the king, stepping into the room. "That's a pleasure dearly paid for."

"Yes," Sully replied icily. "The merchandise is certainly a bit dear."[44]

Having pocketed the cash, Henriette now declared that before the king consummated his passion for her, he must furnish written proof that he intended to marry her when possible. An outrageous proposition—especially in light of his ongoing negotiations with the House of Tuscany—but Henri so burned with desire for Henriette that he wrote with his own hand, "We, Henri IV . . . promise and swear on our faith and word as a king . . . that should the said Henriette-Catherine de Balzac within six months, beginning from this day, become pregnant and should she bear a son, then at that time we shall solemnize the marriage publicly in holy church according to the required customary ritual."[45]

Before sending it, Henri showed his promise to the duc de Sully and asked his opinion of it. The duke grabbed the missive and ripped it to shreds. The king, aghast, asked his adviser if he was mad. To which the duke replied he wished that he were "the only madman in France!"[46] Undeterred, the king had a secretary write out an identical promise and sent it to his lady love.

Henriette gloated over the compromising letter, which at the time was a legitimate contract and could in a court of law nullify Henri's subsequent marriage to another. Now all she had to do was bear a healthy son and she would become queen of France. Her joy was diminished somewhat as Henri continued to pursue his marriage with Marie de Medici. By late April 1600—when Henriette was seven months pregnant and well on her way to fulfilling her side of the bargain—Henri signed the marriage contract with Tuscany. Henriette's feigned veneer of generous goodwill cracked, and for the first time the calculating monster behind showed itself.

Tossing her an expensive bone, Henri quickly created Henriette the marquise de Verneuil, bestowing on her a large territory and castle. The lady was not appeased. She threatened to make public his promise of marriage if he continued with the Tuscan union. Henri became aware that his foolish promise could result in international scandal and loss of prestige to his realm. He fired off a letter to her. "Mademoiselle," he wrote, "Love, Honor, as well as all the favors you have received from me would have sufficed for the most frivolous soul in the world, unless she were gifted with a naturally evil character such as yours. . . . I am asking you to return to me the promise in question and not to give me the trouble of recovering it by some other means. Please return also the ring I gave you the other day. . . . I would like an immediate response."[47] The king waited for an immediate response in vain.

Henriette, while refusing to yield the letter, resumed her mask of gentle goodness. At her advanced stage of pregnancy, Henri was loath to provoke her and so brought her to the royal palace of Fontainebleau for her lying-in. While Henriette could not control the sex of the child—a fact which must have irked her immensely—she took great precautions for her health, combining rest, exercise, and a nutritious diet. Although she implored Henri to stay with her for the delivery, Henri—no doubt still angry over her failure to return his written promise—shrugged off her supplications and rode to Lyons on business.

Unfortunately for Henriette, her labor started during a violent thunderstorm. Lightning flashed outside the palace; then a bolt entered her room and passed beneath her bed. Henriette became hysterical. For hours she screamed uncontrollably, and by morning she had delivered a son, stillborn. When told that her ticket to the throne lay cold and lifeless, Henriette plunged into a deep despair. For weeks she lay listless in her bed. She had come close, so very close. The duc de Sully, however, painfully aware of Henri's foolish promise, thought the bolt of lightning had been sent by God to prevent them all from falling into the nasty clutches of Queen Henriette.

The king, relieved at the outcome, became a caring and consoling lover. Henriette, finally accepting she would never be queen, hardened into an even more coldly calculating courtesan, demanding at least the perks of a throne. When she recovered, she visited Henri in Lyons "in an uncovered litter as if she were the Queen," one witness reported.[48] The English ambassador wrote, "The King hath brought his mistress hither whom he doth embrace with more kindness than kings commonly do their wives, and doth honor with as much respect as if she were his queen."[49]

On November 3, 1600, Marie de Medici was welcomed into the port of Marseilles as queen of France. The bride was rather long in the tooth at the advanced age of twenty-six, and inclined toward heaviness. She boasted a sterling virtue, a queenly bearing, and a calm temperament. The French people approved of her dignified appearance. Her heaviness made her appear queenly in her thick, jewel-encrusted robes. Her lethargy seemed regal. One duchess wrote of the new queen, "Marie de Medici has large eyes, a full round face. . . . Her skin is dark but clear. . . . she is inclined to be a little heavy. There is a great kindness in her face but," she added darkly, recalling the beauty of the king's dead mistress, "there is nothing that even approaches Gabrielle d'Estrées."[50]

"I have been deceived! She is not beautiful!" the groom grumbled to a friend after meeting Marie.[51] Henri IV had been duped by the old portrait trick and was expecting a slender beauty with elegant features, not this heavy woman with a flat farmer's face. He managed to fulfill his dynastic duties, however, and made Marie pregnant on his honeymoon. Soon after, Henri left Marie—to attend to urgent state business, he said— and visited Henriette, whom he also made pregnant. When Marie made her official entrance into Paris alone, she was surprised at the lack of pomp. Worse, when she arrived at the Louvre she found the queen's apartments dark and empty. The king had forgotten to arrange for her furniture.

Conniving Henriette badgered Henri into having her presented to the queen as soon as possible, as such a presentation would raise Henriette's prestige at court. Ladies had to be presented by a noblewoman of good standing, and the unfortunate duchesse de Nemours was given the job, knowing the new queen would never forgive her. Trembling, the duchess introduced

Henriette. Though Marie's French was not yet perfect, she had already heard the name and its unpleasant associations. Henri, with his soldier's frankness, added brusquely, "This is my mistress who now wishes to be your servant."[52] This statement only poured salt on the wound of the poor bride clutching to the last vestiges of her dignity.

Simmering with resentment at the interloper, Henriette bowed to the queen, but not low enough, so Henri shoved her head down farther. She showed great distaste when kissing the hem of Marie's gown. The Tuscan ambassador, in his report to Marie's uncle, the grand duke, reported every detail of the historic event. He wrote proudly of Marie's royal composure, "The Queen received her in the usual manner and treated her thus throughout the evening without showing any displeasure."[53]

But the mask of learned dignity covered an anguished heart. Marie's Italian blood boiled at the insult. Quick where Marie was slow, lithe where Marie was clumsy, Henriette used every trick possible to punish the woman who had usurped what she considered to be her rightful place. One courtier wrote, "The Marquise, believing herself to have all kinds of power over the King, and availing herself as usual of her vivacity and the sharp barbs of her words, so pricked and offended the Queen time after time that at first coldness, then indignation and anger formed between them, and the King was constrained to separate them in order to maintain peace on both sides."[54]

Henriette loved to mimic the queen's Italian accent and clumsy French, as well as her awkward gait. Henri and his courtiers laughed heartily at these performances, which got back to Marie and irked her greatly. Henriette, referring to Marie's merchant ancestors, called her "the fat Florentine banker." The queen called Henriette "the King's whore."[55]

As the months passed, Queen Marie, fat and pregnant, watched her husband and his mistress, also fat and pregnant, laugh and flirt with each other. Silent, angry, unable to understand their double entendres, their rapid exchanges of wit, Marie brooded. A little more than nine months after their wedding night, she fulfilled her primary duty and presented Henri, now a tired and aging forty-eight, with an heir. Marie basked in her husband's praise. For four weeks, her stock was far higher than Henriette's, and she loved it.

But then Henriette, too, gave birth to a boy, dimming some of the luster of the queen's accomplishment. Despite the national outpouring of love and respect for Marie's timely gift of a prince and heir, Marie could clearly see that even the birth of a son could not make her husband love her. His attraction to Henriette was too strong. Marie's thwarted love twisted into black pain, lashed out in red anger.

Marie was delighted to receive a packet of Henriette's love letters to a courtier in which she made fun of her lover the king. The queen, hiding a smile of triumph, delivered the letters to her husband. He grew red and trembled with rage as he read them. He then sent a messenger to arrest Henriette for treason and strip her of all her privileges. But cunning Henriette convinced Henri that the letters were a clever forgery, probably manufactured at the instigation of Queen Marie herself. Henriette deigned to forgive him for the whopping sum of six thousand pounds. Now the king was furious at his wife for presenting him with such outrageous forgeries.

After this episode Marie lost her husband's love entirely. The marriage, which was to produce a total of five children that lived to adulthood, was reduced to violent arguments, and copulation as a political duty. After Henriette's rehabilitation, the English ambassador reported that the queen "kept herself retired in her chamber, either spending the whole day in bed, in tears and lamentations, or if she did rise, yet would not be persuaded to put on other clothes but those of her bed chamber. She refused to open the door to the King when he knocked."[56]

In 1602 Marie gave birth to a princess, and true to form, Henriette gave birth to a daughter shortly thereafter. Upon hearing the news, the queen's fury knew no bounds. The duc de Sully witnessed the queen scratching the king's face in an argument. When she raised her arm to strike her husband, the duke grabbed it to prevent the blow.

Henri confessed, "I receive from my wife neither companionship nor gaiety nor consolation, she either cannot or will not show me any kindness or pleasant conversation, neither will she accommodate herself to my moods and disposition. Instead, she shows such a cold and disdainful expression when I come in and go to kiss and embrace her and laugh a little with her, that I am forced to leave her in vexation and go look for my relaxation elsewhere."[57]

Henriette finally fell from Henri's favor in 1608 after traitorous dealings with the Spanish, whom she hoped would topple Henri and place her royal bastard on the throne. Rejected by the king, Henriette waited on the sidelines for an eventual recall. But when Henri was assassinated in 1610, the new regent of France, Queen Marie de Medici, could freely indulge her hatred of Henriette, and exiled her from court. Here the former favorite took out her frustrations in food and grew tremendously fat. Henriette lived twenty-three years after Henri's death, until 1633, when she died at the age of about fifty-five, alone and unmourned.

FOUR

CUCKOLD TO THE KING— THE MISTRESS'S HUSBAND

*You cannot pluck roses without fear of thorns
Nor enjoy a fair wife without danger of horns.*

—BENJAMIN FRANKLIN

❋

IN MANY CASES THE TRADITIONAL LOVE TRIANGLE—KING, queen, and mistress—was in fact a love quadrangle. Many of the royal mistresses were married, either before their liaisons with the king or during the affair at the behest of the monarch himself. A perfect contradiction in light of our twenty-first-century morality, marriage was thought to pull a veil of respectability over a royal mistress. A husband's tacit approval gave legitimacy to an illicit relationship. Moreover, a pregnant unmarried woman was automatically a focus of social stigma. Even if the pregnant royal mistress had not slept with her husband in years, she was—after all—married.

Some kings, however, notably Louis XIV and his great-grandson Louis XV, fretted about committing a double adultery and, from the standpoint of mortal sin, would have preferred unmarried mistresses, thereby halving their carnal transgressions. Louis XIV was content with single Louise de La Vallière for seven years—during which time she scandalously provided him with four children. When he fell for the very married Athénaïs de Montespan—who provided him with seven—he grew more worried about the salvation of his soul. So worried, in fact, that after the queen died he secretly married the formidable old virgin Madame de Maintenon to enjoy sex without guilt.

In the footsteps of his great-grandfather, Louis XV, who didn't seem horribly concerned about betraying his own wife, suffered for the sin of bedding another man's wife, Madame de Pompadour. His pangs of conscience were especially keen during Lent, the time to weigh one's trespasses throughout the preceding year.

But Louis had no qualms about marrying off his final mistress, the ravishing prostitute Jeanne Becu, to an impoverished nobleman to raise her status. Louis had the taverns and brothels of France searched for her pimp's brother, the comte du Barry. At the altar, the man was given a bag of gold, a pension for life, and a horse to ride away on. This respectable married woman, now a countess, could be presented at court despite the sneers behind painted fans.

The phony marriage would come back to haunt the lovers, however. Four years later, in 1773, the ailing and now widowed monarch considered marrying his favorite and so dying in a state of sanctified grace as had his great-grandfather Louis XIV with Madame de Maintenon. For her part, Madame du Barry was ecstatic. After suffering constant humiliation at court, she saw herself as queen of France before whom all her enemies would have to scrape and bow. But then it was remembered that she had a husband of sorts, drinking somewhere, who about that time sent word to the king that he would make an embarrassing appearance at Versailles unless sufficiently reimbursed. He was speedily paid off with several thousand livres and made a knight of the Order of St. Louis—a medal given for outstanding merit, though in this case outstanding blackmail. All thoughts of marriage were dropped.

In the tenth century B.C., King David rid himself of Bathsheba's inconvenient husband Uriah the Hittite by sending him into the front lines of battle. By the seventeenth century, kings had adopted a slightly more humane solution—exiling the husband to foreign parts under the cover of a diplomatic mission. Such was the case of Roger Palmer, the husband of Charles II's Barbara, Lady Castlemaine. Roger trudged grudgingly about the courts of Europe on Charles's orders. He was yanked back whenever Barbara was about to give birth to a royal bastard, and he was expected to hover solicitously until after the birth as if the child were his.

Two centuries later Nicholas von Kiss, the dashing but ineffectual husband of Katharina Schratt, mistress of emperor Franz Josef of Austria, was invited by the emperor to join the diplomatic service—a request he dare not refuse. When Nicholas complained of boredom in one locale, Katharina would ask the emperor to transfer him to another. Nicholas periodically visited his wife in Vienna to stuff his pockets with her money before going abroad once more.

THE REWARDS OF COMPLIANCE

In 1855 the compliant husband of Napoleon III's mistress Virginie di Castiglione summed up the traditional role of king's cuckold when he said, "I am a model husband. I never see or hear anything."[1] And indeed, many a man was willing to lay down his wife for the good of his country.

In the 1670s, the princesse de Soubise enjoyed a brief liaison with Louis XIV with the aid of her husband the prince. One evening the king's valet, Bontemps, knocked on the princess's apartment door to summon her to her rendezvous with the king. All the while, the prince pretended to snore loudly. Although the affair was brief, the prince found himself the object of uproarious ridicule at court. But the betrayed husband laughed at courtiers' disdain all the way to the bank. "Never was so prodigious a family fortune founded so speedily," wrote the duc de Saint-Simon.[2] The Hôtel de Soubise became the grandest house in Paris and today serves as the home of the French national archives. It is clear why so many courtiers encouraged their wives to sleep with the king—the wages of sin were high.

In the 1820s King George IV flirted with his mistress Lady Conyngham in the presence of her obliging husband. The king held her hand beneath the table and never drank from his glass unless he touched her glass with it first. He had the appalling habit of taking snuff from her generous bosom. During these displays of affection Lord Conyngham often sat next to the happy couple, quite contentedly drinking. He must have relished the riches his family reaped so quickly. The king nominated this compliant gentleman as lord chamberlain of the household, a nomination that was quickly shot down by his morally outraged cabinet.

The fate of Polish count Anastase Walewski—who pushed his wife Maria into the eager arms of Napoleon Bonaparte—was not as happy. The wealthy count had married Maria when she was sixteen and he sixty-eight. It was an excellent bargain for the bride's family, whose fortunes had recently failed as the result of war and partition. Poland was no longer a sovereign nation, having lost its territory starting in 1786 to Russia, Prussia, and Austria, in a kind of international gang rape.

But Maria's young heart withered in the old man's arms. On the altar of self-immolation, Maria plaintively wrote to a friend, "He is kind. He paid all of my mother's farm debts. . . . I must be a good wife to him. . . . Does one ever get *all* one wants in this life?"[3]

The count, who had been surprisingly youthful for his years, aged quickly after the wedding. He grew querulous, criticizing his wife's appearance and behavior and throwing jealous scenes when men spoke to her. Yet her socially ambitious husband dragged Maria to balls and dinner parties, where her beauty constantly attracted admirers. In the social whirl of scheming women, Maria's genuine modesty was perhaps her greatest asset—greater even than her long blonde hair, her large, innocent blue eyes, and her flawless white complexion.

In December 1806, Napoleon and the French army entered Warsaw and were welcomed with open arms by an adoring populace. The Poles were convinced that Napoleon would liberate them from foreign occupation and re-create Poland as a free and sovereign nation. Tens of thousands of young Poles flocked to join the imperial armies, to advance, with their blood, the debt Napoleon would owe Poland and would undoubtedly repay.

In January 1807, Napoleon gave a brilliant ball for Warsaw society. Count Anastase Walewski and his young wife were invited. Maria was extremely nervous about meeting her hero, the man she was convinced would save Poland. She asked her husband's permission to stay home. Not only did he refuse, but he instructed her to wear her most beautiful gown and ordered his family's diamond and sapphire necklace to be brought in from their country estate. The count, though peevishly jealous of the male attention his wife's beauty aroused, wanted to show her off to the emperor.

Wearing a narrow gown of cornflower blue to match her eyes, a silver cord twisted under the high waist, Maria was presented to Napoleon. He looked at her closely and silently passed on. Afterward, he turned to Minister Talleyrand and uttered those ancient, fateful words which have changed so many women's lives: "Who is she?"[4]

Maria went home that evening pleased to have met her hero and thought nothing more of it. Everyone but Maria knew that the Conqueror of Europe was dazzled by her beauty, and that his comment "There are many beautiful women in Warsaw" referred to Maria.[5]

A few days later at the foreign minister's ball, Napoleon wasted no time in singling Maria out and dancing with her. He was seen to squeeze her hand after the dance and to watch her closely from across the room. Indeed, it seemed as if Napoleon did nothing else but stare at Maria the entire night.

The poor woman suddenly became the chief object of interest at the ball. Hundreds of pairs of aristocratic lips whispered about her behind fans. Hundreds of pairs of hawklike eyes fastened on her. Maria was humiliated by all the attention, but her husband preened himself like a vain peacock. Finally she had done something to make him proud.

The following day Marshal Duroc, chief of the imperial household, called on Maria with a bouquet of flowers and a letter fastened with the imperial green seals. It said, "I saw no one but you, I admired only you; I want no one but you; I beg you to reply promptly to calm my ardor and my impatience. Napoleon."[6]

Stunned, Maria told the marshal there would be no reply. That evening came another bouquet and another letter. This one read, "Did I displease you, Madame? Your interest in me seems to have waned, while mine is growing every moment. . . . You have destroyed my peace. . . . I beg you to give a little joy to my poor heart, so ready to adore you. Is it so difficult to send a reply? You owe me two. Napole."[7] Again, Maria declined to send a reply.

Soon after, a third missive arrived in which Napoleon threw his heart at her feet and cleverly added, "Oh come, come . . . all your desires will be granted. *Your country will be so much dearer to me* if you take pity on my poor heart."[8]

The last was a cunning ruse, for it spoke to patriotic Maria in a language she heard. Poland. She could use her influence with the Great Man to save Poland. What Maria did not know was Napoleon's opinion of women meddling in politics. "States are lost as soon as women interfere in public affairs," he said. ". . . If a woman were to advocate some political move, that would seem to me sufficient reason for taking the opposite course."[9] In a message to his army he wrote, "How unhappy are those princes who, in political matters, allow themselves to be guided by women."[10]

Soon everyone in Warsaw knew of Napoleon's infatuation with Maria. Many guests dropped by her house to offer advice. Society ladies offered unwanted congratulations on Maria's conquest, even congratulated her husband. Her oldest brother, Benedict, who had already served ten years with the French army, regarded it as her patriotic duty to have sex with the emperor. The count felt honored that Napoleon wanted to make love to his wife and prodded her to visit him as he requested.

Indeed, it seemed everyone wanted Maria to sleep with Napoleon except Maria. They chided her: What would happen if the emperor, spurned by Maria, turned against Poland as well? It would be Maria's fault! And so trembling Maria, pushed into the carriage by her insistent husband, visited Napoleon in his suite at Warsaw Castle. The first night he talked with her for four hours and nothing more. The second night she became "the unwilling victim of his passion," she wrote a decade later in her memoirs, which sounds alarmingly like rape.[11] But tenderness must have come afterward, for he awakened a sexuality in Maria that she had never known with a sick and aging husband.

The old count had set in motion a love affair that he could not halt. Maria fell in love with Napoleon, and her gratitude to her husband dried up when he forced her into another man's arms. They separated and eventually divorced. Maria fell deeply in love with Napoleon and for the three years of their torrid love affair followed him around Europe on campaign. But when she became pregnant with his child, Napoleon—who had always believed he was sterile—realized he could sire a prince and heir. He divorced the barren Josephine, dumped the heartbroken Maria, and married an eighteen-year-old Austrian princess.

Maria's sacrifice on behalf of her beloved nation was as doomed as her love affair with the emperor had been. Even as Napoleon was promising her he would restore Poland, he had instructed his ambassador to Russia to tell the czar, "His Majesty was prepared to see the words Poland and Polish people disappear from all current political transactions," and "would agree that the kingdom of Poland would *never* be restored."[12]

Doubly betrayed by Napoleon, Maria did not hesitate to visit him in his disgrace and exile on the island of Elba. Bringing their five-year-old son and all her jewels to help him with his financial difficulties, she arrived prepared to stay as his companion. But Napoleon, fearing that scandal would prevent his wife, Empress Maria Louisa, and their son from joining him, sent

Maria packing after only three days. Maria and all of Europe knew that the empress was having an affair with a handsome equerry in Vienna and would never trade in her lavish lifestyle for exile on a rock. Not wishing to disillusion Napoleon, Maria kept her peace and boarded the ship, never to see him again.

LONG-SUFFERING ACCEPTANCE

Not every husband jumped for joy when the king ogled his wife. In 1716, the new mistress of Philippe d'Orléans, regent of France, bore an inconvenient accessory—a loving and jealous husband. While Marie-Madeleine de Parabère reveled in the expensive jewels the regent gave her and ached to wear them, she needed to come up with an explanation for her husband as to how she had obtained them.

Madame de Parabère told her husband that some friends in financial embarrassment wanted to sell the items at a ridiculously low price. Her generous spouse immediately gave her the money to buy them. When she displayed her glittering gems proudly in public and courtiers asked her where she had obtained them, she replied that her kind husband had bought them for her. No one was fooled except her husband. Basking in his wife's seeming fidelity, Monsieur de Parabère replied that a husband should be generous to a wife who loved no one but himself. The room erupted into guffaws of laughter. Monsieur de Parabère considerately died afterward, sparing his wife traumatic scenes when he would inevitably discover the truth. Relieved of this burden, Madame de Parabère could flaunt the regent's gifts more freely.

But most married royal mistresses did not have husbands who thoughtfully provided them with the freedoms of an early widowhood. In the 1740s Madame de Pompadour was forced to unharness herself from an adoring husband when she became the mistress of Louis XV. Born Jeanne Poisson, she had married—rather above her station—a wealthy and handsome bourgeois named Le Normant d'Etioles. Monsieur d'Etioles was the nephew of Le Normant de Tournehem, Jeanne's mother's lover, who was also presumed to be Jeanne's father. Monsieur d'Etioles idolized his bride and gave her a large allowance to beautify herself and their homes, and to secure her social position, which had been dimmed by her mother's shady past.

Since childhood, Madame d'Etioles's sole ambition had been to become the king's mistress. It is likely that her marriage to Monsieur d'Etioles fulfilled a dual purpose—to enjoy the fruits of improved social status, and to use that status as a springboard to meet the king. While the pretty young wife had many admirers, she took no lovers, a rare phenomenon in eighteenth-century Paris. She was known to remark at lively dinner parties that the king alone could make her unfaithful to her husband. The room would always ring with laughter at this remark, her husband laughing loudest of all. Little did he know the cold truth that lurked behind the witticism and the pain it would cause him.

The d'Etioles had been married four years when Jeanne achieved her desire of meeting—and winning—the king. Monsieur de Tournehem occupied the position of farmer-general—a wealthy tax collector—and, showing more loyalty to his presumed daughter Jeanne than to his nephew, quickly packed her husband off on a long tour of the provinces. When Monsieur d'Etioles returned some two months later, his uncle broke the unwelcome news that his pretty wife had become the king's mistress. Monsieur d'Etioles fainted from the shock.

When he came to, he reacted so violently that his uncle feared he would try to kill himself and had all guns removed from the house. Monsieur d'Etioles threatened to go to Versailles to reclaim his wife. His uncle pointed out the folly of such a venture.

Meanwhile, Madame d'Etioles was using her husband's violent reaction to urge the king to commit, to make her the official *maîtresse-en-titre*. Fed up with being smuggled into side doors and up secret stairs at night, she wanted her position recognized; she wanted to taste the power, to enjoy the luxuries of Versailles in all their daylight splendor. Madame d'Etioles told the king that she was in danger of an insanely jealous husband and only he could protect her. She wept copious shimmering tears into a silken handkerchief. Louis, shaken, was won over by her tears and assented to all her demands. As a sign of accepting her as *maîtresse-en-titre,* he created her the marquise de Pompadour.

Monsieur d'Etioles was sent on a business trip to Provence in the hopes that a change of scene would dispel his grief. In 1747 the king rewarded Monsieur d'Etioles for his grudging acquiescence by giving him his uncle's newly vacated post of farmer-general, a position that brought him the enormous income of four hundred thousand livres a year. He took as mistress a singer from the opera, Mademoiselle Raime, and lived with her in a marriage-type relationship for many years, bringing several children into the world. When offered the post of French ambassador to Constantinople, he turned it down because he would not be allowed to bring his mistress and their children and, as long as Madame de Pompadour was alive, could not remarry.

In 1756 Madame de Pompadour ached for the respectability of becoming a lady-in-waiting to the queen, but her romance with the king, which had opened up such glorious possibilities, now stood in her way. The queen's ladies were required to take Holy Communion daily, but the church forbade Madame de Pompadour the sacraments because of her previous adulterous relationship with the king and her continued estrangement from her husband. Although she had not slept with Louis for years, she was still banned from the altar. Madame de Pompadour, who had no wish to reconcile with her husband but now needed to reconcile herself with the church, followed her confessor's instructions and wrote Monsieur d'Etioles a letter requesting him to take her back. "Already my sin has ceased," she explained, "and all that is necessary is to end the appearance of it—something which I ardently desire. I am resolved by my future conduct to atone for my past wrongs. Take me back; you will find me anxious to edify the world by the harmony of our life as much as I scandalized it by leaving you."[13] This conscious-stricken missive was accompanied by another message informing Monsieur d'Etioles that the king would be quite irritated if he accepted Madame de Pompadour's offer.

But Monsieur d'Etioles had no inclination whatsoever to take back the wife who had so publicly shamed him. "I have received, Madame, your letter in which you inform me of your determination to return to me and your desire to surrender yourself to God," he replied. "I cannot but admire such a resolution. I can well understand that it would be very embarrassing for you to see me, and you must agree that my feelings would be the same. Your presence can only intensify painful memories. Therefore, the best course for us is to live apart. No matter how much dissatisfaction you have caused me, I believe that you are concerned for my honor, and I should regard it as compromised if I received you in my house and lived with you as my wife. You are aware that time cannot alter what honor demands."[14]

Breathing a huge sigh of relief, Madame de Pompadour showed her husband's letter to an obliging priest, and was purified of her carnal sins and allowed to take the holy sacraments. Reconciled with the Church, she was now permitted to fulfill her dream of becoming lady-in-waiting to the queen.

Monsieur d'Etioles's story had a happy ending. When Madame de Pompadour died at forty-two, her spurned husband married Mademoiselle Raime, legitimizing their children, and they lived happily for many years. He survived the Revolution and died at the age of eighty-three in 1800.

Some husbands who were initially horrified at the loss of their wives to the king became quickly reconciled. Augustus the Strong, elector of Saxony, had such good fortune with the husbands of several of his mistresses. Tall, handsome, his brute strength only partially tempered by the refinements of the time, Augustus had become elector in 1694 at the age of twenty-four. He dutifully married a princess and sired an heir, but his restless nature compelled him to continue the travels he had enjoyed before he mounted the throne. A crowned king wandering across Europe was a rarity in those days, and the itinerant monarch found throngs of willing noblewomen throwing themselves into his bed when he visited foreign courts.

In Vienna, at the court of the Holy Roman Emperor Joseph I, Augustus fell in love with Madame d'Esterle, whose resistance was conquered by the gift of a pair of earrings worth 40,000 florins. Thrilled with such valuable proof of royal desire, Madame d'Esterle threw caution to the winds and ended up seducing the king rather than the other way around. Soon after, her husband entered her bedroom one morning to find his wife asleep, with the thick curly head of the king of Saxony resting on her naked breast. The distraught husband cried out, "O thou perfidious wretch!"[15] As the shaken king jumped out of bed and grabbed his sword, Monsieur d'Esterle ran away. Dressing hastily, Augustus sent his mistress to the inviolable home of his envoy to Vienna, clutching a case full of her jewels.

Nearly out of his mind, Monsieur d'Esterle raced to the emperor's antechamber, where courtiers dallied, and poured out his shame and rage to his friends. But the courtiers could not agree that Monsieur d'Esterle had a right to be angry. According to Augustus's biographer, "His friends afforded him what comfort they were capable of, in telling him that he had no reason to be so highly afflicted at so trifling a matter. They quoted instances from the fiction of the poets and both ancient and modern history."[16]

His friends pointed out that according to ancient myth, Amphitryon was furious at discovering his wife was having an affair. But when he learned that his rival was Jupiter, king of the gods, he calmed down instantly. They reminded him that many noble Romans gave their wives for the emperors' use. When Monsieur d'Esterle replied that his wife had slept with neither a god nor his own sovereign, the Austrian ambassador to Rome advised him, "That you may imitate the examples of those husbands we mentioned to you, enter into the Elector of Saxony's service; and he may lie with your wife without your being obstructed by any person on that account."[17]

The cuckolded husband felt so much better at the thought of lending his wife to Jupiter that he immediately wrote the elector seeking employment. Confused at such a turn of events, Augustus asked Madame d'Esterle her opinion. She was horrified at the idea of her husband returning with the elector to his court, always being in close proximity to them and in position to make trouble. She advised the elector instead to grant her husband a generous pension upon several conditions which would bestow upon her both freedom and respectability. Her husband would renounce all his marital rights, but give his name to any royal bastards his wife might bear. In return for his annual stipend, the cuckold rigorously observed the terms of this contract.

Another husband who did not resist lending his wife to Jupiter was Edward Langtry, whose brilliant wife, Lillie, became the first official mistress of Edward, Prince of Wales, in 1877. Edward Langtry trailed in Lillie's shining wake as she sailed to fame and glory, never able to catch up. When Lillie sparkled at a party, Edward sat sullenly in the corner drinking.

Edward never publicly showed any resentment toward the Prince of Wales, but he did sometimes vent his frustrations in sudden violent rages at his wife. One day, Lillie and Edward were guests along with the prince at the home of Lord Malmesbury. She wrote her royal lover a suggestive letter, which her husband deciphered by holding her blotting paper up to a mirror. Edward was so angry he reduced the normally tough Lillie to a puddle of tears. The whole house heard their argument. Lord Malmesbury, too, was furious—at the servants for not changing the blotting paper every day in all the guest rooms as they had been instructed, to prevent just such an inconvenience.

After three years as royal mistress, Lillie lost her position to actress Sarah Bernhardt, who took London, and the Prince of Wales, by storm. Lillie turned her attentions to the German prince Louis Battenburg and soon became pregnant. The Prince of Wales, still fond of Lillie, arranged for her to give birth in France, away from prying eyes. Even Edward Langtry was unaware that his wife had had a child.

Lillie, separated now from her nearly bankrupt husband, found herself cut off from the prince's financial largesse. To support herself and her daughter, she decided to emulate her rival Sarah Bernhardt and earn her living on the stage. Her notoriety as the prince's former mistress ensured good box-office receipts, and the Prince and Princess of Wales pointedly attended her London plays. Traveling coast to coast in her own luxurious ten-room railway car, she performed throughout the

United States for six years and met with huge success in the mining towns of the Wild West.

Edward, grasping at some memory of love, refused to divorce Lillie despite her pleas, and without the consent of both parties the British courts refused to grant the divorce. Because American courts were more flexible, Lillie became an American citizen to rid herself of her humiliating husband. Having lost his wife to a prince and a subsequent dazzling career, Edward sank into an irretrievable pit of alcoholism and depression. Lillie, though thrilled to be freed of him, faithfully sent him money four times a year until the day he died.

THE PENALTIES OF DEFIANCE

While some husbands leaped for joy as their monarchs bedded their wives, and others suffered dutifully, a few had the backbone to stand up to such adulterous intrusions. One of the earliest records of such defiance occurred during the reign of England's King John of Magna Carta fame (1167–1216). One Eustace de Vesci, an aristocrat, was hated by King John "because he had placed a common woman instead of his wife in the royal bed."[18]

Thirteenth-century records such as this often offer us more questions than answers. Let us, however, imagine King John rutting joyously in the inutterable darkness of a feudal four-poster with what he presumes is a beautiful virtuous noblewoman. And then, as the first cold fingers of dawn illumine the person in his bed, he finds to his chagrin a scullery maid or washerwoman.

In the 1520s, King François I went to a lady's bedchamber to find her husband waiting next to the bed, guarding his wife's honor with a sword. In a royal rage, the king informed the husband that if he harmed his wife he would lose his head. The king then kicked the unfortunate man out of the room and climbed into bed with his wife.

Henri IV of France suffered resistance from not one, but two of his mistresses' stubborn husbands. When Gabrielle d'Estrées gave him a son, Henri was afraid that her aged husband Nicolas d'Amerval could claim paternity and remove the boy from his mother. Henri decided to press for a divorce. One of the few reasons the Catholic Church would grant a divorce was in the case of the husband's impotence.

Poor d'Amerval found himself in a highly unenviable position. Admitting impotence—unpleasant for a man even in our own day—was almost a fate worse than death in the sixteenth century. On the other hand, angering the king could jeopardize his property and even his life if Henri wanted to have this inconvenient little man assassinated. D'Amerval testified, "To obey the King and in fear of my life, I am about to consent to the dissolution of my marriage with the Dame d'Estrées. . . . I declare and protest before God that if the dissolution be ordered and brought to pass, it will be done by force, against my will, and only out of respect for the King, seeing that the assertion, confession, and declaration that I am impotent and incapable is untrue."[19] Indeed, d'Amerval had sired no less than fourteen children with his first wife.

A few days into the proceeding, d'Amerval suddenly reversed his position and admitted he was indeed impotent. The reason behind his reversal is not known. Henri was not known to threaten but may have bribed. D'Amerval's servants were called as additional witnesses and testified that his sheets were never stained. The divorce was granted.

After Gabrielle's death in 1599, and his subsequent unhappy marriage to Marie de Medici the following year, Henri had an even tougher time with a cuckolded husband when he fell in love with the beautiful Charlotte de Montmorency in 1609. The ardor of the ever-romantic monarch was not dampened by his fifty-four years, nor by the difference in ages; the object of his desires was fourteen and had recently stopped playing with dolls. Charlotte was engaged to a virile and handsome young buck. The king broke the engagement and instructed her to marry the unthreatening prince de Condé, a weak and skinny soul thought to be a homosexual.

In May Charlotte celebrated her fifteenth birthday and was married to the prince de Condé in a glittering ceremony. The king was conspicuous by his absence but lavished princely gifts on the new bride. Unfortunately for Henri, the insignificant little groom was not as pliable as he had believed. The prince's pride was pricked by the sharp and public pain of being a royal cuckold. A month after the wedding, he requested the king's permission to retire with his wife to his estates. The answer was a firm no.

Enraged, Condé confronted the king and called him a tyrant. Henri threatened to stop the prince's pension if he left court without permission. Uncowed, the prince took his wife and fled. Henri disguised himself as a hunter—complete with a patch over one eye—and spied out the prince's estate hoping for a glimpse of his beloved. This romantic trick of disguise had been the stuff of legends in his younger years—crossing enemy lines to visit his mistress Gabrielle for a few precious hours—but was now seen as pitiful in an old roué. Charlotte, at any rate, did not appreciate it. While walking in the gardens she saw the king in his hunter's rags and began to scream at the top of her lungs until he ran away. Upon hearing of the king's visit, Condé realized he must take Charlotte out of France.

Soon thereafter, Henri received the news that the prince had fled with Charlotte to the safety of the Netherlands. Henri's adviser the duc de Sully reported, "When I came to the Louvre I found the King in the Queen's chamber, walking back and forth, with his head reclined and his hands folded behind his back." The king said, "Well, our man is gone and has carried all with him." He added, "I am lost."[20] Henri kept to his rooms for several days after this, locked in deep depression, seeing no one.

Meanwhile, Spain's Philip III, continuing his kingdom's tradition of stirring up trouble with France, assured the prince de Condé of Spain's support in his just struggle against the lascivious king. Philip offered Condé a home in Spain or, if he wished, in the sections of Italy under Spanish domination. Meanwhile, the pope—appealed to by Henri, Philip of Spain, and the prince de Condé, and unwilling to anger either Spain or France—attempted to play the peacemaker. For several months, European politics were roiled by Henri's infatuation with a fifteen-year-old girl and the stubborn refusal of her husband to deliver her up to his king.

As the weeks grew into months Henri's eagerness to reclaim Charlotte became an obsession. He wrote to his agent in Brussels, "I am so tortured by my anguish that I am only skin and bone. Everything bothers me; I avoid company, and if, in order to do justice to other people, I do let myself be drawn into some gathering, instead of cheering me, it only succeeds in deadening me."[21]

The envoy from the court of Spain wrote to his master, "I have been told that the King of France would give the Dauphin and all his other sons for the Princess de Condé which leads me to believe that he will risk everything for his love. His health is altered; he has lost sleep and some people are beginning to believe that he is starting to go mad. He who has so much loved society now remains alone for hours at a time, walking up and down in his melancholy."[22]

In March came an about-face. Charlotte's father sued the prince de Condé for a divorce from his daughter. Her husband agreed to the divorce, and Charlotte decided to return to France and become the king's mistress. Condé had grown weary of fighting the king of France, and perhaps Charlotte preferred a glittering life at court to a dull exile. But Henri's enemies were unwilling to permit such a prize as Charlotte to return to France. They refused her permission to travel. Henri declared war on them and raised an army.

But Henri was destined never to see his Charlotte again. On May 14, 1610, while sitting in his carriage with his counselors, Henri was stabbed in the chest by the madman Ravaillac and died moments later. Charlotte quickly returned to her husband with her tail between her legs and through abject self-abasement made amends with Henri's widow, Queen Marie, the new queen regent and now the most powerful person in France.

Some sixty years later, Henri's grandson, Louis XIV, also suffered the recriminations of a defiant husband. Athénaïs de Mortemart, who had been angling in vain for the position of Louis XIV's mistress, gave up the chase and married the marquis de Montespan in 1663. It was not an advantageous match for the bride, who was already the daughter of a marquis far wealthier than her husband. Dark and dashing, the marquis de Montespan's finer qualities were unaccompanied by good breeding or common sense. Soon after the wedding he spent his small fortune—and his wife's dowry—and ran headlong into debt.

The marquis was a soldier, enjoying to the full a seventeenth-century soldier's perquisites—looting, raping, and burning. He was on campaign months at a time, rarely going long periods without getting himself into scrapes. On one occasion he seduced a girl, dressed her in a man's uniform, and assigned her a position in the cavalry—until her family showed up with the local bailiff. Despite his long absences, his wife gave him two children in rapid succession, a girl in 1664 and a boy the following year. She quickly dumped both children on her husband's relatives so she could devote herself fully to the pleasures of court.

In 1666 her swashbuckler husband departed on a long campaign in the south of France. By this time, the marquis's garish charms must have worn thin on his polished wife. By 1667 she had succeeded in becoming the king's *maîtresse-en-titre*.

Though the marquis must surely have heard of his wife's exalted position as king's mistress, he at first made no noise about it. Perhaps he was eager to see what financial rewards and honors would come his way. When he returned to Versailles in 1668, he found his wife pregnant by the king. Worse, Madame de Montespan had, as one courtier put it, "in acquiring a taste for the King's caresses, developed a distaste for her husband's."[23]

The marquis reacted like the madman which he was commonly thought to be. He ranted and raved to anyone who would listen about the immorality of the king's affair with his wife—though many thought this newfound piety odd in a man known to have stormed convents to deflower girls. Some court ladies were so shocked at his language that they took to their beds with the vapors. He once entered his wife's apartments, soundly boxed her ears, and disappeared. Rumor had it that the marquis was frequenting the vilest whorehouses to catch a disease and pass it on through his wife to the king. If this was true, there was a major flaw in his logic. Madame de Montespan refused to sleep with her embarrassing husband.

One day the marquis drove up to the royal château of Saint-Germain in a carriage draped in black—mourning for his wife, he explained—decorated on the corners with four giant pairs of stags' horns, the traditional symbol of a cuckolded husband. The king had him imprisoned briefly and then exiled to his estates in the south. But the marquis was not finished. He invited all his friends and relatives to his castle for an elaborate mock funeral for Madame de Montespan, mourning her death "from coquetry and ambition."[24] He stood by the main door with his two small children, all clad in black, somberly accepting condolences on their loss.

Elizabeth Charlotte, duchesse d'Orléans, noted that the king could have bribed the marquis into complacence. "Monsieur de Montespan is an arrant opportunist," she wrote. "Had the King been willing to pay off more handsomely, he would have been reconciled."[25]

A year after the mock funeral, the crazed marquis attacked a convent to debauch a young girl who was hiding from him. In the scuffle, the girl, her mother, the father superior, and several peasants were hurt. Louis took this opportunity to send the marquis to prison, from which he escaped south into Spain, as the king had hoped. But at the pious Spanish court, the marquis complained so loudly of his wife's adultery with the king of France that Louis decided he had better pardon him and let him come back to France, where he could not damage his reputation internationally.

This brush with the law effectively subdued the marquis. He remained in the exile prescribed for him in the south of France, managing his estates, farms, and vineyards, hunting, gaming, drinking, and carousing. But Louis had his spies keep a careful eye on him. The king heard rumors that he intended to claim Athénaïs's numerous royal bastards as his own, born within their marriage, and carry all of them off to Spain, where even Louis's long reach would not be able to dislodge them. In 1670, when the marquis was permitted to visit Paris, Louis wrote to his minister Colbert, "Monsieur de Montespan is a madman. Keep a close watch on him . . . in order to deprive him of any pretext for lingering on in Paris. . . . I know that he has threatened to see his wife. . . . Get him out of Paris as quickly as possible."[26]

That same year, Athénaïs petitioned the courts to grant her a legal separation from her husband so that an abduction, or a claim to her children with the king, would be illegal. The court dragged its feet for four years despite, or perhaps because of, the king's insistence on a speedy resolution. These moral arbiters were not impressed with the king's profligate lifestyle. When in 1674 the decree did come through, it read, in part, that Madame de Montespan, "the high and mighty dame . . . does and shall continue to domicile separately from her husband. . . . he, furthermore, henceforward . . . [is] forbidden to frequent or haunt his lady."[27]

History must chuckle over the twists and turns of fate. By 1680 Madame de Montespan had lost her position as king's mistress but stubbornly remained at court. In 1691, at age fifty, she was banished from Versailles and languished at her estates in the country.

Chastened by her long exile, the former royal mistress was persuaded by her confessor to "ask pardon of her husband and submit herself into his hands," wrote the duc de Saint-Simon. "She wrote to him, by her own pen, in terms of total submission, offering to return to his roof if he deigned to receive her; and if not, to betake herself to whatever destination he should prescribe to her."[28]

Madame de Montespan was as fortunate with her request as Madame de Pompadour would be a century later. The duc de Saint-Simon reported, "She got credit for the gesture without having to suffer the consequences. Monsieur de Montespan sent back word that he wanted neither to receive her under his roof nor to make any prescription to her; neither to hear from or of her ever again in his life."[29]

Surely the most bitter pill that Madame de Montespan had to swallow was her husband's welcome at court in the late 1690s. While she continued to suffer humiliating exile, the marquis de

Montespan, his former recklessness tempered with age, moved to Versailles. The marquis's son with his wife, born in 1665, was favored by the king, and for the son's sake the father was welcomed. Court gossips clucked over the amusing spectacle of the marquis, who had created such a ruckus about his wife's affair, calmly playing cards with her two bastard daughters by the king. As Elizabeth Charlotte wrote, "Even he must have seen the humor of the situation because he would occasionally turn around and give a little smirk."[30]

FIVE

UNCEASING VIGILANCE— THE PRICE OF SUCCESS

They lay siege to the heart of a Prince as to a citadel.

—LOUIS XIV

❋

UNLIKE THE QUEEN, WHOSE POSITION WAS CAST IN STONE, the mistress's was made of far flimsier stuff. There would be no peace for her, no rest. Having obtained the great prize, the new mistress could not sit back and enjoy her rewards. She could not look around her magnificent rooms with satisfaction, or smile contentedly as she toyed with her glittering jewelry—not if it meant letting her guard down for a moment.

"Every woman was born with the ambition to become the King's Favorite," wrote Primi Visconti, an Italian fortune-teller who lived at Louis XIV's court.[1] There were hundreds, perhaps thousands, of women hoping to attain the position, which meant toppling the current *maîtresse-en-titre*, even as she had unseated her predecessor. Retaining the position usually took more effort than winning it. In fact, the position of royal mistress was like a marathon where the finish line kept moving.

To defend her turf, the *maîtresse-en-titre* kept an unblinking eye on pretty women attempting to gain the king's attention. Prostitutes, chambermaids, and the like had no hope of rising to the lofty position of royal mistress and therefore posed no threat. Though these minor infidelities might hurt, the *maîtresse-en-titre* had to pretend that they were too insignificant for her to notice. Some royal mistresses even procured lower-class women for the king to distract his attention from the real menace of beautiful noblewomen.

But when a smiling countess insinuated her way into the king's company, the savvy royal mistress would call in her troops. She had a bevy of friendly courtiers and well-paid servants ready to whisper to the king that the woman in question had a venereal disease, a greedy family, or total lack of discretion. Such whispers usually shrank the size of the king's interest.

Most of the mistress's work to seek and destroy her enemies had to be conducted behind the king's back. The mistress could not afford to degenerate into a nagging jealous wife. The monarch already had one of those whom he could not get rid of. But a nagging jealous mistress could be banished at a snap of the king's fingers.

"There is the scent of fresh meat," wrote Madame de Sévigné to her daughter with acidic candor.[2] When the royal eye wandered, as it did with alarming frequency, there was great speculation as to whether the object of kingly desires would prove a meaningless flirtation or if she would completely replace the existing power structure at court. Whatever the king's decision, there was always celebration on the winning side. In 1677 Madame de Sévigné wrote of yet another victory of ten-year veteran Madame de Montespan over fleeting rivals for the affections of Louis XIV.

"Ah, my daughter, what a triumph at Versailles!" Madame de Sévigné gushed. "What pride redoubled! What a solid reestablishment of favor! . . . There is evidence of added zest in the relation—all the sweeter, now, after lovers' quarrels and reconciliations. What a reaffirmation of possession! I spent an hour in her—Madame de Montespan's—chamber . . . the very air charged with joy and prosperity!"[3]

Royal mistresses maneuvered adeptly in an environment rife with intrigue, where the fundamental human matters of life and death and love meant little compared to the crumbs of success or specks of failure at court. To courtiers a little nod from the king in passing spelled exultant victory, the lack of a nod humiliating defeat. The court was a world of twisted values, strange honor, and disgraces incomprehensible to later generations.

In 1671 François Vatel, the chief butler for the prince de Condé, was instructed to prepare a lavish feast for Louis XIV. Before the royal visit, Vatel hadn't slept for twelve nights running after he had been two roasts short of a full banquet for hundreds. "I have lost my honor," he said to a friend who had noticed his disquiet. "This is a disgrace which is more than I can bear."[4] Then the next morning, when his order of fish did not arrive at the expected time to prepare for the king's feast, Vatel ran himself through with his sword. The cart that took his body to the parish church was passed on the road by the cart delivering the fish.

Just as exquisite satins and fine lace hid the reeking flea-bitten bodies of courtiers, so did warm smiles and polite words conceal the razor-sharp weapons brandished on the battlefield of the court. Women, encased in the deceiving armor of beauty and charm, were ready to wreak the most ruthless vengeance against rivals, and all who strode smiling down the gilded halls had fear stabbing at their hearts.

Some courtiers, at least, were authentic about their inauthenticity. One wrote, "It is a country where the joys are visible but false, and the sorrows are hidden but real."[5] And a visitor to Versailles remarked, "A genuine sentiment is so rare, that when I leave Versailles, I sometimes stand still in the street to see a dog gnaw a bone."[6]

The royal mistress who went to the greatest lengths to obtain and then retain her position against rivals was Athénaïs de Montespan. Ravishingly beautiful, venomously cunning, Madame de Montespan hoped for several years to replace Louis XIV's *maîtresse-en-titre* Louise de La Vallière. But the king was unmoved by Madame de Montespan's flirtation. "She tries hard," he told his brother, "but I'm not interested."[7] In 1667, hoping to break up the relationship, Madame de Montespan visited a witch for assistance.

La Voisin, as she was called, looked much older than her thirty-five years. She lived in a dark and crumbling house on the outskirts of Paris, surrounded by a large, unkempt garden. Garbed in flowing robes embroidered with ancient symbols, La Voisin, along with her colleagues, performed magic tricks, read palms and tarot cards, cast horoscopes, babbled in tongues, and held séances for a steep fee.

Her more innocuous services included offering lotions to beautify the skin and spells to increase breast size or firm up sagging thighs. Her more sinister services included sticking pins in dolls to incapacitate and kill an enemy, performing abortions, providing poison to slip to annoying husbands, and celebrating Black Masses with a dead baby's blood while preparing her magic potions. For years the carriages of the rich and famous lined up outside her house as her patrons vied with each other for her services, offering her rich rewards. But Madame de Montespan had no need of potions to improve her breasts or thighs. She wanted the king to forsake Louise and fall in love with her.

Louise de La Vallière was an unlikely object of black magic. Extremely religious, she came from a noble but obscure family and by a stroke of good fortune, found herself at Versailles and soon after in the young king's arms. The abbé de Choisy reported that Louise "had an exquisite complexion, blond hair, blue eyes, a sweet smile . . . an expression once tender and modest."[8] Though all agreed she was a lovely girl, tenderness and modesty did not fare well on the bloody battlefield of Versailles, a court where a healthy slathering of etiquette and a splash of perfume barely disguised savage ambition and vicious greed.

After five years as royal mistress, Louise sensed Louis was growing restless. Heavily pregnant with her fourth child, she invited her good friend Athénaïs de Montespan to join her private meals with the king. Louise knew that her friend was a witty, scintillating conversationalist—all that she, Louise, was not. Ironically, dull Queen Marie-Thérèse was also pregnant and likewise needed help in amusing the king. She considered all the ladies she knew and also selected her dear friend Madame de Montespan to entertain the king during meals. Both queen and mistress committed a naive and deadly mistake.

Madame de Montespan used these opportunities of dining with the king to slip love potions into his wine and onto his meat—disgusting concoctions of dead baby's blood, bones, and intestines, along with parts of toads and bats. Suddenly Louis— either because of her sparkling conversation or her potions—fell in love with Madame de Montespan. With no remorse toward the queen or Louise, she triumphantly affixed the seal of betrayal upon the altar of friendship.

After the birth of Louise's fourth royal bastard in 1667, she never became pregnant again, while Madame de Montespan remained almost constantly in this interesting condition. In order to protect his new mistress from the legal maneuvers of her insanely jealous husband, Louis arranged for Louise de La Vallière and Madame de Montespan to share a joint apartment in the palace. A court joke became, "His Majesty has gone to join the ladies."[9] No one knew for sure which one he visited. Or did he visit both at once? Malicious tongues wagged.

It gradually became crystal clear at court that Madame de Montespan was now the real mistress, and poor Louise just a decoy. Madame de Montespan demanded, with the king's apparent acquiescence, that Louise assist her with her toilette. Only Louise, she said, could tame an unruly curl, clasp a necklace, adjust some lace to make her exquisite for the king. Though the former favorite must have been humiliated performing these duties for her imperious successor, she never complained.

Kind, gentle, as assiduous as any lady's maid, Louise would send the radiant Madame de Montespan bouncing on her way to meet her royal lover.

The king's sister-in-law Elizabeth Charlotte, safely removed from romantic intrigues, looked on eagerly from the sidelines as if watching a horse race. "La Montespan was whiter complexioned than La Vallière," she wrote, "she had a beautiful mouth and fine teeth, but her expression was always insolent. One had only to look at her to see that she was scheming something. She had beautiful blonde hair and lovely hands and arms, which La Vallière did not have, but at least La Vallière was clean in her person, whereas La Montespan was filthy."[10]

Elizabeth Charlotte noted that "Madame de Montespan mocked Madame de La Vallière in public, treated her exceedingly ill, and influenced the King to do likewise. . . . The King had to go through La Vallière's rooms to reach La Montespan's. He had a fine spaniel called Malice; at Madame de Montespan's instigation he tossed that little dog into La Vallière's lap as he passed her, saying, 'Here, now, I'm leaving you in good company. . . . So don't mope.' "[11] And he left her alone with Malice.

Louise wrote in her autobiography, "I stay on in this world of flesh in order to expiate my sins upon the same scaffold upon which I offended Thee. Out of my sin shall come my penance. . . . Those whom I adored now act as my executioners."[12]

In 1674, either because of Madame de Montespan's potions or Louise's humiliation, the rejected mistress retired to a convent. But Madame de Montespan could not afford to stop her potions. The king's eye continued to wander. His valet Bontemps brought willing young ladies to the royal chambers, many of them pushed there by ambitious mothers and aunts. The chief aim was, of course, for the girl to replace Madame de Montespan as *maîtresse-en-titre*. But the consolation prizes were not bad. Even after a brief interlude with the king, girls of inconspicuous lineage would find themselves married off into illustrious noble houses.

In 1675 Madame de Montespan—aware of the king's interest in several of the queen's lovely young maids of honor—successfully intrigued to have them dismissed and replaced with older dames. According to Primi Visconti, the king's mistress, who had given birth to seven illegitimate children, was "shocked, claiming that these young ladies were bringing the Court into ill repute."[13]

By the late 1670s Louis had been with his mistress for more than a decade. She had grown heavy and lost her bloom; this fragrant rose was overblown, its petals were splayed; but its thorns were sharper than ever. As the duc de Saint-Simon put it, "Madame de Montespan's ill humors finished it off. . . . She had never learned to control her moods . . . of which the King was most often the target. He was still in love with her, but he was suffering for it."[14]

Madame de Sévigné wrote that Madame de Montespan sulked petulantly at the success of her rivals, locking herself in her apartments. Sometimes she threw open her doors in desperate fits of sparkling gaiety. Madame de Sévigné predicted the end was near, for "so much pride and so much beauty are not easily reconciled to take second place. Jealousy runs high, but when has jealousy ever changed the course of events?"[15]

In 1676, the princesse de Soubise was the object of that jealousy. Though tall and beautiful, the princess suffered the misfortune of flaming red hair. Redheads were thought to be the product of sex during menstruation and were believed to exhibit the lack of sexual self-discipline inherent in the ill-timed copulation of their parents. Madame de Montespan's eagle eyes noticed that the princess always wore the same pair of emerald pendant earrings whenever her husband left court for Paris. The royal mistress instructed her spies to watch the king's movements as soon as the emerald earrings appeared, and she was furious to discover that they were a signal for a sexual rendezvous. But the king, though initially aroused by the lascivious proclivities advertised in the princess's hair, quickly lost interest.

The next rival was the beautiful Madame de Ludres, who considered herself Madame de Montespan's replacement and gave herself airs. She pretended to be pregnant. The great nobles rose when she passed, an honor reserved by court etiquette for princes of the blood and by practice for the king's *maîtresse-en-titre*. It was this hubbub of nobles rising when Madame de Ludres passed that caused the queen to realize that her husband had yet another one.

Madame de Ludres's pompous airs soon alienated her royal lover, who then promptly fell in love with the very beautiful, very young Marie-Angélique de Fontanges. Suddenly Madame de Montespan found herself in the unenviable position occupied by Louise de La Vallière a decade earlier—curling the hair and lacing the stays of Louis's new mistress. But fiery Athénaïs de Montespan did not acquiesce meekly as Louise de La Vallière had. The marquis de La Fare reported that "Madame de Montespan was close to bursting with spite, and like another Medea, threatened to tear their children limb from limb before the very eyes of the King."[16]

Since childhood, the breathtaking blonde Mademoiselle de Fontanges was deemed by her family to be fit for a king. When this scion of the petty nobility turned seventeen, her impoverished relatives contributed a purse to deck the girl out in finery and send her to Versailles with this sole purpose. Her family's investment had paid off handsomely—she was created a duchess and given an annual pension of forty thousand ecus.

But Athénaïs de Montespan's ultimate replacement was not to be the short-lived Mademoiselle de Fontanges. Justice, balancing her scales, would bestow the king on someone Athénaïs herself had introduced to him. When Madame de Montespan needed to find a nurse and governess for her children with Louis, a woman with whom he might spend a great deal of time, she would never have selected a beautiful young woman. As she cast her long, narrow eyes about, her gaze rested on the pious virgin widow of an invalid poet, the formidable Madame Françoise Scarron. Rattling with rosaries and crucifixes, Widow Scarron always wore black, relieved by trimmings of silver or gold only because court etiquette demanded it. When the Sun

King, center of beauty, color, art, and scandal, first met the woman his mistress had chosen to look after his children, he was horrified by the bristling batlike apparition. "I do not like your *bel esprit*," he told Madame de Montespan, which must have confirmed her in her choice.[17]

But soon Louis grew to admire this intelligent, kindhearted woman. While his mistress took little notice of her growing clutch of children, it was Madame Scarron who nursed them tirelessly through their illnesses and began their education. She was witty, she was sensible, she was efficient, and her rigid piety appealed to the monarch's suppressed yearning for religion. In gratitude for her efforts, the king gave her the estate of Maintenon, a moated castle and lands, and she took the name Madame de Maintenon.

As Madame de Montespan's jealous temper tantrums and rapacious inroads into the royal treasury increased, the king began to see the greater beauty of his children's governess. "Madame de Maintenon knows how to love," he once said wistfully. "There would be great pleasure in being loved by her."[18]

One day the amorous monarch approached this unlikely object of his desires with the offer to make her his mistress and, for what was probably the only time in his life, was refused on religious grounds. Though her piety was genuine, there was perhaps a bit of cunning behind her refusal. "Nothing is so clever as to conduct one's self irreproachably," Madame de Maintenon wrote a friend.[19] Her irreproachable conduct merely increased his ardor—as well she knew it would—and by the late 1670s he spent every spare moment with Madame de Maintenon in her exquisite rooms in Versailles, talking about politics, religion, economics, heavy subjects that even the brilliant Madame de Montespan could barely discuss.

The king's glamorous mistress was positively baffled by her lover's fascination with such a dry bag of bones as Madame de Maintenon. There were countless stormy scenes between the two former friends, as the once omnipotent mistress felt her power slipping through her perfumed white fingers. One courtier reported hearing Madame de Montespan saying to Madame de

Maintenon, "The King has three mistresses. That young hussy [Mademoiselle de Fontanges] performs the actual functions of a mistress; I hold the title; you, the heart."[20]

The beginning of the end of Madame de Montespan occurred in 1679, when the Paris police launched an investigation into numerous allegations of poison in the city. Suspects were some of the highest ladies of the land, who—after visiting the witch La Voisin—had become wealthy widows after the sudden demise of disagreeable husbands. Some of the ladies in question fled France immediately rather than face interrogation.

Over the next year, 218 people were interrogated—some under torture—and 36 were executed by sword, rope, or stake. The police investigation was like a giant spiderweb that grew not only wider, but higher. There was one great lady in particular, several of the accused intimated, who was so high and mighty they dared not name her. In 1680 the witch La Voisin went to her death at the stake, categorically denying that any such woman had ever been her client. But shortly afterward her daughter admitted that the lady in question was none other than Madame de Montespan, the king's mistress of thirteen years, the mother of his children.

The girl reported, "Every time something new came up to upset Madame de Montespan, every time she feared a diminution of the King's good graces, she came running to my mother for a remedy, and then my mother would call in one of the priests to celebrate a Mass and then she would send Madame de Montespan the powders which were to be used on the King."[21]

She described Black Masses in the early years 1666–1668 to win the king's favor, held in abandoned chapels and officiated over by the defrocked abbé de Guiborg, the holy chalice held on Madame de Montespan's groin. "At one of Madame de Montespan's Masses, I saw my mother bring in an infant . . . obviously premature . . . and place it in a basin over which Guiborg slit its throat, draining the blood into the chalice . . . where he consecrated the blood and the wafer . . . speaking the names of Madame de Montespan and the King. . . . The body of the infant was incinerated in the garden oven, and the entrails were taken the next day by my mother . . . for distillation, along with the blood and the consecrated Host . . . all of which was then poured into a glass vial which Madame de Montespan came by, later, to pick up and take away . . ."[22]

At another Black Mass, according to the La Voisin girl, Madame de Montespan called on the demons of hell to assist her. "Hail Ashtaroth and Asmodeus, Princes of Friendship," she reportedly chanted. "I conjure you to accept the sacrifice of this child in return for favors asked of you, that I should have and keep the love of the King . . . that the Queen should become barren . . . that the King should leave her bed and board to come to mine . . . that he should grant whatever I ask of him, for me and mine . . . that I should be included in the councils of the King, a party to all state business . . . and that the King's love for me should wax and flourish . . . so that he shall abandon and no longer look upon the face of La Vallière . . . so that the Queen shall be repudiated . . . so that the King may marry me."[23] At this point the child's throat was slit with a knife and its blood drained into the chalice.

Given reports of babies' bones in La Voisin's garden, the police started digging. And digging. And digging. They uncovered the remains of twenty-five hundred infants—aborted, stillborn, premature, and those who had been sacrificed alive. There was a small oven in the garden pavilion where La Voisin would burn an infant's body if it was too large to bury easily.

Louis finally understood why for thirteen years he had awoken with a headache every morning after having dined with Athénaïs de Montespan the night before. He was revolted at the quantities of noxious potions he had consumed over the years, but perhaps he was even more disgusted at the behavior of the woman he had loved. There was no question of allowing the police to interrogate Madame de Montespan—Louis would be the laughingstock of Europe if word got out. Witnesses who had even mentioned her name were either executed or locked in solitary confinement in distant fortresses until their deaths. The former favorite remained at Versailles for another decade, throwing parties and dazzling guests with her brilliant wit. But the king's visits to her were rare and always in the company of others, and he never ate or drank anything she offered him.

The revelation of Madame de Montespan's witchcraft sent the king fleeing to Madame de Maintenon for religious consolation. She advised him to return to his wife's bed, which he did, making the last three years of Queen Marie-Thérèse's life the happiest ever. After her death in 1683, he secretly married Madame de Maintenon, who otherwise would never have slept with him. The poor widow, the children's nanny, was now the uncrowned queen of France.

Vipers Nourished in the Breast

Certain royal mistresses, adept at quietly seeking and destroying potential rivals, were blindsided by their own relatives, often poor young women from the country invited to enjoy the pleasures of court.

Madame de Mailly, the first mistress of Louis XV, won the dubious distinction of being unseated by her three sisters in succession. Born Louise-Julie de Mailly-Nesle, she had married her cousin the comte de Mailly and been appointed lady-in-waiting to the queen. Madame de Mailly was a plain, sweet woman who for seven years in the 1730s helped the young king grow out of his painful shyness. Paradoxically, one of her greatest assets in Louis's eyes was her lack of beauty and grandeur—the bold advances of countless stunning women at court actually frightened the introverted monarch.

According to a contemporary, Madame de Mailly had "a long face, long nose . . . a large mouth. . . . [She was] tall, without grace or presence . . . amusing, cheerful, good-tempered, a good friend, generous and kind."[24]

Her scheming younger sister Pauline-Félicité was equally plain but not equally kind. Green with envy that her sister was royal mistress while she stewed in the country, Pauline-Félicité begged for an invitation to Versailles to enjoy court life. As her carriage rattled for days from her country estate over the rutted dirt roads toward the palace, she had ample time to plot and connive how she would steal the king from her sister.

Taller, louder, wittier than her older sister, Pauline-Félicité soon sparkled at the king's intimate dinner parties. Her adept intrigue, combined with Madame de Mailly's naïveté, secured her the prize, and Louis soon fell head over heels in love with the younger sister. When she became pregnant with his child, he married her to a nobleman, Monsieur de Ventimille, who was immediately sent to the provinces. Madame de Mailly, though still officially the *maîtresse-en-titre*, stood awkwardly by wringing her hands as her sister rose in favor. The king visited Madame de Ventimille daily, leaving his official mistress alone in such penury that courtiers noticed her petticoats had holes in them. While the younger sister was given a beautiful château furnished in blue and gold, Madame de Mailly was crammed into two small, cold rooms in Versailles.

A few days after Madame de Ventimille gave birth to the king's son she went into convulsions and died. Louis, devastated, returned for solace to Madame de Mailly's arms. For two years she reigned again as undisputed mistress. As naive as ever, Madame de Mailly acceded to another sister's wish to be summoned to Versailles. Marie-Anne, the widowed marquise de La Tournelle, schemed to throw off her widow's weeds and take Versailles—and the king—by storm. Armed with a cunning intelligence, she was the most beautiful of all the Mailly-Nesle girls, with wide blue eyes and a ravishing figure.

Madame de La Tournelle used all her wiles to attract Louis away from her sister and soon succeeded. But she would never suffer Madame de Mailly to mope about the palace in her shredded petticoats still clinging to the title of *maîtresse-en-titre*. Before she relinquished her honor to the king, Madame de La Tournelle demanded that he send away the tiresome Madame de Mailly, and he complied. Her second demand was to be created a duchess, and he made her the duchesse de Châteauroux. Only then, when the act of love had been prepaid with the cold clanking of coins and the hollow braying of trumpets, did the newly minted duchess welcome the king into her soft white bed.

The cunning Madame de Châteauroux brought along yet another sister, Madame de Lauragais, fat and jolly. But she knew that this sister would be no true rival. While the king did sleep with Madame de Lauragais now and then, it was Madame de Châteauroux who ruled the roost. Amused at Louis's fascination for the Mailly-Nesle sisters, court pundits asked whether it was inconstancy or fidelity when a man chose all his mistresses from the same family.

Madame de Châteauroux's success was as brief as it was spectacular. After only two years at the pinnacle, she succumbed to a sudden fever. Unwilling to cede her position even to death, Madame de Châteauroux continued to walk the marble halls of Versailles as a ghost, seen by no less a personage than the queen herself. And poor Madame de Mailly, banished from court, replaced in her lover's bed by all three sisters, wore a hair shirt the rest of her life and haunted cold marble altars on bruised and bleeding knees.

Having run through all four Mailly sisters, Louis suddenly found himself with no royal mistress at all and began actively seeking a suitable replacement. His choice fell on Jeanne-Antoinette d'Etioles, whom he created the marquise de Pompadour. And so Madame de Pompadour had the luck to start off her career as royal mistress by appearing on an empty stage, rather than having to force another leading lady off the boards.

But if, at the beginning, Madame de Pompadour's only rival was a ghost, the field was soon teeming with women of flesh and blood. These rivals became more alarming when, after seven or eight years as royal mistress, Madame de Pompadour's dewy beauty had faded and her increasing frigidity prevented her from having sexual relations with the king. She continued to meet the king's every other need and subcontracted the sexual services to others by establishing a tiny bordello called Le Parc aux Cerfs on the edge of Versailles. Here one or two teenagers at a time—taken from the gutters and scrubbed with soap and water—would be ready to receive the king.

"All these little uneducated girls would never take him from me," she said of the Parc aux Cerfs girls.[25] But her greatest fear was being supplanted by a worthy rival. Madame de Pompadour once told her maid that she was engaged in "perpetual warfare"—like a weary gladiator in the ring, fighting off an unceasing stream of challengers, forced to thrust and parry until her dying day.[26] Her fear of rivals caused her to paint over her pallor and leave her sickbed countless times during her nineteen years as *maîtresse-en-titre*. For Louis XV had little patience with illness, and Madame de Pompadour worried he might turn to another woman to lift his spirits if she allowed herself a long recuperation.

Should the king die or dismiss her, Madame de Pompadour kept as her refuge a sumptuous Paris mansion—which currently serves as home of the president of France. She would have loved to relax there a few weeks each year, outside the "tissue of malice."[27] But she rarely visited it for fear of leaving the king alone. And with good reason. Younger, prettier candidates popped up like mushrooms in the king's path. One ambitious rival caused Madame de Pompadour particular concern. Marie-Anne de Coislin was a cousin of the Mailly family, and Madame de Pompadour well knew that the king had an irresistible fascination for Mailly women.

One evening Madame de Pompadour returned to her Versailles apartments and, throwing down her muff, told her lady's maid, Madame du Hausset, "I never saw such insolence as that of Madame de Coislin. I was at the same table as her for a game of *brelan* this evening; and you can't imagine what I suffered. The men and women seemed to take turns looking us over. Once or twice Madame de Coislin looked at me and said, 'I take the lot!' in the most insulting manner. And I thought I would faint when she said triumphantly, 'I have a hand full of kings.' I wish you could have seen her curtsey when she left me."[28]

Madame du Hausset asked, "And the King, did he greet her warmly?" Madame de Pompadour replied, "You don't know him, my dear. If he was going to move her into my apartment tonight, he would treat her coldly in public and be extremely friendly with me."[29]

But Madame de Coislin made a strategic error. According to

Madame de Pompadour's friend, the writer Charles Duclos, "she could have succeeded but instead of leading her lover by degrees to the final conquest, which would have meant the downfall of her rival, instead of inviting his desires by withholding herself, she surrendered so quickly that she extinguished the desires of the King; she gave herself like a whore, and was taken and abandoned like a whore."[30]

One of Madame de Pompadour's best advisers was Madame de Mirapoix, who told her, "It is your staircase that the King loves; he has grown accustomed to going up and down it. But if he found another woman to whom he could talk of hunting and business, it would all be the same to him after three days."[31]

Madame de Pompadour—who had moved into the grand Versailles apartments used by Madame de Montespan eighty years earlier—studied the lives of Louis XIV's mistresses, seeking to learn lessons from their triumphs and failures. "Madame de La Vallière allowed herself to be duped by Madame de Montespan," she told her lady's maid, "but it was her own fault, or rather, the product of her good nature. Initially, she had no inkling because she could not believe in her friend's treachery. Madame de Montespan was dislodged by Madame de Fontanges and supplanted by Madame de Maintenon; but her haughtiness and capriciousness had alienated the King."[32]

Despite Madame de Pompadour's knowledge that Louise de La Vallière had been duped into losing Louis XIV by her best friend, her closest call to losing Louis XV was orchestrated by her own cousin. Madame d'Estrades was a witty but ungainly woman who owed her position at court to Madame de Pompadour's friendship and generosity. Madame d'Estrades was appointed lady-in-waiting to the king's daughter and wormed her way into Louis's affection as an amusing friend. She tried to seduce him, but as Louis could only be seduced by beauty, her attempt fell flat. Her cousin's success continued to eat away at her, and she devised a new plan to unseat Madame de Pompadour.

Madame d'Estrades brought her beautiful nineteen-year-old niece Charlotte-Rosalie de Choiseul-Romanet to court. Madame de Pompadour arranged the girl's brilliant marriage and obtained a plum position for her as supernumerary lady-in-waiting to the king's daughters. The girl's aunt pumped up her aspirations of replacing the rather worn Madame de Pompadour and winning for herself riches, power, and glory.

Madame d'Estrades would invite her niece to play cards in Madame de Pompadour's apartments during her intimate evenings with the king and a few friends. Madame de Pompadour's friends pointed out uneasily that the young woman seemed hell-bent on seducing Louis, but in this case she naively refused to suspect that sweet, pretty Charlotte-Rosalie could be so underhanded. As the months passed, Madame de Pompadour continued inviting the girl to events where the king would be present.

Gradually Louis became more interested in the flirtatious bride and made several secret appointments with her, during which she steadfastly refused to have sex with him. Madame d'Estrades and her lover the comte d'Argenson had coached Charlotte-Rosalie to refuse the king's advances until she was assured of becoming his *maîtresse-en titre*—and ousting Madame de Pompadour. One day as Madame d'Estrades and d'Argenson sat together, Charlotte-Rosalie rushed in quite disheveled, having evidently just been ravished by the king. She cried, "It has happened. He loves me, he is happy, and she is to be dismissed. He gave me his word."[33] She had even obtained a letter from the king promising to get rid of Madame de Pompadour.

The silly girl, proud of her great accomplishment, showed her letter triumphantly to her cousin the comte de Stainville. The count, though no friend of Madame de Pompadour's, cleverly decided to win the eternal gratitude of so powerful a woman. He convinced Charlotte-Rosalie to allow him to keep the letter a few hours, then visited Madame de Pompadour immediately. He informed her that his cousin was too immature to fill so important a position, one for which Madame de Pompadour was so eminently suited. He gave her the letter and politely departed.

For once Madame de Pompadour vented her rage at her royal lover. When Louis visited her that evening, she showed him the letter and—for the only time in their relationship—threw a shocking temper tantrum. The king, horrified that the indiscreet Charlotte-Rosalie had let his passionate letter out of her possession, agreed to banish her from court that very night. Seven months later she died after giving birth. She was twenty-one.

By way of an apology, a few days later he raised Madame de Pompadour's status from that of marquise to duchess. When she was officially presented to the king and queen as duchess, she made her venomous cousin Madame d'Estrades witness her triumph and later banished her from court. Comte de Stainville had bet on the winning horse; although the king could not bear to see his face—a reminder of the painful episode—Madame de Pompadour had him appointed ambassador to the Vatican and he later became foreign minister of France.

Sometimes the Parc aux Cerfs girls, hired to keep serious rivals from bothering Madame de Pompadour, made trouble themselves. One such girl, the nubile fourteen-year-old Louise O'Murphy, was being coached by Madame de Pompadour's enemies. One evening Louise asked Louis how things were between him and his "old woman," referring to Madame de Pompadour.[34] The king was shocked, and his "old woman" quickly had Louise married off with a large dowry, shortly before she gave birth to a royal bastard.

After this episode the king visited Le Parc aux Cerfs incognito as a Polish nobleman. But one girl searched through her lover's pockets as he lay sleeping and discovered that he was not a Polish nobleman but the king of France himself. Throwing herself at his feet she proclaimed her undying love for him. This poor girl was taken to an insane asylum—a surefire method of invalidating whatever stories she might relate about the king—and after a suitable period of incarceration married off in the country.

Another girl, a stunning prostitute displayed by Paris's premier pimp, was seeking to ensnare the king with her sexual talents and hoped for far more than a stint at Le Parc aux Cerfs. The king's valet and procurer, Lebel, a true friend of Madame de Pompadour's, informed Louis that the girl was eaten up by venereal disease, putting an immediate end to her chances.

When Louis was clearly in love with the beautiful Mademoiselle de Romans, Madame de Pompadour again feared for her position. But she truly trembled when she learned that her rival was pregnant. Mademoiselle de Romans, quite sure that by means of her pregnancy she would oust Madame de Pompadour, took to bragging openly. The king, horrified at the noise she made, had her house searched and seized his love letters to her—proof that he had fathered her child.

Mademoiselle de Romans, certain her child would become a powerful duke, would often carry him in a basket to the Bois de Boulogne, sit down on the grass in her rich lace, and nurse him. Watching the king's former mistress nurse a royal bastard soon became a Parisian pastime. One day Madame de Pompadour took her maid to see the young woman and her child. So that Mademoiselle de Romans would not recognize her, she pulled her bonnet down over her eyes and held a handkerchief to her jaw as if she had a toothache.

It was a sad scene: the aging mistress, who had suffered so many miscarriages in her efforts to give Louis a child, watching the young mother, her raven hair confined by a diamond comb, nursing the king's baby. Madame de Pompadour and her maid exchanged some pleasantries and commented on the beauty of the infant before scurrying away. She seemed deeply distressed by the visit.

Toward the end of her life, Madame de Pompadour appeared to be giving up the struggle against rivals. The price of constant vigilance was poor health. In 1763, a year before her death at the age of forty-two, she retired twice from court for brief periods of rest, something she had never done in her eighteen years with the king.

POLITICAL RIVALS

While most rivals hoping to supplant a royal mistress were ambitious individuals seeking financial rewards, some were candidates backed by powerful political coalitions bent on placing a malleable woman in the bed of power.

One mistress who ultimately lost to a political coalition was Madame Cosel, mistress of Augustus the Strong, elector of Saxony and king of Poland. This lady of towering powdered white curls and unblinking black eyes held on to her position by paying a bevy of spies to inform her of his every move. In the end, however, she was no match for a coalition of the king's ministers.

Madame Cosel stuck to Augustus like glue almost twenty-four hours a day, except when he protested that he must meet alone with advisers to deal with matters of state. These meetings always made her extremely nervous, and with good reason. They were usually excuses to have sex with other women. So watchful was Madame Cosel that, heavily pregnant, she insisted on going into battle with him against the Swedes. But this time the king prevailed and sent her back to the safety of Dresden, though much against her will.

According to Augustus's biographer Karl von Pöllnitz, when Madame Cosel discovered that the king had profited by her absence by having an affair with a wine merchant's daughter in Warsaw, she thundered, "I am resolved not to undergo the fate of your other mistresses. I have for your sake quitted a husband, lost my reputation, and done all this, because you promised me upon oath an everlasting fidelity. I will not suffer your abuses, except your life pays for them. I am resolved to break your head with a pistol, and then to make use of it upon myself, as a punishment for my folly in loving you."[35]

Another unfortunate scene occurred as she was recuperating from childbirth at Augustus's court in Dresden. A note was passed to the king as he sat at Madame Cosel's bedside along with his secretary of state, Mr. Caspar Bose. He read it and turned bright red. His mistress was so curious to read the missive that when she jumped out of bed, according to the report, "she showed the King and Mr. Bose on that occasion what no modest woman would have shown her husband without many persuasions."[36]

Grabbing the letter, Madame Cosel found it was from Henrietta, the wine merchant's daughter in Warsaw. Worse, it informed the king that she had given birth to his daughter.

Madame Cosel went into a purple rage, crying, "Let her drown it! And would to God it was in my power to drown the mother too!"[37] Augustus laughed, but Madame Cosel informed him that if he answered the letter or acknowledged the child, she would, still bleeding from childbirth, take the next stage coach to Warsaw to strangle both mother and child.

Madame Cosel's bad temper was aimed not only at rivals for the king's love, but at courtiers and officials as well, and worse, she meddled in political affairs. After suffering nine years of her tyranny, in 1713 a coalition of ministers decided she had to be replaced with a more compliant mistress. When Madame Cosel was again heavily pregnant at Dresden and the king was required to ride to Warsaw, his advisers used this opportunity to find him another mistress. They held a meeting, discussing all the possible candidates at the court of Warsaw. They finally settled on Countess Maria Magdalena von Denhoff because "she is sufficiently amiable to be capable of pleasing, but her mind is not so exalted as to be able to rule."[38]

The new mistress having been chosen, the cabal had only to make the king and countess fall into each other's arms. They first went to work on Madame Denhoff, using her mother to counter any qualms she might have about betraying her husband to become a royal mistress. Fortunately, Madame Denhoff readily agreed to the plan.

The cabal knew the king would be more difficult. "A brisk and lively disposition could only captivate him," wrote his biographer, "and this was the chief quality Madame Denhoff was deficient in, who with a dull, heavy air affected the modesty of a virgin, which was directly opposite to the character the King required of his mistresses." The advisers "were sensible that she would not suit their monarch's fancy, but knew no lady at Court more proper to propose to him."[39]

Augustus expressed a hearty interest at seeing the beauty so lauded by his friends but was predictably disappointed at their first meeting. He "liked not her dancing" and "his heart could not yet be affected by her beauty." By this time he had figured out that his ministers wanted him to take a new mistress. He told one, "I am to be forced to love but till they find me a better than Madame Denhoff, I doubt whether I shall be unfaithful to Madame Cosel."[40]

Undaunted, the king's advisers threw him so often into the company of Madame Denhoff—who cast him "tender and languishing looks"—that slowly his heart became "enslaved."[41] But back in Dresden, Madame Cosel's spies informed her of her rival. No sooner had she dropped a son than she got in a carriage to Warsaw to confront her faithless lover. Madame Denhoff's supporters, hearing that the imperious mistress was on her way to foil their carefully laid plans, decided her arrival in Warsaw must be prevented at all costs. They quickly advised Madame Denhoff to create a scene that evening, pretending to be afraid for her life if Madame Cosel arrived in Warsaw.

Shedding a great many crocodile tears, Madame Denhoff told Augustus she would leave town rather than face her violent rival. Accordingly, the king gave orders to prevent Madame Cosel from entering the town. True to her reputation, when Madame Cosel was approaching Warsaw and given the message that she must turn back on the king's orders, she took out a pistol and threatened to shoot the messenger if he tried to prevent her from going ahead. She was finally persuaded to go home rather than risk the royal displeasure, and instead seek to win back the king's love upon his return to Dresden.

But the political cabal made sure that reconciliation was impossible. The king allowed his former mistress to live in luxurious retirement, giving her Pillnitz Palace. But Madame Cosel was not one to live peacefully. After political intrigues against Augustus, she fled to Berlin, where the king of Prussia seized her and returned her to Saxony. Augustus, finally realizing she would always stir up trouble, locked her in a fortress despite her shrill cries for clemency. There she remained even after his death in 1733, until her own death in 1765, after forty-nine years of genteel imprisonment.

Sprightly Nell Gwynn, a comic actress born and bred in the London gutters, maintained her place in the harem of Charles II for nearly two decades despite bitter rivalry from duchesses and countesses. In 1667 seventeen-year-old Nell graduated from selling oranges in the theater pit to performing leading parts on stage. Shortly thereafter, she received her first invitation to Whitehall Palace to entertain at royal parties. The French ambassador reported to Louis XIV that Charles laughed to see her "buffooneries."[42]

Though we can assume she began sleeping with the king around this time, she was not given a full-time position as royal mistress with its honors and financial rewards. Whatever remuneration Charles gave her was little enough, as Nell didn't quit the stage for nearly three years. After she had given the king a son in 1670, Nell went back to the theater in protest. She wanted all her fans to know how shabbily Charles was treating her in comparison with his higher-born mistresses. Her ploy worked. After Charles moved her into a modest town house, bought her furniture, and agreed to pay for her living expenses, she retired from the stage.

Nell's low birth was a severe handicap. The tempestuous Lady Castlemaine, whom Charles had recently created the duchess of Cleveland, was losing her influence after a decade as royal mistress; but instead of making spunky Nell a duchess and installing her in the palace, Charles started casting about for a nobly born woman. Even among the lowborn London performers, Nell had a strong rival in Moll Davis, a charming singer and dancer.

The competition between Nell and Moll Davis grew fierce. The king *bought* a fine house for Moll whereas he only rented one for Nell. He lavished Moll with horses, a carriage, and valuable jewelry. Feeling miffed, Nell invited her rival to lunch on the day Moll had an evening rendezvous with Charles. Nell put a strong laxative in Moll's food, and afflicted with painful diarrhea, the poor woman spent the evening with a chamber pot instead of the king.

In 1671, Louise de Kéroualle, the twenty-two-year-old French-born lady-in-waiting to the queen, finally relented and allowed the king to crack open the glass of her virginity. Though tending toward frigidity, she had a strong hold over him and offered the education and courtly polish which Nell utterly lacked. With Lady Castlemaine now languishing on the sidelines, Louise became the king's *maîtresse-en-titre*. But if her powerful position at court was a bed of roses, the thorn that came with it was Nell Gwynn.

In 1674 Louise had her portrait painted in a white smock, one breast exposed, leaning on pillows against a background of draperies, with her young son hovering as Cupid. Nell went to the same artist, posed in the same smock with the same background, had her two sons hovering as Cupid with ridiculous grins, and the king pictured in the background looking at her longingly.

Louise formed the affected habit of donning mourning whenever a great personage in France died, as if to show she were a near relation. Nell couldn't resist poking fun at this, swearing that she would don mourning when the next khan of Tartary died. Nell said, "She claims that everyone in France is her relation; the moment some great one dies she puts on mourning. Well! If she is of such high quality, why does she play the whore? She ought to die of shame. As for me, it's my profession. I do not pretend to anything else."[43]

Nell loved to point out that for all her rivals' blue blood, they were the king's whores just the same as she, a sentiment these noble ladies trembled to hear. One day she called on Lady Castlemaine and felt snubbed by her coolness. Nell "clapped her on the shoulder and said she presumed that persons of one trade loved not one another!"[44]

To put Nell in her place, Lady Castlemaine drove her luxurious new coach drawn by six horses back and forth in front of Nell's house—the king had never given Nell anything half so valuable. The following day Nell drove a broken-down cart pulled by six oxen in front of Barbara's house, crying, "Whores to market, ho!"[45]

Nell offered Charles what his other mistresses could not—

bawdy jokes and unfailing good humor. One day the king, Nell, and several others went fishing. Charles grew frustrated that he was not catching anything. Nell had someone distract him while she tied fried smelt—which had been in their picnic basket—to his line and threw it back in the water. When the king returned, Nell suggested he check his line. To his surprise he found that he had indeed caught a fish—a fried fish.

In addition to her practical jokes, Nell had a great talent for biting mimicry. Bishop Burnet noted that "she acted all persons in so lively a manner and was such a constant diversion to the King that even a new mistress could not drive her away."[46] Nell especially loved to mimic Louise's lisping French accent for the king's entertainment.

When Charles graced Louise with the titles of Baroness Petersfield, countess of Farnham, and duchess of Portsmouth at one stroke, Nell was livid. All she had of the royal largesse was a rented house, a few sticks of furniture, and some pin money. When she asked the king to do more for her and their two sons, he pleaded poverty caused by the war with France. To which Nell replied hotly, "I will tell you how you shall never want. Send the French [Louise de Kéroualle] into France again, set me on the stage again, and lock up your own cod-piece."[47]

If Louise was a Goliath of noble birth, fine manners, and political power, Nell was a little David slinging stones with deadly accuracy. One day soon after her ennoblement, Louise ran into Nell and condescendingly admired her fine dress. "Nelly," she cooed, "you are grown rich, I believe, by your dress; why, woman, you are fine enough to be a queen." To which Nell replied tartly, "You are entirely right, Madam. And I am whore enough to be a duchess."[48]

Another story relates that one evening Nell, the king, and Louise were partaking of a painful supper together. In a rare effort at wit, Louise said she could make three chickens out of the two set before them on the table. "There's one," she said, "and there's two, and one and two makes three."[49]

Nell then lifted one chicken onto the King's plate, the second onto her own, and suggested that Louise eat the third one.

Bereft of anything resembling a sense of humor, sluggish Louise was utterly incapable of parrying Nell's biting one-liners. Skewered alive, her only defense was to call upon every ounce of her formidable dignity.

Sometimes even Charles enjoyed jabbing the humorless and defenseless Louise. The French ambassador reported that the king had provoked Louise by "drinking twice in 24 hours to the health of Nell Gwynn" who "still made the Duchess of Portsmouth the butt of her tickling sarcasms."[50]

By 1674 Moll Davis had retired and Lady Castlemaine had moved to France. These changes in the royal harem made no difference to Nell, but Louise de Kéroualle was delighted with her virtual free run of the palace. Her delight was short-lived, however. Soon a new rival appeared on the scene: hot-blooded, raven-haired Hortense Mancini, duchess of Mazarin. The king was soon heatedly pursuing the sensual seductress who had enjoyed affairs with the handsomest men and most beautiful women in Europe. Louise, prone to melodrama, became thin and pale, moping and weeping almost constantly. Now it was Nell's turn to don black weeds. The actress, who knew how to ride out Charles's infatuations, said she mourned for the "weeping willow" and her dead hopes.[51]

Sometimes fighting her rival's intrigues was more than Louise could bear. One evening Honoré Courtin, the French ambassador, visited her and found her shattered by the strain. "The mistress wept bitterly," he wrote in his dispatch to Louis XIV. "Sighs and sobs strangled her words. Indeed I have never seen so sad a sight, so moving. I remained with her till midnight, and tried in every way to restore her courage and make her understand how essential it was to her position that she should hide her suffering."[52]

Courtiers loved to witness the equivalent of a seventeenth-century female mud-wrestling bout, and clapped their ring-bedecked hands together in glee at the thought of it. By the end of the year, the king's fiery passion for Hortense was waning because of her flagrant infidelity—she even had an affair with Anne

Palmer, Charles's teenage bastard daughter with Lady Castlemaine. The sleekly insinuating Hortense, however, was permitted to remain officially in his harem.

While most men dream of a woman who plays the lady in the parlor and the whore in bed, Charles effortlessly attained this fantasy by spending his days with cold, refined Louise and his evenings with lusty, bouncing Nell. Try as she might, Louise could not expel Nell from the game. Sexually restrained to begin with, Louise had caught a virulent strain of venereal disease from Charles in 1674 which caused her untold suffering for months. She made Charles repay her in the form of two magnificent necklaces, one diamond and the other pearl, but was warned by doctors never again to have sexual relations with the king. It is a testament to Charles's love for Louise that he kept her as his official mistress with little or no sex. But there were the king's sexual needs to be met, and Nell was more than happy to provide these services.

One day Nell stopped by the apartments of Hortense Mancini and found Louise de Kéroualle there with her close friend the French ambassador. It was an odd group. Lady Harvey reported, "I do not suppose that in all England it would be possible to get together three women more obnoxious to one another."[53] Before Nell could prick Louise with her pointed barbs, the duchess haughtily swept out of the room. Nell turned to the ambassador and demanded to know why the king of France "did not send presents to her instead of to the weeping willow who had just gone out?"[54] She said Louis XIV would spend his money more wisely in sending her gifts, as King Charles preferred her to Louise. As a matter of fact, he had sex with her—Nell—every night! The ambassador mumbled, turned red, and cringed.

Hortense adroitly changed the subject to the reputed beauty of Nell's undergarments. In a heartbeat, Nell raised her skirts and showed the ambassador her petticoats, stockings, and garters. It is interesting to contemplate what else she might have shown him, as underpants were not worn. Whatever he saw, the ambassador was evidently delighted. In his official report to the foreign office in Paris, this worthy gentleman lavished ample praise on Nell's undergarments "and certain other things that were shown to us all,"[55] and proclaimed he had never seen anything "more magnificent."[56]

LOVING PROFITABLY— THE WAGES OF SIN

Beauty is potent, but money is omnipotent.

—JOHN RAY, ENGLISH PROVERBS

ONE DAY IN THE LATE 1850S A GROUP OF FRENCH COURTIERS visited an old castle under restoration. Among the group was Napoleon III's mistress, Marie-Anne de Ricci, Countess Walewska, an Italian charmer who had married the son of Maria Walewska, and Napoleon. The countess pointed to a lizard gargoyle and remarked, "It is very well executed, but such a water pipe must be very expensive." The emperor's minister of the household, Marshal Vaillant, replied angrily, "Less expensive than yours, Madame." When another member of the party remonstrated with him for his rudeness, he continued, "This drainage has cost us four million francs!"[1]

The mistress, as opposed to the wife, could be dismissed at any moment with no financial settlement. Her powerful friends at court supported her only while she retained power, expecting favors in return. Exiled and reviled, the former royal mistress could find herself flying from the zenith of magnificence to the depths of poverty and disgrace at a moment's notice.

The wise royal mistress, therefore, began to collect for her retirement as soon as she was appointed, ensuring a lavish lifestyle to cushion her inevitable fall. Cash was always handy, as well as jewels, gilded carriages, fine horses, and gold and silver plate—objects which could easily be converted into cash should the deposed mistress suddenly find herself sent packing into exile.

Royal mistresses also coveted titles—countess, marquise, and duchess—which gave them an official position at court on a par with other courtiers. The titles came with castles and rent-producing lands, which also provided cash if managed well. Additionally, most royal mistresses received annual pensions for their services. The problem with titles, lands, and pensions was that they could always be revoked if the political winds reversed direction. Cash and its equivalent were always preferable in times of emergency.

Ironically, this lining of the royal mistress's pockets with taxpayer money so enraged the king's family, court, and subjects that she had to line them even more quickly.

Athénaïs de Montespan loved profitably indeed. When she began her affair with Louis XIV, her best pair of diamond earrings was in hock. Within a short time, she built three navy vessels for the king at her own expense, and recruited the crews from her native region of Poitou.

English royal mistresses did not have it quite as easy as their fair French counterparts. While the Sun King's word was law, his contemporary Charles II often found his gifts to royal mistresses blocked by court officials. Lord Chancellor Clarendon—who controlled much of Charles's money—made known that he was "an implacable enemy to the power and interest she [Barbara, Lady Castlemaine] had with the King, and had used all the endeavors he could to destroy it."[2] He knew that Lady Castlemaine's "principal business was to get an estate for her and her children,"[3] and "to pay her debts, which she had in few years contracted to unimaginable greatness, and to defray her constant expenses, which were very excessive in coaches and horses, clothes and jewels."[4] The king's requests for gifts to Lady Castlemaine never seemed to make it past Lord Clarendon's desk, and the king had to find other paths by which to route his largesse.

JEWELS

Most royal mistresses were known for their greedy love of fine jewelry, and many flaunted finer gems than the queen. It was not only vanity which prompted the mistress to weigh down her neck and ears, wrists and fingers with diamonds, but the omnipresent fear of sudden disgrace. Indeed, jewelry was the commodity closest to cash. A king's ransom could be stuffed into a small sack or sewn into hems and bodices if the mistress needed a hasty escape—as some did.

In 1662 when the Muscovite ambassador brought Charles II rich presents from the czar—furs and jewels amounting to £150,000—Lord Chancellor Clarendon begged the king not to give them away to "anyone." By "anyone" the chancellor meant the grasping Lady Castlemaine. Charles promised. Stymied here, Lady Castlemaine then persuaded her royal lover to give her every Christmas present he had received from the peers—many were jewels intended for Charles to pass on to his queen. Soon Lady Castlemaine was loaded down with jewels "far outshining the Queen," according to diarist John Evelyn, who saw her at a palace celebration.[5] Courtiers were not pleased to see their gifts to the king adorn his nasty mistress.

Lady Castlemaine had excellent credit with London jewelers, as they knew the king would pay her bills. There are some records of her purchases—a ring for £850 and two diamond rings for a total of £2,000.

In 1666—a year when sailors in the Royal Navy were given worthless vouchers instead of pay—the king cleared Lady Castlemaine's debts to the amount of thirty thousand pounds, which included jewelry and gold and silver plate—and bought her more jewelry. Unsatisfied with such bounty, Lady Castlemaine helped herself to the king's Jewel House in the Tower of London, signing documents agreeing to return the jewelry and plate that she had borrowed. But somehow she always managed to turn the loan into a gift.

England's prince regent, who later became George IV, was so generous in dispensing valuable jewelry to his lady friends that he single-handedly made his jeweler a multimillionaire. Horribly in debt, chased by creditors, the heir to the throne made monthly visits to the London showroom of Rundell and Bridge. In October 1807 the prince spent nearly two thousand pounds (approximately two hundred thousand dollars in today's money) on more than thirty pieces of jewelry inlaid with precious gems, including eight bracelets, four brooches, several silver serving dishes, and fine snuffboxes. It was his habit, when wooing a new mistress, to present her first with a miniature portrait of himself or a lock of his hair in a locket surrounded by diamonds. As the affair progressed he would lavish her with emerald rings, ruby necklaces, and a matched pair of sapphire bracelets.

It should come as no surprise that it was a mistress of George IV who amassed the greatest heap of gemstones during her tenure. Lady Conyngham was an unlikely royal mistress—fat and kind, rich and rapacious. In 1820, at the age of fifty, she found her way into the bed of the far heavier sixty-year-old king.

Lady Conyngham immediately reaped the rewards of her services in jewelry. The king gave her a large sapphire surrounded by diamonds which had belonged to the Stuart monarchs. When taking it from the Royal Treasury, the king had said the sapphire must go in his coronation crown. Instead, it appeared on Lady Conyngham's ample waist. Upon King George's death in 1830, Lady Conyngham—having been reminded by the government of Madame du Barry's unfortunate death on the guillotine—very decently returned the sapphire and other royal gems to the keeper of the privy purse, saying she was not certain that the late king should have given them to her.

Lady Conyngham was always aglitter with gems at parties. One witness described her as being very dull and very brilliant at the same time. George's bills at jewelers at this time included £3,150 for a necklace of remarkably large oriental pearls, £400 for a pair of diamond earrings, £437 for a pair of pearl bracelets, £530 for an emerald necklace, and £740 for another pearl necklace. Some estimated that the king had given his mistress £100,000 worth of jewelry, or $10 million in today's money.

Louis XV's Madame de Pompadour preferred collecting estates to jewelry. She had little taste for jewels, though her position required her to wear them daily. Her gems were of the finest quality. A portion of her collection consisted of a diamond necklace with 547 stones, a set of emerald jewelry, and forty-two priceless rings. But they meant little to her; she twice turned in her jewels to the treasury to help out in time of war.

Her successor, Madame du Barry, would never have been so generous. She positively adored her gems and launched new fashions in jewelry. Throughout the first seven decades of the eighteenth century, court women usually wore diamonds or pearls alone, or sometimes emeralds or rubies outlined by small rows of diamonds, but never two conflicting colors. When she became royal mistress in 1769, Madame du Barry encouraged jewelers to experiment with setting different-colored stones together—amethysts and sapphires, rubies and emeralds, aquamarines and garnets.

The infamous diamond necklace which would cause Queen Marie Antoinette such trouble a decade later was originally made for Madame du Barry. A veritable yoke of the largest and finest gems collected throughout Europe, the necklace consisted of a collar of huge stones from which hung intertwined ropes of diamonds. In a time of national financial disaster, this necklace outraged even the frivolous courtiers of Versailles. Despite the quality of its stones, many found the necklace to be incredibly ugly and compared it to an animal halter. Madame du Barry would have worn it with pride, however, if Louis had not died before purchasing it for her.

In 1847 Lola Montez had wrapped King Ludwig I of Bavaria so tightly around her little finger that the miserly monarch—who made his queen wear old dresses to the theater—showered her with jewels. One night at the opera haughty Lola appeared shining in thirteen thousand florins' worth of glittering diamonds—including a tiara—far outstripping the queen, who sat glumly in her old-fashioned heirlooms and rusty dress.

Of all royal mistresses, Lola Montez was so hated that she truly needed plenty of jewels to make a quick escape. Ironically, Lola's expulsion happened so quickly that she had no time to grab her jewel box. Threatened by an angry mob in front of her house, Lola was pushed by her friends against her will into a carriage, which raced out of town. Wearing a plain dress and no cloak on the cold February night, Lola went into exile.

Ludwig stopped the mob from ransacking her house and arranged for the sale of the building and her furniture, dresses, and jewels to pay her debts. The king sent Lola the little that remained, for her debts in Munich were significant. She should have grabbed the jewels and run.

Royal Apartments, Real Estate, and Furnishings

One of the greatest benefits given a royal mistress—though only during her tenure—was luxurious apartments in all the royal palaces, usually attached to those of the king by a secret door or staircase. One's rooms at court proclaimed one's status. Hundreds of noble families vied for the limited space, eager for a single cramped, cheerless room under the eaves. While most courtiers had comfortable homes near the royal palaces, they coveted the honor of lodging under the king's roof.

We can imagine the inexpressible joy of an obscure woman—who under ordinary circumstances would never have been given the coldest garret in the royal household—when she found herself the mistress of not only the king, but a huge suite of palace rooms. Often the mistress had more—and lovelier—rooms at court than the queen. For instance, in the 1670s Queen Marie-Thérèse was given only eleven rooms at Versailles, whereas Madame de Montespan occupied a suite of twenty.

Charles II's mistress Louise de Kéroualle had a lavish suite with furnishings so ostentatious that the queen's apartments looked poverty-stricken in comparison. The diarist John Evelyn visited the royal mistress as she sat in a rich dressing gown, having her hair combed. Looking around her apartment in amazement at "the riches and splendor of this world, purchased with vice and dishonor," he saw "the new fabric of French tapestry, for design, tenderness of work and incomparable imitation of the best paintings, beyond anything I had ever beheld. . . . Japon cabinets, screens, pendule clocks, huge vases of wrought plate, tables, stands, chimney furniture, sconces, branches, braziers, etc. . . . all of massive silver, and without number, besides of His Majesty's best paintings."[6]

As highly coveted as court apartments were, they were the first perquisite a disgraced royal mistress would lose. As she left her suite of finely furnished rooms with head hung low, her replacement would be tripping in eagerly with her luggage. So it made sense for the mistress to acquire property away from court.

Country estates were highly desirable, providing considerable income from tenants and the sale of crops and wine produced on them. In the 1440s Charles VII of France bestowed several castles and manor houses on Agnes Sorel, the first of which was the Château de Beauté—the Castle of Beauty—from which she acquired her nickname, the Lady of Beauty. Other properties were given to her on the births of her children.

Not content with vast suites of rooms in each of the three royal palaces, Athénaïs de Montespan wanted Louis XIV to build her a château of her own. He had already purchased her a fine house near the Louvre in Paris, but she wanted one in the country as well. When Louis had floor plans drawn up for a country house near his Palace of Saint-Germain, she rejected them out of hand as "good only for a chorus girl."[7] So Louis gave her the château of Clagny, which took ten years to build, with up to twelve hundred men working on it at a time, and which cost $11 million in today's money.

In 1668 Charles II gave Barbara, Lady Castlemaine, the lovely Berkshire House. The gift had a dual purpose—to silence her clamoring for money for a while and to remove her termagant presence from Whitehall Palace. Soon the French ambassador reported, "She is busying herself getting her gift valued and having the house furnished."[8] Realizing the value of the land, Lady Castlemaine demolished the venerable mansion, then sold the timber and all the land except a small corner of the property, where she built a new brick house. She pocketed a great deal of cash in the transaction.

In the early 1700s Augustus, elector of Saxony and king of Poland, built a palace for his mistress Madame Cosel. Her two summer apartments were lined with cool marble; her two winter apartments were inlaid with fine wood and adorned with porcelain and brocade hangings. In addition, he filled the palace with silver plates, crystal tables, and beds of exquisitely embroidered brocade.

Over her nineteen-year tenure as Louis XV's mistress, Madame de Pompadour owned seventeen estates, in addition to numerous houses that she bought as investments. She devoted the equivalent of millions of dollars to improving and decorating these estates—mainly for the king's convenience. Linens alone cost her a fortune—one item in the inventory of her estate listed 112 pairs of sheets, 160 tablecloths, 1,600 napkins, and 388 kitchen aprons. Firewood, candles, and food would have cost her additional large sums. But her estate expenses were not as frivolous as they might seem; the properties yielded rents from tenants and income from the sale of wine and crops. Many estates she sold at a profit.

But properties, unlike jewels, could not be hidden in a bodice and spirited away. In the late 1690s Peter the Great gave his mistress Anna Mons 295 farms and a mansion near Moscow. Anna was stripped of all these when Peter learned of her infidelity.

Even a tenure of twenty years could not protect Wilhelmine Rietz from losing her home. In 1775 Frederick the Great was worried about the expensive dissipations in Berlin of his nephew and heir, Prince Frederick William. Hoping to save money in the long run, the king gave his nephew twenty thousand thalers to buy a country estate outside Berlin for himself and his mistress. But in 1797, after King Frederick William's death, Wilhelmine was kicked off the estate by the new king, who grabbed it for himself.

TITLES

One of the greatest privileges for a royal mistress was to be raised into the rarefied air of the nobility, to be created a countess, marquise, or duchess with a stroke of the royal pen.

There were various reasons for a king to upgrade the status of his mistress. In 1450 Charles VII made Agnes Sorel a duchess, but only after her death so she could receive a splendid ducal burial.

A few kings ennobled their mistresses as a preparation for marriage. A king marrying a commoner or a member of the minor nobility would be frowned upon, but marrying a woman of great rank would be more acceptable. Preparing to marry Anne Boleyn, in 1532 Henry VIII created her the marchioness of Pembroke, an English peer in her own right and an unprecedented honor for a woman. The title carried with it large revenues and great privileges. Similarly, Henri IV made his mistress Gabrielle d'Estrées the marquise de Monceaux in 1594 and the duchesse de Beaufort in 1597, gifts strewn on her way to the altar.

Sometimes the ennoblement occurred as a kind of consolation prize when the king decided to replace his mistress with a new face. In 1853 Emperor Napoleon III created his long-suffering mistress Harriet Howard the countess of Beaurégard when he became engaged to the beautiful Spaniard, Eugénie de Montijo. Harriet, who had been angling for the honor of becoming empress of France, suddenly found herself dismissed and exiled. "His Majesty was here last night, offering to pay me off," Harriet wrote sadly to a friend. "Yes, an earldom in my own right, a castle and a decent French husband into the bargain. . . . The Lord Almighty spent two hours arguing with me. . . . Later he fell asleep on the crimson sofa and snored while I wept."[9]

In 1670 Charles II, growing tired of Lady Castlemaine, created her the duchess of Cleveland, an honor which brought with it extensive lands and revenues. The elevated status assuaged the king's conscience as he ardently pursued his next mistress, French-born Louise de Kéroualle.

At about the same time, on the other side of the Channel, Charles's cousin Louis XIV was faced with a similar problem. He created Louise de La Vallière, his mistress of seven years, a duchess, ostensibly as a reward for the birth of her fourth royal bastard. But in reality the king was beginning to tire of her and salivate over her prettier friend, Madame de Montespan. As a duchess, Louise would now be able to wear a train three yards long and sit on a taboret in the presence of the queen.

The much-coveted taboret was a wooden folding stool used by duchesses in France—which boasted the most etiquette-bound court in Europe—upon which the lucky few could sit in the presence of the royal family. The stool consisted of a few pieces of curved wood which served as legs, and a piece of tapestry at the top, which served as the seat, edged with tassels. It was carried pompously about by a bewigged and liveried servant, who snapped it open with a flourish and set it down when the duchess was ready to be seated.

For so small a thing, the taboret was one of the premier honors at the French court. When the Polish nobleman John Sobieski—who would become king of Poland in 1674—married Marie d'Arquien and lived at Versailles, his wife never ceased needling him to use his influence with Louis XIV to make her a duchess, which would automatically give her a taboret. Sobieski called it "this miserable stool."[10] In 1650 Louis XIV's mother Anne the Regent granted taborets to two nonduchesses, raising such a storm of protest that she shamefacedly had to revoke them.

Upon receiving her taboret, however, Louise de La Vallière was not impressed. She said it seemed to her a kind of retirement present given to a servant.

Often mistresses were raised in rank because their status reflected the glory of their royal lovers. Augustus the Strong, elector of Saxony, created his new mistress Madame Lubomirski the

princess of Teschen shortly after he was elected king of Poland in 1704, giving her the certificate of her new status along with a box bursting with jewels of every kind. But soon thereafter Augustus fell in love with a Madame Hoym, who requested a signal honor—she wanted to be made a countess of the Holy Roman Empire. Augustus, who was not the Holy Roman Emperor, had to call in some chips with the emperor and obtained the title of Countess Cosel for his mistress.

In 1745, Louis XV created Jeanne-Antoinette d'Etioles the marquise de Pompadour, giving her the title, estate, and coat of arms of a defunct noble family which had reverted to the crown, along with all the estate's revenues. In 1752 he raised her to the rank of duchess. This new position gave her not only the taboret but in some obfuscation of royal etiquette allowed her to sit on an armchair like a princess with the royal family during public dinners. Her coach, bearing ducal arms, was now permitted to enter the innermost courtyards of the various royal palaces. Lesser mortals were required to get out of their coaches at the outer courtyards, hold up their skirts, and walk around piles of horse manure. But Madame de Pompadour, while enjoying the privileges of her new title, never used it, still proclaiming herself the marquise de Pompadour, out of respect for the queen.

Sometimes kings favored their foreign-born mistresses with titles to help them better fit into their adopted country. George I turned his stiffly Teutonic mistress Ermengarda Melusina von Schulenberg into the smoothly English duchess of Suffolk. Similarly, George II's Hanoverian mistress Amelia von Walmoden became the countess of Yarmouth. Charles II honored French-born Louise de Kéroualle by presenting her with a bouquet of fragrant English titles—Baroness Petersfield, countess of Farnham, and duchess of Portsmouth.

Perhaps Lola Montez cast her glance backward into history and decided that as a royal mistress she, too, should be ennobled. If so, she did not recognize that she lived in a different time, a time when the king's word was not law. The timid mewling of most seventeenth- and eighteenth-century political opposition had swelled into a roar with the French Revolution and would never again be muted. Nevertheless, Lola demanded that Ludwig give her the title of a Bavarian countess, something which she hoped would provide her with an air of respectability, or at least officially elevate her position above that of her angry detractors.

Ludwig succeeded only with great difficulty in pushing Lola's Bavarian citizenship and ennoblement as countess of Landsfeld through his ministry. His entire council resigned in protest. But Lola was now permitted to drive a carriage with the nine-pointed crown of a Bavarian countess, and she gave herself more imperious airs than ever. To her chagrin, the new countess was still not received by Bavarian high society, as Queen Therese made known that *she* would not receive anyone who received Lola.

For two years after her exile from Bavaria Lola traveled about Europe, where her title was ridiculed by true blue bloods. Curiously, her title did her more good in the United States, where she lived in the 1850s. Unlike the ossified European nobility, Americans were thrilled to meet a real Bavarian countess and didn't care how she had come by the title.

GAMBLING DEBTS

In past centuries gambling debts routinely made up a significant part of the cost of living. Those in the upper echelons of society were expected to play cards and dice and wager large sums on the outcome. Those who refused were considered boring or, even worse, poor. Needless to say, many of the players suffered extraordinary losses, which as a matter of honor had to be paid promptly. One of the most satisfying perquisites of a royal mistress was the certainty that the king would pay her gambling debts.

Throughout her decade-long reign at court—and a decade beyond that—Charles II would pay what in today's money would be millions of dollars in gambling debts for Lady Castlemaine. She would lose—and sometimes win—startling amounts, wagering princely sums without blinking an eye. In 1679, Lady Castlemaine returned to England from a long stay in France. One courtier reported that upon hearing this, "His Majesty gave the Commissioners of the Treasury fair warning to look to themselves, for that she would have a bout with them for money, having lately lost 20,000 pounds in money and jewels in one night at play."[11]

Lady Castlemaine's contemporary and French counterpart Athénaïs de Montespan was also an avid card player and gambled heavily, sometimes hazarding several hundred thousand pounds on the play of a single card. She won often, and when she didn't, Louis XIV routinely paid off her debts. One Christmas Day she lost the staggering sum of £230,000, kept playing, and won back £500,000 on one play involving three cards.

Since the beginning of her relationship with Emperor Franz Josef in 1886, Katharina Schratt benefited by having her gambling debts paid. She routinely lost frightful sums at the casino in Monte Carlo and seems to have suffered an addiction to gambling. In 1890 she lost all her travel money and had to borrow her train fare back to Vienna. This happened again in 1906, when she lost no less than two hundred thousand francs and found herself stranded on the Riviera with a nasty red rash all over her body. She immediately contacted the emperor, who was so angry he let her stew awhile before responding. He finally sent her the money and a letter brimming with reproaches.

The imperial mistress replied, "A thousand thanks for your dear kind letter. The doctor, who at first thought I had chicken-pox, is now of the opinion that Monte Carlo is responsible for my rash. My heavy losses appear to have upset my stomach, then my nerves and finally affected my skin. If only your Majesty had inherited the gambling instincts of some of your ancestors, then you would be able to sympathize and understand, and I would not have to go through the world disfigured and misunderstood."[12]

The emperor, so thrifty that he wrote urgent telegrams on old scraps of paper, wrote back, "I am glad you are happy again and so hope that by now you are fully recovered. Medical science has obviously made a new discovery through your illness, for I have never before heard of a rash brought on by bad luck at gambling."[13]

PENSIONS AND CASH

Royal mistresses were usually given monthly allowances—often startling sums—which rapidly vanished, often leaving the mistress in debt at the end of the month. What happened to the royal largesse? Quite simply, the mistress had to keep up appearances— royal appearances. She was required to be a glorious accessory to the glory of the king. Not all her gowns and jewels arrived in gift boxes from her royal lover; the mistress had to keep herself fash- ionable with part of her allowance. There was an unspoken rule that the royal mistress's wardrobe had to outshine that of all the other ladies at court—including the queen.

Even Lillie Langtry, who did not receive a regular allowance from Edward VII, was expected to appear in an astonishing array of new gowns. In her later years, Lillie reported that she had had only one quarrel with Edward during her three-year tenure as his mistress. "I wore a dress of white and silver at two balls in succession," she reminisced. "I did not know that he was going to be present at both balls, but he was. He came up to me on the second night and exclaimed, 'That damned dress again!' He walked away in a temper. . . . It took me a long time to make it up. . . . That was the only quarrel we ever had."[14]

Lillie, who had come to London with just one plain black dress, patronized the fashion houses of Worth and Doucet. Her evening gowns were embroidered with pearls, her tea gowns bor- dered with silver fox, her dressing gowns lined with ermine. For a ball at Marlborough House, Lillie appeared in a confection of yellow tulle over which a gold net held preserved butterflies of various sizes and colors.

In the 1890s Edward's second official mistress, Daisy War- wick, never paid less than five thousand dollars in today's money for a gown, often far more. Society columns gushed about the "violet velvet with two splendid turquoise-and-diamond brooches in her bodice" she wore to a ball; the "gauzy white gown beneath which meandered delicately shaded ribbons" she wore to a dinner party; the "splendid purple-grape-trimmed robes and veil of pearls on white" she wore to a drawing room.[15]

More expensive—and certainly less rewarding than the mistress's own bodily glorification—was the management of a large household of retainers and servants. In the 1590s Gabrielle d'Estrées managed a household consisting of eighty-three ladies and gentlemen, seventeen crown officials, and more than two hundred servants. This large tribe of hangers-on needed to be fed, housed, paid a salary, and in some cases clothed.

A portion of the mistress's cash went to maintain the ultimate status symbol of centuries past: a magnificent coach. The mistress needed to keep her coach in good order—fresh paint and gilding on the outside, plush upholstery and plump pillows on the inside. The carriage was pulled by horses which she needed to feed and stable. In addition, she had to pay the staff that looked after them. Madame de Montespan, the proud owner of a luxurious carriage drawn by six horses, was flabbergasted to see her younger rival, the teenage Mademoiselle de Fontanges, drive by in a grander carriage pulled by *eight* horses.

The mistress arranged entertainments for the king, often lavish ones, where she paid not only for food, cooks, and waiters but for actors, singers, musicians, theatrical sets, costumes, and fireworks. In 1671, for instance, as a token of her gratitude for being created a duchess, Louise de Kéroualle gave a dinner for the entire English court.

A portion of the royal mistress's pension went to purchase expensive gifts for courtiers, ambassadors, and servants, as well as for the king himself. She was expected to contribute to charities—the church poor box, indigent families, wounded soldiers, hospitals, orphanages, and the like. In time of war she might receive hints to donate money back into the royal treasury from whence it had come.

We can understand the financial side of a mistress's life by examining the meticulous records kept by Madame de Pompadour of her expenses from September 9, 1745, when she was officially installed as king's mistress at Versailles, until her death in

April 1764. During those nineteen years, she was given the astonishing amount of 36,827,268 livres, or what today might be valued at $200 million.

But though free-spending, Madame de Pompadour usually spent wisely, buying and renovating estates, which she could rent and sell, and amassing collections of gems and porcelain, which increased in value and were eventually bequeathed to the king. She even invested in what amounted to pirate ships, fitted out to prey on English merchants, and shared in the pirates' treasure. She was a leading force in the revival of French industry, founding the world-renowned Sèvres porcelain factory—still in existence today—and a successful glassworks that produced bottles, carafes, and enameled pieces.

However acquisitive Madame de Pompadour was—she loved buying and beautifying—she always retained a generous heart, contributing dowries to poor brides, even selling diamonds to endow a hospital for the poor. During her disastrous running of the Seven Years' War, she turned in to the treasury most of her jewelry to help pay the soldiers. Because of her generosity and her surprising promptness in paying her contractors' bills—a quality almost unknown in eighteenth-century France—Madame de Pompadour never amassed great quantities of cash. The returns from her many investments went out just as quickly. When she died only a few gold coins were found in her desk.

Her successor, Madame du Barry, was forever in debt despite her huge monthly income from the king—at one point three hundred thousand livres. In addition to exquisite gowns and jewels, she surrounded herself with luxurious furnishings—a chandelier of rock crystal, a mirror made of pure gold, perfume bottles of crystal with solid gold stoppers. She employed sixteen footmen and at least as many maids, whom she had to dress, feed, and house, and paid for the stabling and feeding of her numerous horses.

Charles II—who never concerned himself with paying the salaries of his soldiers and sailors—was constantly thinking about providing his mistresses with financial assistance. By 1674 Lady Castlemaine was receiving annually £15,000 directly from the king, £10,000 from customs taxes, £10,000 from the beer and ale tax, £4,700 from the post office, and £3,500 from wine licenses. Louise de Kéroualle received £18,600 from Charles and, ironically, an annual pension from the taxes paid by the clergy. Gradually her pension increased to about £40,000, though in one year—1681—she received an eye-popping £136,000. Nell Gwynn, always coming in last, received a mere £4,000 for herself and her two sons.

While new monarchs often cut off pensions given to the mistresses of former kings, Lady Castlemaine miraculously retained hers. Many of her pensions continued after Charles's death in 1685, after his brother James II's exile in 1688, throughout the reign of William and Mary, and well into that of Queen Anne. While Lady Castlemaine periodically had to badger monarchs and their officials to send her the money, she retained her pensions until her death in 1709. Her success was no doubt due to the effective combination of her relentless will and the fact that she had married her royal bastards into the best families in England, who supported her quest to retain her pensions.

By the late nineteenth century, a monarch was in no position to give large amounts of cash to his mistress either from public funds or from his personal allowance. Parliament looked carefully into a monarch's spending; tabloid newspapers gleefully printed scandalous rumors, and the king's subjects frowned when reading them. But Emperor Franz Josef and his contemporary Edward VII found a way to help their mistresses financially that would avoid public scrutiny. Both men appointed clever financial advisers to quickly turn the women's meager savings into huge fortunes. Both also found lucrative employment for their mistresses' husbands, serving the dual purpose of earning even more money and getting them out of the house when the royal lovers came calling.

BRIBES AND GIFTS

In addition to benefits bestowed by the king, royal mistresses were often the recipients of legitimate gifts from ambassadors, public officials, and courtiers, and some not so legitimate gifts in the form of bribes to procure influence. Behavior that was acceptable before the French Revolution—the giving of valuables to influential people—was seen as corruption by the following generation.

One African ambassador, having heard about Louis XIV's Madame de Montespan, considered her the second queen of France. In presenting himself to Louis, he brought forth extraordinary gifts for the king, the queen, *and* the royal mistress. Not wanting to commit a faux pas, this honorable gentleman, who had three wives of his own, gave pearls and sapphires to "the King's second wife," which delighted Madame de Montespan but must have infuriated the queen.[16]

Gabrielle d'Estrées received gifts on a regular basis from foreign monarchs and the French nobility. She kept a detailed record of gifts she received when making an official visit with Henri IV to the city of Rouen. Queen Elizabeth I of England sent Gabrielle a large diamond-and-sapphire broach mounted in gold; Archduke Ferdinando de Medici of Tuscany gave her a set of twenty-four goblets of chased silver; a French politician presented an emerald pin; a noblewoman handed her a jar of fine perfumed oil; and a courtier bestowed on her two stags he had just killed.

In 1669, Barbara, Lady Castlemaine's rapacious appetite for gifts and bribes ate up the French ambassador's budget. "I have given away everything I brought from France," he lamented, "not excepting my wife's skirts. . . . As for Lady Castlemaine, if we lavish handsome gifts on her King Charles will understand that we believe she rules him in spite of his denials. We ought to dispense no more than ribbons, dressing gowns and other little fineries."[17]

But Louis XIV had a difficult task in mind for Lady Castlemaine, one that required an ampler reward than mere ribbons. First, Lady Castlemaine was to convince Charles II that he should not extend a general religious indulgence. Second, she should persuade him against reconvening Parliament.

The French foreign minister replied to the ambassador,

"The King highly appreciates the confidence you have cultivated with Lady Castlemaine . . . and since . . . you believe she can put more pressure on King Charles . . . than any other person, His Majesty wishes you to cultivate this good beginning with her. . . . In this regard he has ordered your brother to send you a gift of jewels from France which you may present to her in your own name—and jewels always go down well with ladies, whatever their mood."[18]

The gift of jewels was valued at a thousand pounds. Delighted, Lady Castlemaine showed it to King Charles, who—not seeming to mind his mistress's being bribed to influence him—agreed it was in excellent taste. The French-English alliance took two years to craft, but Barbara abandoned the cause early in the game. She kept the diamonds, however.

The French king had more luck with Lady Castlemaine's replacement, Louise de Kéroualle, who, fortunately for Louis, happened to be French. She rendered her native land such indispensable services in influencing Charles II's pro-French position that in 1675 Louis gave her a pair of earrings worth the astonishing sum of eighteen thousand pounds, his most expensive gift to England that year, and certainly more lavish than anything he had ever given Charles's queen.

In addition to official gifts there were those that smelled faintly of contamination, and others that positively reeked. George I's mistress Ermengarda Melusina, countess of Schulenberg, was delighted at her lover's promotion from a mere elector of Hanover to king of Great Britain, because of the financial rewards she would reap. The new king gave her an annual pension of seventy-five hundred pounds a year and suggested she acquire funds on her own if this income did not suffice. The countess gratefully accepted bribes as large as ten thousand pounds each from courtiers who felt she would influence the king on their behalf. George was aware of her earnings on the side and, with traditional German thriftiness, approved of her tidy income, which did not diminish the royal coffers.

George II probably learned from his father how to keep his mistresses wealthy without draining the treasury. When Lady

Yarmouth asked him for thirty thousand pounds, he tactfully suggested that he sell two peerages with the funds made payable to her. Lady Yarmouth happily pocketed the money, and George was thrilled that it hadn't cost him a cent.

In the 1660s and 1670s, Lady Castlemaine routinely sold political offices, raking in some fifteen thousand pounds a year. Her successor, Louise de Kéroualle, did a brisk business selling royal pardons to wealthy criminals. But times had changed by 1809, when George III's son the duke of York was investigated by Parliament because his mistress, Mary Anne Clark, had been selling military commissions.

Upon making Mary Anne his mistress, the duke had promised her an annual income of twelve thousand pounds. The giddy woman immediately rented a huge house; hired numerous servants; bought horses, carriages, gowns, and jewels; and entertained extravagantly—all on credit. When the duke—kept on a tight allowance by his thrifty parents—could not keep his promise and creditors pressed, Mary Anne went into business for herself, selling promotions to ambitious officers.

Eight charges were brought against the duke but none stuck. Although he had clearly profited from the transactions, it could not be proven that he had actually known about them. Though known to be thoroughly guilty, Mary Anne was not charged and became something of a folk heroine, cheered by people in the street. It was a short-lived victory. The duke of York broke with her, hid himself for shame, and resigned his post as commander in chief, losing the annual income of six thousand pounds, which he so sorely needed. And Mary Anne Clark sank back into the streets from which she had risen.

Tightfisted Kings, Poverty-Stricken Mistresses

Not all mistresses reaped piles of gold and diamonds from their royal lovers. Some actually lost money. Others could make ends meet only with the utmost frugality. When George, elector of Hanover, became king of Great Britain in 1714, he jumped on a

boat to claim his rich inheritance. His mistress Sophia Charlotte Kielmansegge, however, was detained in Hanover by her creditors. When the new king of Great Britain refused to help her out with her debts, she escaped by donning a disguise and followed him to his new land.

Frederick the Great of Prussia kept his nephew and heir, Prince Frederick William, on a tight financial leash. The prince lived in a charming estate outside Berlin with his mistress Wilhelmine Rietz, their children, and his children by several other mistresses. Wilhelmine had to stretch her small pension to keep up appearances. She carefully selected furniture that was elegant but affordable. Once, to provide the prince with an excellent meal, she pawned her silver. Wilhelmine was rewarded for her patience when her lover became King Frederick William II in 1786. She was given a beautiful palace in Berlin, a generous pension, and eye-popping jewels, and was later made a countess.

Of all royal mistresses, the one who fared worst financially was without doubt the English comic actress Dorothy Jordan. When speaking of her former royal lover, the future William IV, she once said, "Had he left me to *starve*, I would never have uttered a word to his disadvantage!"[19] Her statement would prove to be deadly accurate. He *did* leave her to starve, and she *was* too fiercely loyal to utter a word to his disadvantage.

Sprightly Dorothy Jordan, a comic genius, was already the mother of four children from two different men when William, duke of Clarence, saw her on the Drury Lane stage and wanted her for himself. One contemporary described her as follows: "Her face, if not exactly beautiful, was irresistibly agreeable; her person and gait were eminently elastic; her voice in singing perfectly sweet and melodious, and in speaking clear and impressive."[20]

In 1791 Dorothy yielded to William's ardent suit for—it was reported in the papers—the princely sum of three thousand pounds before consummation and one thousand pounds a year. Together with her theatrical earnings, this would have made Dorothy a wealthy woman. But kindhearted Dorothy and her money soon parted ways.

Before long, papers reported that the duke, suffered to live on the pauper's allowance meted out to him by his parsimonious father King George III, not only was withholding Dorothy's allowance, but arranged profitable terms for her performances and actually showed up at the theater to collect her earnings himself. One wit quipped:

> As Jordan's high and mighty squire,
> Her play-house profit deigns to skim,
> Some folks audaciously inquire
> If he keeps her or she keeps him.[21]

Over a period of twenty years, Dorothy bore William ten children. To generate the greatest possible revenues, she performed all over England, often bumping about for days in a carriage on muddy roads. But however generous her acting income, it was immediately siphoned off for the care of her fourteen children—education for the boys, dowries for the girls, and gambling debts for sons and sons-in-law. In 1797 the duke and Dorothy moved into the elegant Bushy House. This venerable mansion was not a gift from William to his mistress, but a gift from the mistress to her prince. In one letter complaining about the pace of her acting engagements, Dorothy wrote, "I have been playing [acting], and fagging myself to death, but it has enabled me to pay a good part of the purchase money of my house."[22]

In 1810, as William ran headlong into debt, Dorothy felt him slipping away from her and worked harder than ever for the cash she hoped would bind him to her; but as she jolted across England for performances, the duke began courting an heiress of twenty-two. When the heiress rejected him, William coldly informed Dorothy that they must part, as he considered his relationship with her a primary obstacle to a successful matrimonial suit.

By 1815, in poor health and besieged by her own creditors and those of impecunious family members, Dorothy escaped to France rather than face debtors' prison. The duke, her lover of twenty years and father of ten of her children, refused to lift a finger. She was not even allowed to write to him.

In France, worn down by disappointment and worry, Dorothy's health took a turn for the worse. She awaited eagerly each day's mail, hoping against hope for news that she could return home to England. Her neighbors in France, including many British expatriates, admired Dorothy's loyalty and fortitude. They never heard her say an unkind word about the duke. One day, when the post failed yet again to bring her a letter, Dorothy collapsed and died. She was buried in a corner of the churchyard through the charity of friends. None of her family was present at her death or burial.

When William became king in 1830, the dark whispers about his treatment of Dorothy rose into a pained cry. One paper lambasted him: "The people . . . have witnessed a man who has inundated his country with bastards, and deserted the deserving but helpless mother of his offspring, and finally left her to perish like a dog in the streets, and to be buried as a pauper at the public charge when she ceased to maintain him by her own exertions."[23]

After her death, one of her daughters revealed that the duke of Clarence had borrowed—and never repaid—some thirty thousand pounds from Dorothy.

SEVEN

POLITICAL POWER BETWEEN THE SHEETS

Hard by Pall Mall lives a wench call'd Nell
King Charles the Second he kept her
She hath got a trick to handle his prick
But never lays hands on his scepter.

—1670S RHYME

❋

IT WAS OFTEN ASSUMED THAT THE KING WAS MOST SUSCEPTI-
ble to political suggestions when lying down, that the royal mistress, having purchased power through sex, hopped out of bed,
smoothed down her rumpled skirts, and victoriously wielded her
omnipotence over court and country alike. This perception is
generally incorrect. With a few notable exceptions, most mistresses exerted political *influence,* the influence of a loved one
persuading the monarch to look at a problem from a different
angle, to consider different solutions. Some mistresses worked
in concert with the king's ministers by informing them of the
royal mood and the best times to present proposals. They
calmed the king down when he was angry and buoyed him up
when he was despondent, thereby oiling the wheels of state.

Many mistresses were either too stupid or too self-absorbed to be interested in politics and limited themselves to appointing their friends and relatives to government positions. Most kings, prickly with pride in their God-given authority, were repelled at the thought of a woman's meddling. After hours of discussing politics with his ministers, the king visited his mistress for a cozy dinner, light conversation, and good sex.

In the 1570s and 1580s, Archduke Francesco de Medici (1541–1587) fumed that he would brook no interference in politics by women. His mistress Bianca Cappello tactfully made Francesco believe her ideas had originated in his own brilliant mind. The archduke sank so frequently into irretrievable pits of depression that Bianca effectively ran Tuscany with her friend Secretary of State Serguidi. Together they made most of the political decisions and appointments to important posts. Even after the archduke married his mistress in 1578, Bianca, now the archduchess of Tuscany, still remained seemingly in her woman's role in the background, quietly pulling all the strings.

Some kings, however, cherished the sage political advice of their clever mistresses, many of whom spoke honestly, unlike the royal ministers. The quiet pillow talk in a curtained four-poster bed often had greater effect than the bobbing and angling of ambitious ministers pushing one self-aggrandizing plan or another. "Ah, and who is left now to tell one the truth?" lamented Louis XV upon hearing of the death of his mistress Madame de Châteauroux.[1]

The first mistress to wield true royal power in her own right was, naturally, French. In the 1550s Diane de Poitiers, the older, wiser mistress of Henri II, signed official documents; appointed ministers; bestowed honors, pensions, and titles; and bequeathed and revoked great estates. She became a member of the privy council and exerted great influence over the other members.

To help fill the empty royal treasury Diane imposed taxes—most notably on salt and church bells. She signed her name simply as Diane—as royalty did—not bothering with the string of ungainly titles most nobles proudly trailed behind their names.

Sometimes both Diane and the king signed a document, their signatures running together as "HenriDiane." When a group of cardinals protested her influence, she sent thirteen of them to Rome, ostensibly to represent French interests, but really to get them out of her way at court.

"PARIS IS WELL WORTH A MASS"

In the 1590s, Henri IV of France issued a royal decree that all foreign ambassadors be presented to his mistress Gabrielle d'Estrées, stipulating that all French nobility, clerics, and officials visiting the court wait on her immediately after speaking to the king himself.

Gabrielle possessed a great gift for using women's weapons—persuasion, conciliation, and charm—rather than men's—battle axes, cannonballs, and swords—to iron out the turbulent conflicts besetting France. Born Catholic, Gabrielle convinced Protestant Henri to convert to Catholicism to end the religious civil war, prompting him to maintain, "Paris is well worth a Mass."[2]

Although the king made Gabrielle the marquise de Monceaux and later the duchesse de Beaufort, she had no official position at court to match her diplomatic duties. No-nonsense Henri, adept at calling a spade a spade, appointed her "Titulary Mistress of His Majesty, the King of France."[3] Armed with her new title, Gabrielle communicated directly with the pope. The Vatican had been supporting the Catholic League led by Spain against Henri and had not stopped supporting it after what they considered to be his fraudulent and politically motivated conversion to Catholicism. Philip II of Spain made routine incursions into the south of France, draining Henri's resources.

Gabrielle, sending the pope copies of her letters patent naming her "titulary mistress," politely requested that His Holiness stop supporting a useless war now that Henri had become a true son of the church. She reminded him that it was she who had convinced Henri to become Catholic, and hinted darkly at the possibility of France breaking with the church completely, as

England had sixty years earlier, if the Vatican continued to support the kingdom's enemies. Two weeks later, the pope instructed all religious houses in France to pray for the health of King Henri IV. When Henri was informed of the pope's acceptance of his conversion he was heard to say, "Gabrielle has succeeded where others have failed."[4]

Gabrielle then set to work settling the differences between Henri and the duc de Mayenne, head of the powerful de Guise family. Mayenne had been the leader of the Catholic League; he still held a large body of troops and refused to make peace with the king. Mayenne's female relatives were close to Gabrielle; a scheme was hatched among the women to force the men to make peace. Gabrielle persuaded Henri to be more conciliatory to his adversary, and the de Guise women set to work on Mayenne to give up a lost cause. Finally, Gabrielle conferred with Mayenne himself for two days in a small château, ironing out the details of his surrender. Henri made many concessions—including a large sum in gold and three châteaus—to pacify his enemy.

Gabrielle had become Henri's most important diplomat but had no official seat in the council, where national policy was made. Yet there was a precedent—only forty years earlier Diane de Poitiers had served on the council. In March 1596, bypassing with royal aplomb the customary steps, Henri bestowed on Gabrielle the set of gold keys which gave her the right to join the council. To deflect criticism, at the same time he wisely gave an identical set to his sister, the devout Catherine. And so he appointed two female council members in one fell swoop, Gabrielle known for her diplomatic skill, and Catherine for her saintliness. On many public occasions after this it was observed that Gabrielle, instead of flaunting her magnificent diamonds, proudly wore her little gold keys on a chain about her neck.

In 1597 the duc de Mercoeur, virtual ruler of the state of Brittany, led the last pocket of rebellion. When war looked inevitable and the two armies faced each other across the battlefield, Gabrielle invited Mercoeur's wife to a tête-à-tête with her in a carriage. The two women arranged Mercoeur's surrender under honorable terms and a marriage between their children.

They then set to work persuading their men to agree to their decision. And so Henri's last victory was achieved without shedding a drop of blood. It was a woman's victory.

The civil war having been finally quelled, Henri looked toward preventing another one. Tensions between Catholics and Protestants ran deep, and Henri looked for a way to reconcile the two groups. Henri's Huguenot sister and Catholic mistress set to work. The duc de Montmorency, constable of France, wrote, "Madame [Catherine] and the Duchess de Beaufort have begun their formidable task of reconciling the unreconcilable. They will need to exercise their command of the arts of persuasion to the utmost and to utilize the natural charms with which they are endowed, for surely no two women have ever undertaken a more difficult task."[5]

Some Catholics resented being lectured on the subject of religion by the king's mistress. These were reminded that it was Gabrielle who had convinced the pope himself to accept Henri into the church. Henri was thrilled at Gabrielle's success in convincing powerful Catholics, one by one, to accept his decree of religious toleration. He wrote, "My mistress has become an orator of unequaled excellence, so fiercely does she argue the cause of the new Edict."[6] Through a combination of warm charm and cold threats Gabrielle pushed her point home. In 1598 the Edict of Nantes was signed granting Huguenots certain rights while deferring to Catholics. The sure sign of the edict's justice was the fact that both sides went away grumbling. But Henri was thrilled and knew he could not have issued the edict without Gabrielle's diplomatic skill.

"WE MUST NEVER YIELD OUR MIND"

Henri's grandson Louis XIV did not permit his mistresses any great exercise of political power. Louis himself in his memoirs, which were intended to help his heir rule after him, wrote, "Time given up to love affairs must never be allowed to prejudice affairs of state. . . . And if we yield our heart, we must never yield our mind or will. . . . We must maintain a rigorous distinction between a lover's tenderness and a sovereign's resolution . . . and we must make sure that the beauty who is the source of our delight never takes the liberty of interfering in political affairs."[7]

Louis's Madame de Montespan had little interest in politics, but she demanded that her views be heard in the realms of art, architecture, literature, and music. Her protégés included Molière, Racine, Boileau-Despréaux, and La Fontaine. Her only success in the political domain was in getting her candidates appointed to high-level positions—and even then, she usually promised much and delivered little.

One courtier, the marquis de Puyguilhem, tired of waiting for her to procure for him a coveted position at the king's disposal, actually hid beneath her bed while she was out having lunch with Louis, knowing they would return to her room for sex afterward. Silent as the grave, the marquis listened to the royal lovemaking and their postcoital conversation. He was furious to hear Madame de Montespan argue *against* his appointment, despite her glittering promises.

Later, as Madame de Montespan and her ladies started walking toward the palace theater, the marquis accosted her, calling her a dog's whore and a liar and repeating word for word what she had said to the king. Shaking with fear—certain that the devil himself was in league with Puyguilhem against her—the royal mistress stumbled to the theater, where she promptly fainted and was revived only with great difficulty.

"LADIES HAVE A GREAT INFLUENCE OVER THE MIND OF THE KING OF ENGLAND"

While Louis XIV did not allow his mistresses political influence, he knew his cousin Charles II was far more susceptible to their blandishments. In 1670 Charles first spotted Louise de Kéroualle among the retinue of his sister Princess Henrietta, who had married Louis XIV's brother, during her visit to England. Thunderstruck with admiration, Charles asked to keep the girl at his court. Knowing her brother's debauchery, Henrietta firmly refused and took Louise back to France. Within weeks Henriette was dead, and the French king, hoping Louise could help France more than Charles's mistress Lady Castlemaine had, agreed that Louise should be sent to England.

The ambassador of Savoy informed his monarch of Louise's arrival at the English court. "Mademoiselle de Kéroualle . . . is a beautiful girl," he related, "and it is thought the plan is to make her mistress to the King of Great Britain. He [Louis XIV] would like to dethrone Lady Castlemaine, who is his enemy, and . . . his Most Christian Majesty would not be sorry to see the position filled by one of his subjects, for it is said the ladies have a great influence over the mind of the King of England."[8]

Louise was in no rush to give her virginity to the English king. She wanted to make sure he appreciated the great gift she was about to bestow on him, and thought that his gratitude would be proportionate to the amount of time he was required to wait. As the months went by, and Charles's admiration for Louise remained encouraged but unsated, the French ambassador began to stir uneasily—Louise was taking so long that she risked losing the king's interest entirely.

A full year after her arrival in England, the envoys were happy to inform the French minister that Louise had been nauseated. The dispatch reported, "The affection of the King of England for Mademoiselle de Kéroualle increases every day, and the little attack of nausea which she had yesterday when dining with me makes me hope that her good fortune will continue."[9]

The French foreign minister replied eagerly, "The King was surprised at what you wrote me concerning Mademoiselle de Kéroualle, whose conduct while she was here, and since she has been in England, did not inspire much expectation that she would succeed in achieving such good fortune. His Majesty is anxious to be informed of the result of the connection which you believe exists between the King and her."[10]

But these royal hopes were inspired, after all, by only a fit of indigestion. There had been no sex between Charles and Louise. Disappointed, the French envoys felt that Louise did not understand the importance of her position and was not doing her duty for her country. They were afraid that another pretty face—one less prudish than Louise—would steal the English king away, and Louise would irrevocably lose her chance. But after applying pressure to her from all sides—including the threat of sending her to a strict convent—the French ambassador wrote, "I believe that I can assure you that if she has made sufficient progress in the King's affection to be of use in some way to his Majesty, she will do her duty."[11]

Louise finally did her duty in late October 1671. It is reported that she lounged around in a state of undress—petticoats and shift, but no stays—and after a mock marriage ceremony, finally bedded the king. The proof was in the pudding—nine months later she gave birth to a son, whom she named Charles.

The French ambassador—and Louis XIV—were ecstatic at their success. Now they finally had King Charles under their thumb. Ambassador Colbert wrote to Minister Louvois, "I have made Mademoiselle de Kéroualle very joyful by assuring her that his Majesty would be very pleased that she maintains herself in the good graces of the King. There is every appearance that she will possess them for a long time, to the exclusion of everyone else."[12]

The ambassador was correct. Louise initially took over the official duties of the queen, and finally, some offices of the worn-out king. By the early 1680s, Charles had passed his fiftieth birthday and was aging rapidly. A lifetime of hard living, combined with the long-term effects of venereal disease, was gently pushing him toward the grave. He often left London to frolic at Windsor with Nell Gwynn, leaving affairs of state in the capable hands of Louise, who, though she had no official power, worked assiduously behind the scenes in elections, appointments, arrests, and foreign policy. Charles, who twenty years earlier had vowed never to allow a woman to hold the reins of power, gratefully handed them to Louise.

It was a wise choice, for Louise had political talents unlike any of the king's other mistresses. Lady Castlemaine was solely concerned with stuffing honors, titles, jewels, and subsidies into her pockets and then howling for more. The fiery Hortense Mancini was too busy conducting love affairs with men and women at court to meddle in affairs of state. Nell Gwynn preferred practical jokes to politics, calling herself "a sleeping partner in the ship of state."[13]

"YOU ARE TURNING THE KING YELLOW"

More powerful even than Louise de Kéroualle, Madame de Pompadour wielded the greatest power of any royal mistress ever. Initially she was interested only in her romance with Louis XV. But once she found herself clawing for survival in the snake pit of Versailles, she was clever enough to know she needed friends in high places. The new mistress started—tentatively at first—sounding out which courtiers were her friends and which were her enemies. She used her influence with Louis to dismiss high-level officials who stood resolutely against her and replace them with her friends. One of her first steps was to replace the comptroller, who had remonstrated against her extravagance, with a friend of hers who immediately paid all her bills without question.

Soon, Madame de Pompadour controlled the plum prizes of pensions, titles, honors, and positions at court. The king, relieved that he did not have to make all the decisions himself, gratefully relied on his mistress to take care of them. The great majority of courtiers, ministers, government officials, and even struggling artists decided to befriend her. In the morning, they were allowed to crowd into her rooms to watch in awestruck admiration as she applied her makeup. A young writer named Marmontel handed her a manuscript he was working on and asked for her comments. Several days later, he wrote, "I presented myself one morning at her toilette when the room was crowded by an assemblage of courtiers." To his surprise, Madame de Pompadour took the young man into her private office to return his manuscript marked with corrections and suggestions. When they returned to the pool of humanity swimming in her drawing room, "All eyes were turned on me," Marmontel relates, "on every side I was greeted by little nods and friendly smiles, and before I left the room I had received enough dinner invitations to last the whole week."[14]

As the sexual relationship between Madame de Pompadour and the king waned, her political power increased. Messages designed for the king's eyes alone first had to pass through the mistress's hands, and it was she who decided if they were important enough to bother Louis. Ambassadors found they could see the king only in the company of the *maîtresse-en-titre*, who carefully observed to see if Louis was turning yellow, a clear indication that the conversation was upsetting him. When Monsieur de Maurepas, minister of Paris as well as secretary of state and secretary of the navy, involved the king in a long, boring discourse, Madame de Pompadour dismissed him smartly by saying, "Monsieur de Maurepas, you are turning the King yellow. Good day to you, Monsieur de Maurepas."[15] The minister waited in vain for the king to countermand his mistress's order. When this did not come he withdrew, seething with anger that a middle-class female nobody should throw him out.

After five years as the king's mistress, Madame de Pompadour moved from her cozy apartments under the eaves of Versailles, directly above the king's chambers, to palatial apartments on the ground floor, directly below them. Again, her suite was connected to the king's with a secret staircase. In these grand rooms, she worked for thirteen years as the unofficial prime minister of France. Indeed, she had far more power than any of Louis's ministers, as it was *she* who appointed *them*. In 1753 the marquis d'Argenson wrote, "The mistress is Prime Minister, and is becoming more and more despotic, such as a favorite has never been in France."[16]

Hearing of Madame de Pompadour's power, the renowned misogynist King Frederick the Great of Prussia was so offended he named his dog—a bitch—after her. According to Countess Lichtenau, the mistress of Frederick's nephew and heir, the king "thought that it did not become the destined ruler of a great and powerful nation to be governed and duped by women and a set of idle parasites. Such creatures were generally connected with a gang of adventurers who had no other aim but that of creeping into favor of the ruling prince, under the protection of a clever courtesan, and as soon as they had obtained that favor they would interfere with the most serious and momentous concerns of the State."[17]

Perhaps it was a self-fulfilling prophecy for Frederick when Madame de Pompadour used her power to spurn Prussia—France's traditional ally—and side with Empress Maria Theresa of Austria during the Seven Years' War (1757–1763). France's support in this territorial catfight between Prussia and Austria was likely to tip the scales in favor of whichever side France weighed in on. And Frederick's caustic comments about Madame de Pompadour convinced her to side with two other powerful women, Maria Theresa and Empress Elizabeth of Russia, after both of whom Frederick had named dogs as well. He sometimes called his brood of powerfully named bitches Petticoats I, II, and III. Frederick was delighted that when he snapped his fingers, Madame de Pompadour, Empress Maria Theresa, and Empress Elizabeth came running, and when they misbehaved he could beat them. But that was only the dogs. The women, claws unsheathed, pounced on him in concert.

The Austrian alliance was not popular among the French people, who until quite recently had lost sons and fathers to Austrian guns and bayonets. But Madame de Pompadour convinced the king that Prussia had become too powerful under Frederick and that an alliance with Austria would create a better balance of European power.

Madame de Pompadour became the unofficial minister of war, personally choosing the generals. Her choices were extremely limited. Generals had to be selected from the nobility, and many of the best French generals were either too old or too ill to participate. Some competent men were available, but these were not admirers of Madame de Pompadour, who insisted on appointing her friends.

The French believed that good breeding and noble blood,

rather than military genius, could win a war. Undisciplined French armies were encumbered by chefs, hairdressers, valets, and courtesans and became a kind of mobile court. Warhorses dragged barrels of hair powder, pomade, and perfume. One evening, after a brilliant Prussian victory, a captured French officer found himself eating a jovial dinner with Frederick the Great. The officer asked the king how he had won such a triumph against the odds. "It is easy," replied Frederick. "The Prince de Soubise," he said, referring to the French general, "has 20 cooks and not a single spy; while I, on my part, have 20 spies and but one cook."[18]

After seven years, both sides were exhausted. The French treasury was empty and, worse, France had lost some two hundred thousand men. In signing the truce, France agreed to give up numerous possessions, including Canada and parts of India. The one case of a royal mistress holding true power in her smooth white hands ended disastrously.

Perhaps it was fortunate that Madame de Pompadour's successor, Madame du Barry, was less interested in politics. It was often remarked that when courtiers discussed political matters with her, hoping to win her influence, she smiled vaguely as if she had not understood a word. Madame du Barry was more successful as a patron of arts and letters, generously doling out the king's money to young artists and writers who sought her assistance. Each morning, as she lay in her perfume-scented bath, her waiting women would read to her petitions and letters begging for help.

The favor seekers waited patiently in her drawing room until the royal mistress emerged wrapped in a beribboned morning gown. As her hairdressers were putting the finishing touches on her coiffure, tradesmen jostled with each other, eager to show her jewelry, porcelain, and bolts of fine fabric. Most important politicians attended her levee, as well as bankers, artists, and philosophers. Many brought proposals with them, seeking her advice or support. Others were armed only with amusing gossip. Even if Madame du Barry had no political influence, visiting the favorite's toilette was the best way of running into the king, who often stopped by to visit his mistress on his way to Mass.

"THE POWER BEHIND THE GERMAN THRONE"

Frederick the Great, who died satisfied that he had trumped Madame de Pompadour during the war and probably hastened her death, would have turned over in his grave if he could have seen his Prussia being ruled by an American courtesan barely a century later. Mary, Countess von Waldersee, was the Bible-thumping daughter of a wealthy New York grocer who married Colonel Alfred von Waldersee, the quartermaster general of the German army. In Berlin, silver-haired Mary created a salon and entertained the right people lavishly, including Prince William, the heir to the throne.

The older, wiser woman had a great calming effect on the nervous young prince, who took great pains to follow her advice. Soon secret diplomatic dispatches sent from Berlin to the corners of Europe contained suspicions as to the nature of the relationship, even though pious Mary was two years older than the prince's *mother*. Ministers and ambassadors suddenly became quite respectful to her. When the French called her a Pompadour, it was the greatest compliment. When the Germans called her a Pompadour, it was the deadliest insult.

In 1888 Prince Willy became Kaiser Wilhelm II and soon referred all political matters to Mary before he announced his opinion. American newspapers went wild. The *New York Tribune* proclaimed, "Former New York Woman Dominates New Emperor."[19] The *New York Transcript* announced, "American Princess Sways the Haughty Kaiser—Romantic Story of Merchant's Daughter Who Is Power Behind the German Throne."[20] A Boston paper declared, "Every step undertaken by the Kaiser is the outcome of her influence and intrigue."[21]

The *New York Tribune* stated, "The Countess von Waldersee is so much Commander-in-Chief that she can toss out general officers filling the highest posts."[22] The *New York Times* reported,

"Fortunate indeed is the incoming Ambassador who succeeds in winning the prestige of her personal interest. To him opens as by magic the door to the charmed inner circle, which otherwise is only to be approached after countless struggles with the all-pervading redtapeism of German official life."[23]

Mary angled for the speedy demise of the all-powerful Chancellor Bismarck. She told the kaiser that he could never truly rule with the popular Bismarck in the way. While this was true, Mary's main objective in removing the Iron Chancellor was to clear the path for her husband to succeed him. Using all her persuasion on the kaiser, Mary worked long and hard to topple the giant.

In March 1890, Bismarck fell. Mary and Alfred waited confidently for the fruit of their seventeen years of joint effort—Alfred's appointment as chancellor. But instead of immediately replacing Bismarck with Count von Waldersee, the kaiser chose another man for the job. Egged on by his new set of debauched friends, Willy decided that with Bismarck gone, *Mary* was the one standing in the way of his exercising complete power. He bristled as he read the newspapers referring to Mary as the power behind the throne.

Instead of promoting Count von Waldersee, the kaiser publicly demoted him from the highest post in the army to commander of a corps in a suburb of Hamburg, making his disgrace the talk of Berlin. Mary and Alfred lived out their lives in dignified exile. Without Mary's calming influence, Willy gradually degenerated into a paranoid megalomaniac, setting the wheels in motion for World War I.

"SHE DOES NOT MEDDLE AND SHALL NOT MEDDLE"
The one royal mistress who never had even a taste of power during a twenty-year tenure was Henrietta Howard, the mistress of George II of Great Britain. Though Henrietta had no political interests, she would have liked to procure positions for her friends and family, the time-honored perk of a royal mistress. "Upon my word," she bemoaned to an old friend, "I have not

had one place to dispose of, or you should not be without one."[24]

Henrietta's friend Lord Hervey wrote that she was keenly aware "that some degree of contempt would attend the not having what in her situation the world would expect her to have, though she had never pretended to be possessed of it, and that a mistress who could not get power was not a much more agreeable or respectable character than a minister who could not keep it."[25]

After gentle Henrietta's retirement, George II's next mistress, Lady Deloraine, unsettled the queen and court. The new favorite was a mincing, scheming little jade who boasted every time the king made love to her. One day Lord Walpole remarked how much he regretted that Lady Deloraine was the king's choice. But Lord Hervey replied, "If she got the ear of anyone in power, it might be of very bad consequence, but since 'tis only the King, I think it of no great signification."[26]

After the queen's death, George assuaged his grief by sending now and then for Lady Deloraine, even though she had taken to drinking strong Spanish wine and offended the king with the stink of it. Afraid of Lady Deloraine's political meddling, the prime minister decided it would be best to bring over from Hanover the king's German mistress, Madame Walmoden, who seemed politically innocuous. In the meantime, he shrugged off the king's sporadic encounters with that little minx Deloraine. "People must wear old gloves until they can get new," he sighed.[27]

To the king's delight, Madame Walmoden came over. To her delight, she was created the duchess of Yarmouth. To the ministers' delight, she did not interfere with politics. Gradually, however, Lady Yarmouth became a conduit of political influence between the king and his ministers, and a wholly beneficial one. She informed the ministers of the right time to approach the king with important matters and how to broach them. She prevented the more irritating politicians from upsetting George.

The French, studying the influence of the English king's mistress, found she suffered in comparison to their own

Madame de Pompadour. A French nobleman in London wrote to Paris sneeringly, "Whereas Madame de Pompadour shares the absolute power of Louis XV, Lady Yarmouth shares the absolute impotence of George II."[28]

Unlike Louis XV, who encouraged his mistress to make political appointments, George was outraged when he learned that then secretary of state William Pitt had requested an interview with Lady Yarmouth to discuss his candidates for various positions. "Mr. Pitt shall not go to that channel anymore," the king thundered. "She does not meddle and shall not meddle."[29]

But if the king remained stubbornly oblivious of his mistress's political influence, his courtiers did not. As the wit Lord Chesterfield noted, Lady Yarmouth must be seen as the keystone of His Majesty's opinion, "for even the wisest man, like the chameleon, takes . . . the hue of what he is often *upon*."[30]

EIGHT

RED WHORES OF BABYLON — PUBLIC OPINION AND THE MISTRESS

Some praise at morning what they damn at night
But always think the last opinion's right.

—ALEXANDER POPE

❋

WE CAN ONLY WONDER HOW WOMEN'S LOT IN WESTERN SOCI-
ety would have improved during the past four thousand years
had Genesis blamed seductive Adam for tempting innocent Eve
with a banana. But since it was Eve who gave Adam the apple,
Sinful Woman became a fair target for tempting Virtuous Man
from the straight and narrow path with her sexual wiles.

This was doubly true for a royal mistress. Whereas most
women conducted their illicit affairs hidden from public view,
maintaining an outward image of chaste propriety, by virtue of
her very position the royal mistress was known by all the world to
be having sex with a man not her husband. Moreover, however
dissatisfied a nation may have been with its king, it was treason to

speak so, and the mistress was a far likelier target of wrath among the people and discontent at court.

Often a royal mistress could not win in the stern court of public opinion no matter what she did. If she bore the king children, she was a harlot bringing expensive bastards into the world. If she did not, she was even worse—a barren harlot. If she was beautiful, her beauty was a gift from the devil to inflame the hapless monarch. If she was plain, the king deserved better. If she lived opulently, she was selfishly spending the poor people's taxes. If she lived simply, she was detracting from the king's glory.

Mistresses from powerful noble families often meddled in politics and turned their relatives into a political faction, causing strife at court. For this reason, some kings avoided the snares of lovely countesses and breathtaking duchesses and sought out mistresses born as commoners. Such women were far more grateful for blessings bestowed and less adept at intrigue. Commoners usually applauded the rise of one of their own, but those born with blue blood pulsating nobly through purple veins turned green with jealousy when an outsider invaded the Holy of Holies.

Native-born mistresses were better tolerated than imports, who were often, and sometimes rightly, suspected as foreign spies. In 1736, when George II insisted on bringing over a German mistress, his English subjects wanted to know why he couldn't content himself with an English whore. After all, they said, "There are enough of them to be had and they are cheaper."[1]

"KÖNIGS HURE! HURE!"

Louis XIV's brilliant mistress Madame de Montespan was disliked by court and populace alike for her vainglorious spending and imperious attitude. She encouraged the king to build palaces, create gardens, and give lavish entertainments. The court, and French life that aped the court, buzzed with music, dancing, fireworks, gambling, the rustle of colorful silks, and the sparkle of priceless gems.

During her thirteen-year tenure, this Red Whore of Babylon was considered a drain on the royal treasury, a burden on the backs of the working poor. Hearing of her sordid reputation, German troops marching past her in a military parade shouted, *"Königs Hure! Hure!"*[2] Unable to understand German, Madame de Montespan asked another spectator what the soldiers were yelling and was informed that they had been calling her the "king's whore." Unfazed, later that evening she told the king that while she had enjoyed the parade she wished the Germans were not so painfully precise in calling everything by its proper name.

Once she was dismissed, Louis secretly married the pious Madame de Maintenon, who had all the virtues the French disliked and none of the vices they admired. Suddenly public opinion veered back in Madame de Montespan's favor. The French wanted their king, and their court, to dazzle the world. They missed the balls, fetes, masquerades. To follow the new fashions, many courtiers traded in dice for rosaries and romance novels for Bibles, but it didn't mean they liked it. As Louis XIV's sister-in-law Elizabeth Charlotte, the duchesse d'Orléans, wrote of Madame de Maintenon, "Not all the King's mistresses together did as much harm as she!"[3]

"If I Die It Will Be of Grief"

Madame de Pompadour, despite her generosity and encouragement of French art and industry, was the subject of harsh lampoons and barbed poems throughout her tenure. Many courtiers were simply jealous that Louis XV had chosen a woman of the middle class for the honor, and they poked cruel fun at her background and her maiden name, Poisson, which means "fish" in French. She once found under her napkin at her dining table a poem accusing her of having venereal disease. Away from the poisoned elegance of court, the French populace enjoyed poking fun at her in taverns and tacking up nasty verses on the lampposts.

Upon her arrival at Versailles, the nobles looked down their long aristocratic noses at her and sniffed. "She is excessively common," the comte de Maurepas wrote, "a bourgeoise out of her place, who will displace all the world if one cannot manage to displace her."[4] Similarly, the duc de Luyne scoffed, "She will probably be just a passing fancy and not a proper mistress."[5]

Her enemies at court delighted in spreading word among the common people of Madame de Pompadour's extravagance, wildly inflating the money she spent. When she set up a tiny theater in Versailles for the king's amusement, word got out in Paris that it had cost an exorbitant sum wrung from them in the form of taxes. When she visited Paris—her childhood home and a place she far preferred to Versailles—her carriage was pelted with eggs and mud, and she was hissed and booed and even threatened with death.

But it was not until Madame de Pompadour took charge of running the Seven Years' War beginning in 1757 that she was truly reviled. Some two hundred thousand Frenchmen were killed or wounded, the national treasury was bled dry, taxes were raised. Madame de Pompadour found herself the recipient of frequent death threats, some mysteriously appearing on the mantelpiece of her apartment.

The detested royal mistress slipped into a profound depression and suffered from insomnia, which she deadened with drugs. When peace was declared in 1763, France lost most of its possessions. The French people did not blame King Louis the Well-Beloved for the devastating losses, but his devilish mistress. Madame de Pompadour, whose health had never been robust, suffered greatly from the barbs and pricks of her unpopularity. "If I die," she sighed, "it will be of grief."[6] She died the following year.

Parisians greeted her death with a jeering verse:

Here lies one who was twenty years a virgin,
Seven years a whore, and eight years a pimp.[7]

Madame de Pompadour's successor, Jeanne du Barry, started off her career as royal courtesan with a dreadful handicap—she had been an infamous Parisian prostitute with whom many of the king's ministers and courtiers had had sex.

To become *maîtresse-en-titre*, Madame du Barry had to be presented officially at court by a noblewoman. And here was the difficulty—no noblewoman would be caught dead facilitating the prostitute's intrusion into their privileged sphere. Finally the king convinced the impoverished comtesse de Béarn to accept the job by paying off her debts and promoting her sons serving in the armed forces.

The day of the presentation ceremony, however, the well-bribed comtesse de Béarn lost her nerve, knowing that if she went through with it no one at court would ever speak to her again. Limping pitifully, she claimed to have sprained her ankle so badly she could hardly walk. Many thought that if she had in fact hurt herself, the injury had been intentional. The ceremony was canceled, to the delight of Versailles courtiers and the French populace.

Under intense pressure from the king and Madame du Barry's cabal, three months later the comtesse de Béarn kept her part of the bargain and presented the royal mistress at Versailles. The rooms were packed with courtiers hoping to witness an utter failure. Madame du Barry was late, but when she did arrive even her most bitter enemies gasped at her beauty. She was wearing one hundred thousand livres worth of diamond jewelry and a court gown of silver and gold cloth, with huge panniers and a long sweeping train which she managed gracefully to kick out of the way to make her three backward curtsies. If they had hoped to see an oafish street urchin, they were disappointed. Madame du Barry's graceful refinement was equal to that of the most inbred duchess.

Nevertheless, for much of her six-year tenure as mistress, Madame du Barry was ostracized by courtiers. When she sat down at a card table, the other seats remained eerily empty.

When she gave a party, no one came. Finally, the king ordered courtiers to attend her parties.

Her greatest challenge came when the king's grandson, the future Louis XVI, received as his bride the fourteen-year-old Marie Antoinette, daughter of the Austrian empress Maria Theresa. Strong-willed, beautiful, and charming, the new dauphine stole the king's heart and despised Jeanne du Barry. She demanded that she, as dauphine, be the first lady at court, and snubbed the king's mistress socially, despite gentle remonstrances from Louis. Courtiers enjoyed this spectacle of two females—a highborn princess and a prostitute—duking it out for the king's affections.

Finally, after two years Marie Antoinette's refusal to say even a word to the favorite became an international scandal. The king, Empress Maria Theresa, and the Austrian ambassador to France finally prevailed on the dauphine to say publicly a few polite words to Madame du Barry. At a carefully orchestrated event, the chastened princess coolly remarked to the *maîtresse-en-titre*, "There are a lot of people today at Versailles."[8] The king and his mistress were gushingly grateful. Strained relations between Austria and France were improved, but Marie Antoinette's hatred of Madame du Barry intensified. She was never invited to join the dauphine's youthful, fun-loving entourage, which soon became the center of court social life.

Madame de Pompadour, detested toward the end, was now sanctified by the white pall of virtue that death often brings to the departed no matter how scandalous their earthly sins. The living, however, are doomed to suffer for their transgressions, and a former prostitute gracing the gilded halls of Versailles revolted the French populace. Writing pornographic poetry and bawdy songs about the favorite became a new national pastime. During her final months as royal mistress in 1774, Madame du Barry had become so unpopular that she feared entering Paris. Mobs, who called her the "Royal Whore," attacked her carriage. They saw her lavish lifestyle as the cause of high unemployment, staggering taxes, and a shortage of bread. One courtier wrote that her entertainments "were carried to such an indecent pitch of luxury as to insult the poverty of the people."9

For many years after the king's death, Madame du Barry lived a quiet life in a country manor outside of Versailles. Rich from her tenure as royal mistress, she entertained visitors from across Europe who came to look at the face that had bewitched a king. A Versailles courtier enjoying her hospitality told her apologetically, "There was no hatred but we all wanted to have your place."10

"I AM THE PROTESTANT WHORE"

When Charles II was invited to ascend the English throne in 1660, his riotous living was a charming contrast to a decade of the deadly dull Puritan Protectorate. But within a few years, many God-fearing Englishmen decried the debauchery of the court, protesting—perhaps with a bit too much ardor—that the king wasted time with his mistresses "feeling and kissing them naked all over their bodies in bed."11

Charles's first royal mistress, Lady Castlemaine, often experienced the stabs of public anger. "Give the King the Countess of Castlemaine and he cares not what the nation suffers," they said.12 After the birth of her fourth child by the king in as many years, some English subjects thought that enough was enough. One evening as she was walking across St. James Park she was accosted by three men who called her a vile whore and reminded her that two hundred years earlier Jane Shore, the mistress of King Edward IV, had died alone and detested on a pile of manure.

In 1665 while staying with the court in Oxford, Lady Castlemaine gave birth to her fifth child and soon after found an insulting verse nailed to her door in Latin and English, referring to the punishment of ducking immoral women in water:

> The reason why she is not duck'd?
> Because by Caesar she is fucked.13

The king posted a reward of one thousand pounds to find the perpetrators, but no one came forward.

In 1668 a group of London apprentices pulled down some infamous brothels and threatened to pull down the biggest brothel of all, Whitehall Palace, home of King Charles. Soon after, a mock petition was published titled "Petition of the Poor Whores to the Most Splendid, Illustrious, Serene and Eminent Lady of Pleasure, the Countess of Castlemaine," begging for her influence on their behalf for "a trade wherein your Ladyship has great experience."[14] As Lady Castlemaine stormed and raged, someone then published a "Gracious Answer" to the poor whores, purportedly written by none other than the king's mistress herself.

Lady Castlemaine's replacement, Louise de Kéroualle, was known to be an avid supporter of French policy, no matter what disadvantages it might offer England, and an agent for French king Louis XIV. The English people were appalled at their king's giving her English citizenship and granting her ducal honors. They deeply resented in wartime the cash, jewels, and subsidies he laid at her feet. One day Louise found the following rhyme tacked to the door of her palace apartments:

Within this place a bed's appointed
For a French bitch and God's annointed.[15]

Louise had the misfortune to be a Catholic mistress in a strongly Protestant country during a time when religious hatred was flaring. King Charles's mother was Catholic, his younger brother James had converted, and it was suspected—rightly—that Charles himself was a secret Catholic. The Protestant populace lived in fear of regressing to the age, only 120 years earlier, when Bloody Mary burned heretics in the marketplace.

Englishmen were infuriated by the idea of a foreign Catholic mistress whispering blandishments into the ear of their wavering king. They looked back wistfully to the time of Lady Castlemaine, remarking with pride that she had been the best whore of all—delivering countless royal bastards, cleverly bleeding the treasury dry, and boasting English birth to boot.

Matters came to a head in 1680 with a firestorm of riots between Catholics and Protestants in the streets. The pope was burned in effigy almost daily. The French ambassador wrote Louis XIV that the new Parliament would demand Louise's exile from court, and that she would very likely be imprisoned in the Tower and possibly executed. Protestant leaders attempted to charge Louise with being a common whore before a grand jury. Luckily for Louise, the judge threw the case out of court.

If English commoners were shocked at Charles's choice of Louise de Kéroualle, courtiers were more shocked at the advent of lowborn Nell Gwynn. The earl of Arlington, one of the king's ministers, told the French ambassador that "it was well for the King's good servants that His Majesty should have a fancy for Mademoiselle Kéroualle, who was not of an evil disposition and was a lady. It was better to have dealings with her than with lewd and bouncing orange-girls and actresses, of whom no man could take the measure."[16]

Many noblewomen who welcomed Charles's other mistresses with open arms refused outright to have Nell among their company because of her base birth. The dowager duchess of Richmond told the king that she "could not abide to converse with Nell," to which the monarch replied that "those he lay with were fit company for the greatest woman in the land."[17]

Commoners, on the other hand, felt that if Charles had to have a mistress, it should be a Protestant Englishwoman like Nell rather than an aristocratic French papist like Louise de Kéroualle. Many of the lower and middle classes admired Nell for dragging herself out of the gutter and through talent, hard work, and humor making a lady of herself.

By the time of the Catholic Panic in the late 1670s and early 1680s, Nell clearly came out on top in the public opinion poll. She was thought to be a "good commonwealth's woman," a Protestant who had never "to make her own private gains endeavored the ruin of a nation."[18] Louise de Kéroualle, on the other hand, was certainly a spy for their historical enemy France and the pope. Stuffing her money bags with their taxes, she became known as one of "Pharaoh's lean kine" who had "almost devoured a nation."[19]

One day Nell's carriage was encircled by a mob who thought it belonged to Louise de Kéroualle and threatened to overturn it. Nell stuck her head out the window and cried, "Pray, good people, be civil, I am the *Protestant* whore."[20] In response, the laughing mob blessed her and bid her be on her way.

"Kill me if you dare!"

In 1848 Lola Montez was so unpopular in Bavaria that she precipitated a revolution. In late 1846 the dancer had visited Munich with the intention of staying a week or two and pulling in some money for her performances. But she enchanted the elderly King Ludwig, who convinced her to stay on as his special friend. The Munich citizens were not blind to their ruler's frequent visits to the dancer's hotel. Whipping out binoculars, they studied her closely in the special opera box she had convinced Ludwig to give her.

As always, the populace was not so much concerned with their monarch's sexual morality, but with the political influences exerted on him by an outside source. This woman was no German, as Ludwig's others had been. Worse, Lola had no clear nationality at all, claiming to be a Spaniard in order to hide her true identity. Born in Ireland, raised in India, married in England and divorced there for adultery, Lola spoke a little Spanish with an Irish-British accent. Who was she? If she was indeed working for a foreign government, which one was it?

Worse than her uncertain nationality and political agenda was Lola's uniquely bad temper. Petulant, fiery, uncontrollable, she frequently slapped and punched shop owners and people on the street who she felt had insulted her. One day, as she walked the streets of Munich, her huge black dog bit a deliveryman's foot. Reaching for a club to protect himself, the poor man was struck hard several times by the king's mistress. A crowd formed and chased Lola into a silver shop. As darkness fell, and some four hundred incensed citizens yelled for her in front of the shop, Lola escaped down a ladder in the back.

The seats near Lola's theater box were usually empty, as no one wanted to be seen near her. During the plays, when Ludwig would abandon his wife, children, and royal guests to visit her, Lola remained seated while the king stood, a shocking breach of protocol.

People in the street jostled her and called her rude names. Boys threw horse manure at her. Though Lola was far from a typical damsel in distress, these incidents soon attracted a group of university students which acted as a personal bodyguard. Her admirers formed their own fraternity, the Alemannia, named for an ancient German tribe, and wore a distinctive red cap.

With Ludwig's money, Lola treated the Alemannen to wild drinking parties—some said orgies—at her stately house. At one dinner, the students, carousing around wearing no pants, carried Lola on their shoulders and knocked her unconscious on a chandelier. The arrogance of the few dozen Alemannen outraged the other two thousand university students, who began to whistle and catcall whenever a red cap appeared in view. When Lola's fraternity boys would attend lectures, the other students would rise and leave. On some occasions, two or three Alemannen would sit alone in a large lecture hall.

Annoyed by the constant reports of disruptions, Ludwig decided to close the university for a semester. A riot ensued, students and ordinary citizens chasing the Alemannen and battling with them in the streets. Lola, hearing about it, threw herself into the midst of the fray with characteristic fearlessness. But she was soon recognized and chased, pelted with manure, and knocked to the ground. She made her way to a church, where the priest promptly threw her out. Finally, several gendarmes encircled her and helped her escape to the royal palace.

Hundreds of protesters stormed the police headquarters, tore up the paving stones, and broke every window in the building. The following day, protests continued. To defuse the ticking time bomb, the city commandant announced to a crowd that Lola Montez would be leaving the city within an hour. Delighted, the mob ran to her house to witness the royal whore's departure. But the statement was false. Lola ran outside with a gun and dared them to kill her. When a hail of stones was the reply, she cried, "Here I am! Kill me if you dare!"[21]

Worried that Lola's foolhardiness would indeed get her killed, her coachman and a lieutenant harnessed her horses to a carriage and threw her inside. The coachman sprang on top and whipped the horses through the jeering crowd. Against her will, Lola left Munich.

Within a few days, Lola, dressed as a man and wearing a false beard, sneaked into Munich and managed to visit Ludwig briefly to secure her financial future. She and Ludwig arranged to meet in Switzerland a few weeks later when things calmed down. But word flew through the city that Lola had visited, and angry crowds, hearing that she was hiding in this building or that, would surround them and threaten to tear them apart.

In the midst of the uproar, Ludwig abdicated the throne, hoping to leave Bavaria and go to his Lola. But Bavarian citizens, furious that he would escape with state funds and crown jewels for his whore, grew riotous when word spread of his intended trip. His son, the new king, begged Ludwig to stay in Bavaria or else he, too, might lose the throne. Despite several efforts over the next two years to meet, the pair were always thwarted. And slowly, as reports filtered in about Lola's lifestyle, Ludwig's heart hardened against her. And he looked back wistfully on his blinding, foolish dream of love.

But the revolutions of 1848 were the last convulsions of the French Revolution. By the late nineteenth century, Western Europe had settled into a more polite form of civilization where society could not be roiled by anything as boring as a king's mistress. When Edward VII became king of Great Britain in 1901, he was labeled "King Edward the Caresser," a pun on his saintly ancestor King Edward the Confessor. Englishmen roared with laughter when they heard a story first reported by a naval officer on the royal yacht who, walking by the porthole of Edward's cabin, heard him cry, "Stop calling me Sir and put another cushion under your back."[22]

NINE

THE FRUITS OF SIN—
ROYAL BASTARDS

This making of bastards great
And duchessing every whore
The Surplus and Treasury cheat
Hath made me damnably poor.

—1680S POEM ABOUT CHARLES II

❈

MORE VALUABLE THAN A TIARA OF DIAMONDS, A LARGE BELLY was the greatest proof of the king's affections. A child bound the king to his mistress long after her disgrace or retirement and usually ensured her a lifetime of generous pensions. It is no wonder that most European courts were littered with royal bastards.

It was generally accepted that bastards were more intelligent and better looking than legitimate children. The belief was that intercourse between a man and his mistress was truly an act of love, or at least genuine desire. And in that moment of conception, the passions of love and desire mingled to form a more impressive child than those wrung from forced copulation. Louis XIV, distressed that five of his six legitimate children died young, while so many of his bastards thrived, was informed by his doctors that he had given his best juice to his mistresses, leaving the queen with only the dregs of the glass. The truth was that compulsory marital sex between inbred cousins often produced another genetically inferior generation, with the poor health, plodding intelligence, and grim appearance of their parents.

One day in the 1670s Louis XIV's Queen Marie-Thérèse, mother of a prince just as dull and unattractive as herself, grew quite peeved when she heard courtiers raving about the king's adorable, precocious sons with Madame de Montespan. "Everybody goes into ecstasies about those children while Monsieur le Dauphin is never even mentioned," she complained.[1]

In addition to superior intelligence and looks, royal bastards were less arrogant than their legitimate half siblings, who sauntered about court prickly with the pride of their fully royal birth. Bastards had no official position other than what their father chose to bestow on them and usually offered him a fierce loyalty in return for his generosity. When Henry II of England lay dying in 1189, of all his children, only his bastard son Geoffrey Plantagenet sat by his side. Henry's surviving legitimate sons, John and Richard, had allied themselves with the king of France and were rebelling against their father. "You alone have proved yourself my lawful and true son," Henry grumbled. "My other sons are really the bastards."[2]

THE LOVE OF KINGS AND BASTARDS

The king often loved his bastards far better than the princes and princesses coerced from his loins in the marriage bed. Nothing devastated Henri IV of France so much as seeing how his heir, the dauphin, was the spitting image of his mother, the unloved Queen Marie de Medici. According to a nobleman, soon after the birth of Henri's bastard with Henriette d'Entragues, the king said that this child was "finer than that of the Queen, who resembles the Medici, being swarthy and fat." When the queen was told of the king's comment, "she wept bitterly."[3] As his bastard son grew up, Henri would point to him and say, "See how good-natured this son is and how much he resembles me. He is not a stubborn child like the Dauphin."[4]

Henri's court physician, Dr. Hérouard, wrote, "The Queen can't understand how . . . the King . . . can give more caresses to the bastards than to the legitimate children . . . [and fears that] all the world will think that they are more loved by their father than the Queen's children."[5]

When the royal family's coach overturned in a flash flood while crossing a river in 1606, Henri grabbed César, his twelve-year-old bastard son with Gabrielle d'Estrées, and raced with him to safety, leaving the rest of the family in danger of drowning. We can picture fat Queen Marie, sputtering water, sinking in her heavy velvets into the muddy current, watching the back of her husband race away from her to carefully deposit his bastard on shore. The queen was fished out by a courtier, who dragged her to safety by the hair. She rewarded the courtier with a casket of jewels, an annual pension, and the position of captain of the Queen's Guards. But she never forgave her husband.

Much to Marie's dismay, Henri IV insisted on raising his eight bastards by various mistresses in the royal nursery along with his six legitimate children. At first Henriette d'Entragues, who had obtained a written promise of marriage from the king and considered herself his true wife, refused to allow her child to join the nursery. "I will not," she stormed, "allow my son to be in the company of all those bastards!"[6] Eventually Henri insisted, hoping that daily contact would result in brotherly love among the children rather than bitter rivalry. The king visited his brood frequently but had a hard time keeping them straight. He wrote a list that he kept in his pocket describing the children, detailing their names, ages, and mothers.

Many royal bastards, well loved by the king, disliked their mothers, who lived in a state of full or partial disgrace. Louis XIV's son with Madame de Montespan, the duc du Maine, had developed infantile paralysis at the age of three which left him with a limp, a tragedy of incalculable proportions in that world of exquisite grace and howling ridicule called Versailles. The duke blamed his mother for this calamity and never forgave her for her subsequent coldness to him. In 1691 the duke was so thrilled when he heard the king had finally exiled her from court that he insisted on taking the news to his mother himself. Within an hour of her sudden departure, he had all her baggage sent after her to Paris. He then ordered her furniture thrown out the windows onto the courtyard below lest she come back to fetch it. The duke immediately took over her prime apartments for himself.

Similarly, the son of Charles II and Louise de Kéroualle, duchess of Portsmouth, was close to his father but disliked his mother. When the king died in 1685 Louise took fourteen-year-old Charles to France, where she compelled this staunch young Protestant to convert to Catholicism. At nineteen Charles fled to England—rumor said with his mother's jewels—bounced back to the Protestant religion, married an English noblewoman, and took his place in the House of Lords—devastating his very French, very Catholic mother.

The saddest case was that of the actress Dorothy Jordan. Her ten children with the future William IV allowed her to die alone in exile and poverty while they were attending parties with their royal father. Their mother had become an embarrassment, but high society welcomed them with open arms when accompanied by William. All eight of the ten children who married did so into English nobility, living lives of luxury and conveniently forgetting that their mother was buried in a pauper's grave in France.

LEGITIMATE BASTARDS

Kings usually legitimized these offspring by royal decree. This legitimization was an official recognition of fatherhood, leaving the children bastards, but bastards with high expectations. In 1360 King Pedro of Portugal wanted to legitimize his children with his mistress Inez de Castro, whom he had married after their births. The pope declared that the children could be legitimate only if their mother was crowned queen—and Inez had died five years earlier. Undeterred, King Pedro dug her up, dressed her skeleton in regal robes, and had it placed in a chair in the cathedral and crowned in an elaborate ceremony which all the nobles were forced to attend. After that no one protested when he legitimized the children.

By the sixteenth century Europe had become somewhat more civilized. When Henri IV of France wanted to legitimize his son with Gabrielle d'Estrées in 1594, he merely issued documents proclaiming César his son. "We accord to him these letters," Henri wrote, "inasmuch as the stigma that is attached to the birth of our son excludes him from all hopes of succeeding to this our Crown. . . . His state would be but a poor one, were it not for this, his legitimation, whereby he is rendered capable of receiving all the gifts and benefits which may be conferred on him both by us and others."[7]

In addition to legitimizing their bastard children, kings often ennobled them, creating a string of infant counts and countesses, dukes and duchesses. While royal bastards were not considered suitable marriage partners for foreign royalty, they were highly sought after in marriage by noble families of the same nationality—thus mixing their blood with the sacred blood of the king. Because of the frequent marriage of bastard dukes and duchesses into established noble families, most of European nobility today is directly related to royal children born on the wrong side of the blanket.

Speaking of Charles II, the courtier George Villiers remarked, "A king is supposed to be a father to his people and Charles certainly was father to a good many of them."[8] Charles acknowledged fourteen bastards—nine sons and five daughters. He created six dukedoms and one earldom for his bastard sons, and made four of the daughters countesses. So many of his illegitimate sons were called Charles that he, like Henri IV before him, had a hard time keeping them straight. Charles kept a keen eye on young heirs and heiresses for his bastards and arranged for them to marry as children—some as young as five years old—to make sure the mouthwatering fortunes didn't slip away.

The fierce rivalry among royal mistresses often extended to the honors the king bestowed on their children. In 1674 Louise de Kéroualle was delighted to learn that Charles II had created her two-year-old son Charles the duke of Richmond. But her joy was almost immediately tempered by the news that he had also named Barbara, Lady Castlemaine's eleven-year-old son Henry the duke of Grafton, and Barbara was demanding that her son have precedence. Officially, precedence was given to the duke whose patent was first signed. Both women hammered poor Charles, who lamely suggested that the patents be signed at precisely the same moment; but neither would hear of it.

Both patents were made out bearing the same date but required a signature by Lord Treasurer Danby to be effective. Danby was planning to leave the next morning for Bath, and Lady Castlemaine instructed her agent to wait upon him very early, before he departed. Louise, however, heard that he had changed plans and would depart the night before. Her agent handed the patent to Danby as he was getting into his coach, and he obligingly went into his house to sign it. The next morning, when Lady Castlemaine's agent arrived, he found that Louise's son would always have precedence over Lady Castlemaine's. It is amusing to picture the blazing fury of the defeated mistress when she heard the news.

Because of her low birth, Nell Gwynn's sons were not included in these fits of generosity. Nell sadly informed her two boys that they "were princes by their father for their elevation, but they had a whore to their mother for their humiliation."[9] One day in 1676 when Charles came to visit, Nell, frustrated by years of waiting for the king to honor her sons, called out to her six-year-old, "Come hither, you little bastard!" When Charles scolded her, she said, "I have no better name to call him by." Laughing, Charles replied. "Then I must give him one," and soon after made the boy the earl of Burford.[10] After another eight years of Nell's lobbying, cajoling, and begging, Charles made him the duke of St. Albans. The handsome thirteen-year-old was given splendid apartments in Whitehall Palace and an annual allowance of fifteen hundred pounds. A lucrative marriage was arranged for him with a young heiress. The duke of St. Albans later served his country as ambassador to France.

PUSHED INTO WAR, SOLD INTO MARRIAGE

While seventeenth-century royal bastards could generally count on a dukedom, their counterparts in the rough-and-tumble medieval world stood a good chance of winning a throne. William the Conqueror, the valiant bastard son of Robert the Devil, duke of Normandy, took up his sword and vanquished English troops in 1066; nearly a thousand years later, his more refined descendant Elizabeth II serenely wears the crown. In twelfth- and thirteenth-century Norway royal bastards were handed the throne when their fathers died without legitimate sons. In the fourteenth century, royal bastards established dynasties in Portugal and Castile. It is ironic that the Renaissance, which ushered in the power of royal mistresses, suppressed the possibilities for their sons. The medieval world, forged by maces and battle axes, boasted few laws of marriage, divorce, and legitimacy compared to the civilized, refined society of later centuries.

It should come as no surprise that some royal bastards of the Renaissance and the Baroque era looked back wistfully to earlier centuries, when courageous bastards could win a kingdom for themselves. James, duke of Monmouth, the favorite son of Charles II, plotted to grab the throne of England. His father had no legitimate children, and Charles's brother and heir, James, was detested for being Catholic. After Charles's death in 1685, the popular duke raised troops and fought against James II. Monmouth was captured sleeping in a ditch and beheaded at the command of his uncle.

Many bastard sons, recognizing the foolhardiness of battling for a throne, found honor and glory fighting on behalf of royal fathers and half brothers. Don Juan of Austria (1547–1578), illegitimate son of the Holy Roman Emperor Charles V and Barbara Blomberg, became an admiral, clearing the seas of pirates and vanquishing the Turks at the Battle of Lepanto for his half brother Philip II.

Maurice, Count de Saxe (1696–1750), bastard son of Augustus the Strong of Saxony and Aurora von Königsmarck, became a great general and military theorist. James Fitzjames, the marshal duke of Berwick (1670–1734), the son of James II of England and his mistress Arabella Churchill, became a general and fought victoriously first for his exiled father and then for his cousin Louis XIV. During the War of the Austrian Succession, when the duke was sixty-four, a cannonball took off his head in a burst of glory.

While the illegitimate sons of kings often won glory on the battlefield, the daughters were used as marriage pawns to placate unruly but powerful noble families. Louis XIV married two of his bastard daughters into the Condé clan, a powerful family with a history of treason going back several generations. Louise-Françoise, Mademoiselle de Nantes, daughter of the king and Madame de Montespan, was only twelve when she married a Condé, a seventeen-year-old dwarf with an enormous head. Because of the bride's tender age, consummation of the marriage would have to wait two or three years. But Madame de Montespan, grasping greedily at such a brilliant match and fearing the marriage might fall through before consummation, pushed for her daughter to lose her virginity that very night.

The groom's family was equally pleased at such a close connection to the king, though they insisted that sex wait. Madame de Caylus wrote, "The nuptials were celebrated at Versailles in the King's state apartments . . . with a glorious illumination of the gardens and with all that magnificence of which the King was capable. The Grand Condé [the groom's grandfather] and his son left nothing undone to signal their delight in the consummation of the betrothal which they had made every effort to bring about."[11]

THE STRANGEST BASTARD OF ALL

The oddest case on record of a royal bastard was that of Don Antonio de Medici, the son—and yet not the son—of Archduke Francesco de Medici of Tuscany and his mistress Bianca Cappello. In 1576 Bianca had been a royal mistress for a full decade but had never conceived. Archduchess Johanna had provided her husband with several useless girls, and Francesco promised his mistress that if she gave him a son he would marry her and make her archduchess as soon as his unloved wife, always in precarious health, breathed her last. This longed-for son, legitimized through marriage, might very well inherit the throne.

Not one to accept defeat, Bianca seized on a bold measure to give Francesco the son he wanted. She sent an accomplice to choose three unmarried pregnant women in need, believing that surely one of the three would have a son, and housed them at her expense in different parts of the city. Bianca then proudly announced to a delighted Francesco that she was finally pregnant. She began padding her gowns and would not let her lover touch her for fear of disturbing her pregnancy.

Two of the women produced girls, much to Bianca's dismay, and were paid off. The third woman, Lucia, chosen for her health and beauty, gave birth to a boy. Immediately upon hearing this, Bianca pretended to go into labor, rending the air with cries of pretended pain. Francesco, hearing the news, raced to comfort her and brought with him his court physician. The baby, who had been unceremoniously nabbed from his mother and brought to Bianca's house in a basket of goods, remained hidden until he could be smuggled into the safety of her four-poster bed with curtains drawn.

The labor lasted many hours until Francesco gave up and returned to the palace. His doctor, however, remained to assist with the birth. When the doctor, who had not been permitted to touch or examine Bianca during her gut-wrenching performance, saw her old serving woman Santi bring in the basket through the garden, he understood what was happening. He tactfully obliged when Bianca instructed him to bring her wine. Upon returning, he was presented with Bianca's newborn child.

And the real mother? Lucia, deprived of her child and still bleeding, was forced to go on horseback on a long journey to Bologna with Gazzi, Bianca's humpbacked doctor, who had cared for her during her pregnancy. Gazzi obtained a position for her as wet nurse to a wealthy family under an assumed name and told her the whole story. Her son, whom Bianca and Francesco named Antonio, would have a brilliant life. But Lucia feared the Medicis would not hesitate to silence her to protect the secret of Antonio's birth. For twelve years she wandered around Italy using false names, always looking over her shoulder for a Medici dagger.

Soon after Antonio's birth, Archduchess Johanna finally gave her husband a son and heir, and temporarily at least, Antonio's importance shrank. Meanwhile Santi, Bianca's accomplice in the phony birth, began to blackmail Bianca. While on a journey with other servants, Santi was attacked and knifed by mysterious bandits who ignored the others in her party. Santi died—we must conclude she was murdered at Bianca's instigation—but not before confessing the whole story to a priest.

Archduchess Johanna died in 1578, and as she lay cooling in the grave, Francesco married Bianca. Rumors about Antonio's strange birth flew on swift wings, even as Europe reeled from the news that the archduke had married his mistress and crowned her. Francesco, Bianca, and Antonio became the butt of sneering jokes across Europe.

When the boy was two years old, Bianca knew that stories of his birth had reached Francesco's ears. Since he had a legitimate son, there seemed little reason to keep the lie about Antonio alive. And so she disclosed her secret as an amusing joke she had played to make him happy. Francesco, content in his legitimate son, accepted her explanation. However, he continued to raise Antonio as his son. He must have grown to love the boy, and moreover, he didn't want to become the laughingstock of Europe by admitting that his mistress had foisted a stranger's bastard upon him as his son.

When Francesco's only legitimate son died at the age of four in 1582, Bianca pushed to have Antonio created heir to the throne. Francesco asked permission from King Philip II of Spain, who wielded great power over the Italian states. It was a shocking request, especially as most of the world knew the child's unique history. With great diplomacy, Philip consented to having the child elevated to prince of Capestrano of the kingdom of Naples, but not heir to the throne of Tuscany.

Without waiting for Philip's response, Francesco legitimized Antonio in a completely illegal maneuver, presented him to his legislative advisory group, the Council of two hundred, as his son, and ordered that he should be addressed as His Highness. He sent the child out in a coach accompanied by an escort of the German Guard, a privilege reserved for princes. The Tuscan people were appalled. Legitimate Medicis had become bad enough, but to foist on them as their prince a commoner's bastard—without a drop of Medici blood—was to foment rebellion.

Francesco's brother Ferdinando, the legitimate heir to the throne, was afraid that Francesco would convince King Philip to recognize Antonio and support him with Spanish firepower. He kept a watchful eye on Bianca and loathed her more than ever.

Both Francesco and Bianca died within a few hours of each other in 1587, apparently from a malarial infection, though many whispered of poison. Ferdinando, the new archduke, immediately stripped eleven-year-old Antonio of all titles and possessions and refused to acknowledge him as his nephew. But the next day Ferdinando, having flexed his muscle and shown the boy's true position, returned all his magnificent estates. He promised to protect and honor him as long as he remained a faithful subject. A loving guardian, Ferdinando personally arranged an excellent education for the boy.

Hearing of the deaths of Bianca and Francesco, Antonio's mother, Lucia, ventured back to Florence and, at archduke Ferdinando's instigation, was reunited with her son. Ferdinando, seeking to avoid a future generation of spurious heirs claiming the Medici throne, forced Antonio to become a Knight of Malta, an order whose members were unable to contract a legally valid marriage. Antonio lived rich and successful and died in 1626, so ending the story of the royal bastard who almost inherited a throne—without a single drop of royal blood.

TEN

DEATH OF THE KING

❋

DEATH IN HIS BLACK ROBES WAS A FREQUENT VISITOR TO royal palaces in centuries past. The highest in the land were often struck down at the peak of their youth and power. A member of the court or royal family could be dancing one night, dead the next.

Even kings must die. Inevitably, the day came when Death, gaunt and hollow-eyed, began to pluck with clawlike fingers at the monarch's soul, patiently plucking until in shrieking agony it tore through bone and sinew. Now indeed was no time for fond memories of candlelit lovemaking, of hazy wine-filled nights, of women's lips and breasts and thighs. Not now, as the king prepared to walk into the gulf alone. For the first time in his life he would be truly alone, with no retinue of fawning courtiers or mincing ministers to strew rose petals in his path. In the end he was crownless, reduced in stature to that of the scurviest beggar, worth no more than any other human soul fleeing rancid human flesh.

Looking Death in the face after a reign of seventy years, Louis XIV soberly reflected, "We do what we choose while we are alive, but when we are dead we have less power than the lowliest individual."[1]

The king's protection of his mistress ceased with the beating of his heart; sometimes, in a desperate fit of repentance, earlier. The mistress was often barred entrance into his sick chamber by angry relatives, unless of course the king had a contagious disease such as smallpox, in which case she would be expected to nurse him. Even if she did make it to the deathbed to bid her lover farewell, she was sent away before the priest came to administer last rites. To the dying monarch, his mistress had become a living accusation of mortal sin, and he was not permitted to sully his newly cleansed soul by even looking at her.

There was no one less pitied than the courtesan of a dead king. Her carefully constructed position—which had been upheld only at the king's insistence—suddenly collapsed, flinging her far below ordinary mortals. She was rarely permitted the right of the poorest citizen to participate in her lover's funeral obsequies or visit the body lying in state.

Retribution from the royal family for perceived insults was often swift and merciless. While former mistresses, long since dismissed by the deceased monarch, were forgotten and permitted to rusticate gracefully, it was the king's final mistress who bore the full resentment of the royal family, courtiers, and commoners. In 1350 when Alfonso XI of Castile died of the black plague, his mistress Leonor de Guzman was imprisoned by Alfonso's long-ignored wife Queen Maria and murdered in her cell by the queen's express order.

The following century was only slightly more civilized. After the death of Edward IV of England in 1483, court and public opinion were so violently hostile to his final mistress, Jane Shore, that she was forced to march through London wearing the white shroud and dunce cap of a penitent, holding a candle. Though there is evidence that she survived another forty years, a legend sprung up that she died on a dunghill, pelted by stones, and many subsequent royal mistresses were heartily wished the death of Jane Shore.

The new king, usually the son of the former monarch, often ached to punish the woman who had hurt his mother the queen. Charles VII's son and heir Louis often bristled at the insults offered his long-suffering mother by his father's mistress Agnes Sorel. One day in 1444, Louis, running into Agnes, cried, "By our Lord's passion, this woman is the cause of all our misfortunes," and punched her in the face.[2] Perhaps it was lucky for Agnes that she predeceased her royal lover; one cannot imagine a peaceful existence for her under Louis XI.

In 1760, as King George II of England lay dying, his beloved mistress was nowhere near his deathbed. Lady Yarmouth, who knew the future George III was no admirer of hers, was quietly stuffing ten thousand pounds into a strongbox to take back to her native land of Hanover, where young George couldn't get her.

Upon hearing of a monarch's serious illness, friends deserted his mistress in waves in an effort to ingratiate themselves with the future king. Madame de Pompadour experienced this in 1757, when a madman stabbed Louis XV as he entered his carriage at Versailles. Though superficial, the wound in his side was bloody, and Louis thought death was imminent. Madame de Pompadour, whose rooms were always filled with simpering courtiers, suddenly found fewer visitors, and those with gloating faces. "They came to see how she took it," wrote her lady's maid.[3] Her enemy the marquis d'Argenson could not conceal his glee when he reported, "She pretends not to feel her disgrace, but little by little people are forsaking her."[4]

Crying, deserted, the royal mistress packed her bags and prepared to flee to her safe haven in Paris in the event of the king's death. But after several days Louis, rallying, grabbed a cane, called "Don't you come" to his son, and hobbled down the private staircase to her rooms.[5] Madame de Pompadour's position was once more secure, and the obsequious courtiers once again waited in her antechamber for an audience.

Death was a friend of sorts to a long-betrayed queen, serving up her husband cold on a platter, all hers for the first time since their honeymoon. She knew where he was, and he was in no position to escape her clutches to visit a mistress. The few days between the king's death and his burial were often sacred to his neglected wife, and the last thing she wanted was his mistress to soil the sanctity.

Shortly after Edward VII's death in 1910, his widow Queen Alexandra invited her friend Lord Esher to take one last look at the king's body before the funeral. He was perplexed by her smiling gaiety until he realized this was the first time in nearly fifty years of marriage that Alexandra completely possessed her husband with no competition in sight. "After all," she said over the corpse, "he always loved me best."[6]

"BITTERNESS . . . WILL BE BUT SWEETNESS BESIDE MY GREAT LOSS"

In 1559 Diane de Poitiers, the most powerful woman in France, lost everything in an instant when a wooden lance shattered the visor and pierced the eye of her lover Henri II in a joust. Both Diane and Queen Catherine had been cheering in the stands for the king when the accident occurred. As Henri's limp body was carried away, blood gushing from his smashed visor and splinters driven deeply into his brain, his unloved queen became monarch in name and fact, ruling for her young son.

Diane tried to push her way through the crowds to see Henri but could not. He was carried on a litter to the palace, where she was barred admittance. Inconsolable, she returned to her house in Paris and tried desperately to get word of the king's condition. None was brought to her. She could not know that her dying lover called out her name unceasingly, but Queen Catherine refused to send for her. Finally, fate had delivered full possession of the wayward king to his neglected wife, and she was not about to share it with the detested Diane.

The king endured several days of agony as surgeons probed his shattered eye socket. The queen coldly had four condemned criminals beheaded so their skulls could be probed in a fruitless effort to save her husband.

Ten days after the accident the queen sent a messenger to Diane demanding the crown jewels Henri had given her. Diane asked quietly, "Is the King dead?" The messenger replied that death was not far off. Diane responded, "So long as there remains a breath of life in him I wish my enemies to know that I do not fear them. As yet there is no one who can command me. I am still of good courage. But when he is dead I do not want to live after him, and all the bitterness that one could wish me will be but sweetness beside my great loss."[7]

Two days later the king died, and another messenger was sent to Diane to retrieve the crown jewels and the keys to the king's cabinets and desk. Diane returned a box containing the jewels and keys, as well as an inventory of its contents and a personal letter to the queen asking her pardon.

Diane was not permitted to attend Henri's funeral but watched the procession pass under the window of her Paris house. Then she sat down and waited to be arrested. But the guards never came for her. Diane had ruled France prudently for the twelve years of Henri's reign and could not be accused of treason. Perhaps more important, she had married her two daughters into families that were powerful allies of the queen. Catherine satisfied herself with claiming Chenonceaux, the fairy-tale castle Henri had given Diane, and defacing the countless "HD" ciphers Henri had placed all over his many châteaus. She either had them removed and burned or hired a wood carver to turn them into an "HC."

Diane retired to the château of Anet, which she had inherited from her long-dead husband. Devoting her last years to good works, she built a hospital and a home for unwed mothers, orphans, and widows. She left money to several convents for Masses to be said for her soul. In 1566, seven years after Henri's death, she died quietly after a brief illness at the age of sixty-five, still lovely. One courtier wrote, "It is sad that earth should hide that beautiful body."[8]

"Let not poor Nelly starve"

Unlike most kings, who left behind a single declared mistress on their deaths, Charles II left behind a harem in 1685. His two principal mistresses met with very different fates.

As the fifty-five-year-old king lay dying of a stroke, possibly the result of syphilis, it was Louise de Kéroualle who provided Charles with a last great service. One of the few who knew him to be a secret Catholic who, for political reasons, had never officially converted, she wanted him to receive the sacrament and last rites according to the Catholic Church. He had refused the Protestant sacrament on his deathbed, and no one was certain why—except Louise and his brother James. But James was lost in the fog of thought that descends when one is about to become king.

Louise felt herself forbidden by decency to visit the king's chamber, where the unhappy queen kept vigil. She went instead to the French ambassador and requested that he speak with James and find a priest. According to the ambassador, she said, "Go and tell him that I have implored you to warn him to consider what can be done to save the King, his brother's, soul."[9] James, recollecting his duty, visited Charles at once and asked him if he should send for a priest, to which the king replied, "For God's sake, brother, do, and lose no time!"[10]

Shortly thereafter, up the secret staircase, the same way the prostitutes had crept to visit the king, came a priest, who administered the last rites. Afterward, Charles said of Louise, "I have always loved her, and I die loving her."[11]

Upon hearing the news of Charles's death, a panicked Louise found sanctuary in the house of the French ambassador. Knowing she had never been popular, had meddled in politics, and was hated as a Whig, a papist, and a foreign spy, Louise feared the new government as well as the mob. She tried to sail for France at once. King James, fearing the wrath of her powerful protector Louis XIV, ensured her safety and guaranteed her a pension of three thousand pounds a year. But he also demanded that she stay in England to pay her creditors and return certain of the crown jewels in her possession.

Smoothing down her ruffled feathers, Louise returned to court squawking for the pensions Charles had awarded her—nineteen thousand pounds yearly as his mistress as well as twenty-five thousand a year from the Irish revenue. James allowed her to keep the nineteen thousand but pocketed the twenty-five thousand himself. Six months after Charles's death, she sailed for France in an armada stuffed with her possessions—two hundred thousand gold francs, oaken chests of jewels and plate, furniture, coaches, sedan chairs, and works of art.

Used to living extravagantly and gambling wildly, Louise soon parted ways with her riches. Pressed by creditors, she bounced between London and Versailles, clamoring for pensions from both nations for services rendered, and usually obtaining them. But Charles's death had forced her from the stage; in one instant she went from leading lady to reluctant spectator. Much to her chagrin, for nearly fifty years she lived as an interesting artifact from a bygone reign, still attractive but indisputably irrelevant. The initial virulent bout of venereal disease she had caught from the king seems never to have returned. She died in 1734 at the age of eighty-five.

Unlike Louise de Kéroualle, Nell Gwynn's pensions were set up to end upon Charles's death. She had no ducal estates or income in perpetuity. As Charles lay dying, he must have wished he had rewarded her better for her seventeen years of faithful service. "Let not poor Nelly starve," Charles implored his brother James shortly before he expired.[12]

Nell suffered financial problems immediately after Charles's death. Her creditors, a variety of shopkeepers with whom she had kept large accounts, beat against her door demanding payment. Initially King James turned a deaf ear to her urgent pleas for assistance. While Nell owned numerous valuable properties, they were entailed to her son with Charles and she was not permitted to sell them.

Finally, Nell mortgaged some of her properties and borrowed against her jewels and plate to obtain cash to pay the creditors. She believed that James would honor his brother's deathbed request. She was right—three months after Charles's death, James sent Nell cash for her most pressing needs and promises of additional help. By the end of the year he had paid numerous merchants' bills and given her an additional twenty-three hundred pounds in cash. Most important, in January 1686 James settled on Nell an annual pension of fifteen hundred pounds—a fraction of what she had received from Charles, but enough to live on comfortably as a private person.

In the two years after Charles's death, Nell enjoyed her life in London. She visited friends, gave dinner parties, and went to the theater. Over the years she had spells of illness but usually bounced back quickly. It is likely that Nell had caught from Charles the same venereal disease that Louise had, but in Nell's case it slowly hardened her arteries and increased her blood pressure.

In March 1687, Nell had a stroke. She seemed to be slowly recuperating when two months later she suffered one even more devastating. Paralyzed, she lay in her great silver bed, the one royal Charles had christened so many times, and there she breathed her last at the age of thirty-seven.

"MORE IN NEED OF PITY THAN ANYONE ELSE"
It was not Madame de Pompadour but her successor, Madame du Barry, who had the misfortune to lose Louis XV to death while she was still maîtresse-en-titre.

At sixty-four the king, who had always enjoyed a morbid fascination with dead bodies, caught smallpox after examining the coffin of a girl about to be buried. His face, covered with boils, turned the color of bronze, and he suffered horribly.

After Madame du Barry had nursed her royal lover through

the ravages of the disease at great risk to herself, she was dismissed from the stench of sweat and putrefaction so the king could receive absolution for his earthly sins. When the king, roused from a feverish sleep, asked for her and was told she had left, he asked, "What, already?" and wept.[13] Before administering the comforting rites, the priests forced the dying monarch to sign a letter imprisoning his faithful mistress in the moldering convent of the Pont aux Dames. The faithless lover, trembling before the gates of hell, signed the despicable document.

The new king, young Louis XVI, at his wife's prodding, banished everyone with the name of du Barry from court, and many relatives who had been the objects of her bounty quickly changed their names. But Marie Antoinette's mother, Maria Theresa of Austria, reproached her daughter for gloating over an "*unfortunate creature* who had lost everything and was more in need of pity than anyone else."[14]

As Louis's stinking corpse, packed with aromatic herbs into a lead casket, was carried to its final resting place, the former favorite went with a heavy heart to her imprisonment. A few loyal friends at court arranged for her to have a maid and a wagonload of plain furniture—a bed, a couple of chairs, a little rug, and a screen to shield her from drafts. Armed with these small comforts Madame du Barry was confined to a narrow room in a dank thousand-year-old convent.

Though the nuns were scandalized to have such a notorious woman in their midst—some were afraid that even looking at her would blemish their souls—they soon grew to admire Madame du Barry's pleasing ways. Her convent education assisted her in falling right into place. She gladly helped with chores, was never late to prayers, and within weeks of her incarceration had wrapped the prudish nuns around her little finger. A year later, when she was released, they wept as her wagon rumbled away.

She was initially banished from coming within ten leagues of both Paris and Versailles, but her exile was soon lifted, and she returned to the small château of Louveciennes, outside Versailles, which her royal lover had given her. She became the patroness of the neighborhood, dispensing charity to the poor and sick and entertaining lavishly.

But Jeanne du Barry was not destined to live out her life in bourgeois luxury. The French peasants who starved while she played with the king had long memories. In 1789 her world began to fall apart. The Bastille fell, Louis XVI was guillotined, and Madame du Barry's lover the duc de Brissac was torn apart on the streets, his head affixed to a pike. Sweet, naive, and stupid, Madame du Barry lived in a fantasy world at Louveciennes. She ordered statues for the garden, gowns for herself, new furnishings. When her jewels were stolen and turned up in London, she obtained papers from the revolutionary government to sail to England to identify the items. At a time when thousands were trying to escape France by any means to avoid the guillotine, Madame du Barry *sailed back to France*. She returned to her château to soak in scented baths and meet with her dressmaker.

But shortly after her return Madame du Barry was taken prisoner, found guilty of trumped-up charges of treason and espionage, and sentenced to be guillotined. She made a bargain with her executioners—she would tell them where all her valuables at Louveciennes were hidden in return for her life. For three hours they dutifully recorded her statements about jewels buried in the garden, silver concealed in the pond, paintings secreted in the old mill.

And then they sent the man to cut her hair and bind her hands. Fainting, this king's darling was loaded onto a tumbrel with other prisoners. Moaning and sobbing, she was forcibly dragged up the steps to the guillotine, crying, "You are going to hurt me! Please don't hurt me!"[15]

As her shorn head fell into the basket, a cry went up of *"Vive la révolution!"* The most beautiful woman in Europe, the last great *maîtresse-en-titre*, was dumped in an unmarked grave beside other victims of the French Revolution.

While touring Italy in 1796 Wilhelmine Rietz, countess of Lichtenau, was informed that her lover of twenty-six years, King Frederick William II of Prussia, was dangerously ill. A high-level official wrote her that "only the presence of Countess Lichtenau could perhaps save the King, who was anxious to see her."[16] She set out at once for Berlin.

Upon her return, Wilhelmine found the king greatly altered by his severe illness. Upon seeing his beloved companion, however, he began to feel better at once. She nursed Frederick William faithfully, arranging for plays to be performed in his sickroom, instructing the cooks to prepare his favorite meals. The pain-ravaged king was irritable unless his countess was by his side. Most courtiers agreed that she prolonged his life.

But after eighteen months of gradual recuperation his condition worsened, and it became obvious to all that he was dying. Wilhelmine's friends recommended that she flee the country with her jewels worth 50,000 crowns, and her drafts upon the Bank of England, worth another £120,000. But Wilhelmine was literally faithful until death. She wanted to be there, at her lover's side, at the moment of passing. Only then would she look to her own concerns.

Frederick William's legs swelled horribly. Plays and music were no longer appropriate diversions for the dying man. Wilhelmine brought in courtiers whose conversation amused him. She read to him from books he found interesting. As the king's agonies increased, Wilhelmine fell into convulsions. The doctors in attendance advised her to return home and get some rest. They would notify her if the king either improved or deteriorated. Drained, Wilhelmine complied. When she approached the crown prince, Frederick William's twenty-seven-year-old son and heir, he cried, "Take that woman away out of my sight."[17] It was a sign of things to come.

The crown prince had word sent to Wilhelmine that his father was doing well to prevent her from returning. And so King Frederick William II, at the last, strode into the abyss without her hand in his.

Wallowing in a bed of sorrow, Wilhelmine soon learned that additional blows awaited her. Friends disappeared overnight. No one called to console her. Her own servants abused her. Worse, the new king sent agents to search her house for state papers and demanded the keys to her desk and cupboards. The papers so sought after proved to be romantic poems, songs, and love letters.

Nonetheless, three days after the king's death she was put under house arrest. Her ailing mother was removed, along with her faithful maid. Her frightened children threw themselves into her arms but were dragged away. For six weeks soldiers guarded Wilhelmine as she remained alone inside her shuttered house mourning her lost lover. Finally, the commission investigating her crimes permitted her a two-hour daily walk. When she walked near her lover's palace, she burst into tears.

Wilhelmine was charged with numerous crimes, including taking rings from the fingers of the dying king, as well as a large diamond known as the Solitaire. In response, Wilhelmine described the cabinet in the king's bedroom where the Solitaire and other jewelry could be found. She had removed the rings at the king's request so he could wash his hands. Afterward, when she wanted to put them back on, she noticed how swollen Frederick William's fingers had become. Not wishing to alarm him, she deposited them in the cabinet.

Wilhelmine languished under house arrest a total of three months from the day of Frederick William's death. Finally, a messenger visited her one evening with the decision of Frederick William III. She was permitted to retain any furniture and jewelry the dead king had given her and keep a small pension of four thousand talers a year. However, she would trade her country estate and Berlin palace for a fortress prison in Silesia. Without shedding a tear, she packed her bags and left immediately.

But Wilhelmine had some influential friends willing to stand up for her against the tide of royal displeasure. They reminded the new king of how poorly Louis XVI's treatment of Madame du Barry had reflected on him. A friend of hers, the Italian poet Filistri, frequently cautioned the new king about dishonoring his father's memory. He also set to work on the queen mother—

the dead king's neglected wife—the young queen, the princes, and the ministers to free Wilhelmine from her fortress. After only two months' incarceration she was set free. A few years later Napoleon, visiting the court of Berlin, interested himself in her case and, hearing that she was living in great poverty, persuaded Frederick William III to return a part of her confiscated fortune.

But the chastened mistress did not go quietly into retirement; she had a series of lovers. At the age of fifty she married a young artist, who left her only two years later. She moved to Vienna and then to Paris, and died in obscurity in 1822 at the age of sixty-eight.

"I WAS NEVER A POMPADOUR, STILL LESS A MAINTENON"

Because of her age and the length of her relationship with Austro-Hungarian emperor Franz Josef, Katharina Schratt was accorded the greatest deference upon the death of her lover. She had assuaged his grief in 1889 when his only son, Crown Prince Rudolf, murdered his seventeen-year-old mistress, Maria Vetsera, and committed suicide at the royal hunting lodge of Mayerling. She had been his only solace when his beloved wife, the empress Elizabeth, was assassinated in 1898. And for thirty-three years she had comforted him as his unwieldy empire fell apart at the seams.

In 1916, when the emperor expired at the age of eighty-six, his mistress was sixty-six. No longer the tempting actress the emperor had first seen in the imperial theater, Katharina had grown stout and matronly. During World War I, good-hearted Katharina opened a hospital for wounded soldiers, personally supervising the preparation of nourishing food, which was becoming increasingly difficult to find.

During her visits to the widowed emperor, the two were seen tottering around the garden. Sometimes she read imperial documents to him, as his eyes were failing. She soothed the shattered little man who had borne an empire on his slender shoulders for nearly seventy years, sinking now under the weight of a world war.

As soon as the emperor died, Katharina was called to the palace. She cut two white roses from her greenhouse and took a carriage the short distance. Her former enemy, the emperor's daughter Archduchess Valerie, ran to her weeping, thanking her for her lifetime of care of her father. Katharina entered the death chamber, saw Franz Josef on his narrow bed, his body shrunken and empty without its spark, and placed the roses in his folded hands.

With the real estate and jewels she had earned as imperial mistress Katharina supported her family and dependents in the awful period between the wars. Known for her generosity, she took in numerous dogs abandoned by owners who were no longer able to feed them.

In the 1930s journalists pestered her for a statement about her relationship with the late emperor. Publishers begged her to write her memoirs. Katharina would always reply, "I am an actress not a writer and I have nothing to say, for I was never a Pompadour, still less a Maintenon."[18]

One day when she was eighty-six, Katharina—who had lived in the glittering twilight of the Habsburg Empire, a time of horse-drawn carriages, elegant waltzes, and bustled ball gowns—looked out her window and saw Hitler's motorcade in a triumphant procession through Vienna, passing right in front of her home. Finally, fifty-six years after becoming imperial mistress, Katharina made a political statement. She pulled down all the blinds.

"WHAT IS TO BECOME OF ME?"

In 1910 sixty-eight-year-old King Edward VII lay dying, his ox-like constitution finally broken by a lifetime of dissipation. Hearing the news, his mistress Alice Keppel rifled through her papers to retrieve a letter he had written her eight years earlier after he had recovered from a severe attack of appendicitis—during which her path to the sickroom had been firmly barred by Queen Alexandra. In this letter the king requested that Alice be allowed to visit him should he suffer a serious illness again.

And so, permitted but unwanted, Alice slipped into the death room, sat next to the dying monarch, and stroked his hand. Alexandra looked out the window, turning her slender royal back on this touching scene between her husband and his mistress. Edward whispered hoarsely to his wife, "You must kiss her. You must kiss Alice."[19] We can imagine the revulsion with which the queen presented her marble lips. Such revulsion, in fact, that she later denied the kiss had been bestowed.

When Edward lapsed into a coma, Alexandra took aside Sir Francis Laking, the king's friend, and instructed him, "Get that woman away." Alice grew hysterical and refused to leave her lover's side. As she was being dragged from the room she cried, "I never did any harm. There was nothing wrong between us. What is to become of me?"[20]

With the door safely shut, in the presence of her husband's corpse, Alexandra finally vented to Sir Francis the feelings she had sealed in for nearly five decades. "I would not have kissed her, if he had not bade me," the queen cried. "But I would have done anything he asked of me. Twelve years ago, when I was so angry about Lady Warwick, and the King expostulated with me and said I should get him into the divorce court, I told him once for all that he might have all the women he wished, and I would not say a word; and I have done everything since that he desired me to do about them. He was the whole of my life and, now he is dead, nothing matters."[21]

Having composed herself, Alice returned home and reported to all her friends that Queen Alexandra had not only kissed her but had assured her that the royal family would look after her, a statement denied by all other deathbed witnesses. Alice went in full mourning to Edward's funeral, swathed in floor-length black veils and plumed with black ostrich feathers like his widow, but slipped into the chapel by a side door. After the period of mourning, Alice decided that her disappearance might be appreciated by the new king. With her ill-gotten gains, Alice took her husband and children on a two-year tour of India and China. When they returned to England, the family entertained lavishly.

In 1936, sixty-seven-year-old Alice was lunching at the Ritz in London when an announcement was made that King Edward VIII was abdicating to marry his mistress, Wallis Warfield Simpson. She winced. "Things were done much better in *my* day," she sniffed loudly.[22]

ELEVEN

THE END OF A BRILLIANT
CAREER AND BEYOND

*Decay's effacing fingers have swept
the lines where beauty lingers.*

—LORD BYRON

❋

PADDING SILENTLY THROUGH GILDED CORRIDORS, SOME-
times Death slipped past the king's chamber and glided on to
another, where he visited a mistress. The dead royal mistress was
scooped up still warm, thrown in a grave, and promptly forgotten by courtiers, who focused immediately on her replacement.

Most mistresses, however, were not fated to die tragically
young or suffer dramatic punishment after the death of their
royal lovers. Most were destined for a more mundane fate—they
lived to despise their mirrors, were dismissed and replaced by
younger, prettier faces. In centuries past the cruel hand of time
swooped down earlier to wreak its ravages on female beauty.
Louis XIV's beautiful blonde Louise de La Vallière immured
her fading looks in a convent at the ripe old age of twenty-nine.

Samuel Pepys described one of Charles II's mistresses, a venerable twenty-three, as beginning to "decay."[1]

One day when Lady Castlemaine ran into her enemy the duke of Ormonde at court, she vociferously wished him disfigurement, dismemberment, and a last gasp at the end of the hangman's rope. The duke looked coolly at the twenty-nine year old and replied, "I am not in so much haste to put an end to your days, Madam, for all I wish is that I may live to see you old."[2]

What happened to rejected mistresses as they aged? Many continued active lives away from court, marrying, bearing children, visiting friends, enjoying their ill-gotten gains in lovely country homes filled with fine furnishings.

In their later years, many former royal mistresses found in religion the antidote to their youthful sins. And while most surrendered their beauty wearily to that most puissant enemy, time, a few battled bravely until the last.

DEATH TAKES A MISTRESS

It is not surprising that Death took many royal mistresses at the peak of their youth and beauty. Their doleful end was often presaged months earlier in the happy news of a longed-for pregnancy, a tangible tie to the king forever.

Death must have laughed as he looked for Gabrielle d'Estrées, for he timed his visit with exquisite irony—only hours before she was to wed her lover Henri IV, becoming queen of France and clearing the way for her son César to inherit the throne. By March 1599 Gabrielle was five months pregnant. She had sailed through her three previous pregnancies in glowing health. This one was markedly different, however. She was peevish, fretful, depressed. She complained often of feeling unwell, feared some impending disaster. She spent many sleepless nights and suffered horrible nightmares when she did sleep.

Three days before the wedding, which was to take place on Easter Sunday, Gabrielle traveled to Paris by barge to prepare for the ceremony while Henri remained at the palace of Fontainebleau. When Henri bid her farewell on the bank of the river, she burst into tears and clung to him. The king thought Gabrielle was suffering from nerves; but perhaps in some secret part of her soul she knew it was the last time she would ever see Henri, feel his flesh warm and solid against hers.

Landing in Paris, Gabrielle ate at the house of her friend the banker Zamet, where dinner included a lemon. Feeling unwell, Gabrielle canceled her appearance at several gala events. By the next afternoon she was in labor—four months early. Her birth pangs were keener than they had ever been. She twisted in agony as doctors dismembered the dead child inside her and drew it out. Despite the presence of two surgeons, three apothecaries, and a priest, Gabrielle died on Easter Saturday, the day before she was to have become queen of France.

The timing of Gabrielle's death was so strange that—naturally— rumors swept France that she had been poisoned. The likely culprits were the Vatican or the House of Medici, which had been violently opposed to Henri's marriage to Gabrielle, hoping he would marry Tuscan duchess Marie de Medici instead. The doctors—baffled despite a careful autopsy—concluded she had been killed by a "corrupt" lemon.[3] Modern doctors, reading reports of Gabrielle's symptoms and suffering, believe she died of a septic pregnancy. Whatever the cause of Gabrielle's death, many Catholics thought God had struck her down in the nick of time, saving them the indignity of having a whore as queen.

Hearing of her sudden grave illness, Henri raced to see her but was stopped on the way with the news of her death. Devastated, he went into mourning, immediately donning black instead of the traditional white or violet, something which French monarchs had never done before. His love had been deep; initially his grief was extreme. During a long life of philandering, Henri was faithful to only one woman, and that woman was Gabrielle.

The royal mistress who had found such honor in life received strange indignities in death. Household servants stole valuable rings from her dead fingers. Upon hearing the news of her death, Gabrielle's father harnessed his horses and carted off from storage the royal furniture she had ordered for her queenly apartments. Gabrielle had grimaced so in agony that her mouth twisted around toward the back of her head and, at her death, stuck there as if in concrete; neither the doctor nor her attendants could push it back into its proper place. Her mangled body, exhibiting no traces of her former beauty, was in no condition to view. Nailed in a coffin, it was pushed under the bed in her Paris town house while mourners visited her wax effigy, propped up on the bed, offering it food according to custom. Henri—prevented from holding her funeral at Notre Dame, as Gabrielle had not been royal—was forced to settle for a lesser church.

After the funeral, Gabrielle's effigy was placed in a small chamber in the king's private apartments in the Louvre and dressed in a new gown daily. Henri wrote, "The root of my love is dead; it will not spring up again."[4] He visited the figure for many years, even after he had caved in to the pope's wishes and married Marie de Medici and—perhaps as a protest—taken a nubile young mistress. Despite the king's genuine sadness at the loss of Gabrielle, the root of his love continued to spring up until his dying day.

The gloriously beautiful Mademoiselle de Fontanges also died as a result of a pregnancy. In 1680 she gave birth to Louis XIV's child, who died shortly thereafter. While she survived the delivery, her bleeding did not stop. After several weeks the wan, weakened woman left Versailles to recuperate in a convent. The king had little patience with illness, and his mistress hoped to vanquish his heart once again by returning bursting with health and beauty.

Madame de Sévigné described the touching contrast between Mademoiselle de Fontange's rich emoluments and her deadly illness. "Mademoiselle de Fontanges has left for Chelles," she wrote. "She had four carriages, drawn by six horses, each, her own carriage drawn by eight, and all her sisters with her, but all so sad that it was pitiful to see—that great beauty losing all her blood, pale, changed, overwhelmed with sorrow, despising the 40,000 *ecus* annual pension and the *tabouret* which she has, and wishing for her health and the heart of the King which she has lost."[5]

The former favorite bled to death slowly, each day losing a bit more strength, a bit more color, until a year later Mademoiselle de Fontanges was dead at the age of twenty-two. There is a story in which Louis visited in her final hours and sat crying at her bed. "Having seen tears in the eyes of my King," she is supposed to have said, "I can die happy."[6] But this story was deemed untrue by many at Versailles because the king had, in fact, already forgotten her.

In 1743 Louis XV's mistress Madame de Ventimille gave him a healthy son and a few days later suffered sudden fatal convulsions. The body of the unpopular "king's whore" was laid out in a house in the town of Versailles watched over by guards. When they left their posts to drink, an enraged mob broke in and insulted the corpse.

Louis's next mistress, Madame de Châteauroux, also died young. A few weeks before her sudden demise, the king had nearly died from fever while on campaign and had submitted to his priests' demands to send Madame de Châteauroux away in disgrace, stripping her of all her titles and privileges. As he recovered, Madame de Châteauroux waited on tenterhooks for her summons to return to court. Finally the summons came. Triumphant, the favorite packed her bags ready to race back to her lavish apartments in the palace and take up where she had left off. She eagerly planned suitable punishments for those who had gloated over her downfall.

But before she could enter her carriage, she was struck with a blinding headache and took to her bed. Impatient at the delay of her victorious return, she waited for the headache to disappear. Then fever set in. She went into convulsions, sending soul-wrenching shrieks through her house. Her burning ambitions, which had enflamed the entire court, dwindled to a tiny spark, then to a cold ash.

The king was devastated. The marquis d'Argenson wrote, "Our poor Master has a look which makes one tremble for his life."[7]

Louis had lost two mistresses in two years. He was to lose his next and best-loved mistress to death as well. For nineteen years,

Madame de Pompadour had reigned supreme over a king and a nation. But in 1763, her health rapidly deteriorating, she confided her long years of suffering to her old friend Madame de La Ferté-Imbault. "I have never heard a finer sermon on the nemesis of ambition," the friend wrote. "She seemed so wretched, so proud, so violently shaken and so suffocated by her own enormous power that I came away after an hour's talk feeling that death was the only refuge left to her."[8]

At the age of forty-one, probably suffering from tuberculosis and congestive heart failure, Madame de Pompadour had such difficulty climbing steps that a mechanical chair was installed on the staircase in Versailles. By early 1764 it was clear to all that the royal mistress was a dying woman. In February of that year she suffered a lung hemorrhage, followed by chills and fever. The king visited her every day. By April, the cold wet spring in the drafty palace had exacerbated her illness. In her last days, she rouged her deathly pale cheeks, put on a brocade dressing gown over white taffeta petticoats, and had her hair combed. When the king visited her, she, knowing he hated sickness, refused to talk about her illness and pretended she was actually quite well. Dying, she listened to his boring stories and injected the witty remark at just the right moment.

On April 13, the king, having spoken with Madame de Pompadour's doctors, broke the news to her that she had days, perhaps hours, left. She asked him if he wished her to see a priest, and he nodded. She was not eager to do so, because she knew that once a priest arrived Louis would have to leave, given the sinful nature of their early relationship, and she would never see him again. Catholic mistresses were doomed to die without their lovers by their side.

As if an ordinary mortal's death would pollute the ambrosial atmosphere of the gods, it was not permitted for anyone but a member of the royal family to die at Versailles. But Louis insisted that Madame de Pompadour stay there unmolested, in as much comfort as possible.

Slipping from life, she made her will, leaving many bequests to faithful friends and servants. That last night she slept sitting up in a chair because her rotting lungs could inhale a bit of air only in that position. The following afternoon the dauphin wrote, "She is dying with a courage rare in either sex. Every time she draws a breath, she thinks it is her last. It is one of the saddest and most cruel endings one can imagine. . . . The King has not seen her since yesterday."[9]

At the very end, Madame de Pompadour soiled her linen. When her maids wanted to shift her to change it she replied, "I know you are very skillful, but I am so feeble that you could not help hurting me, and it is not worth it for the little time I have left."[10]

As her priest rose to go, she gave one last, shining smile and said, "One moment, Monsieur le Curé, and we will go away together."[11] Her lungs—never strong, now utterly defeated—rattled out the last breath of air. And then there was the awful silence.

When the king was informed that his mistress had died, he shut himself up in his apartments with some of her best friends. Meanwhile, the duchesse de Praslin, looking out her window, saw the corpse of a woman, "covered only with a sheet wrapped so tightly that the shape of the head, the breasts, the stomach and legs were distinctly outlined."[12] Moments after Madame de Pompadour's death, her body had been whisked away.

The day of her funeral, a cold wind howled around Versailles. As the solemn procession passed in front of the palace, the king—who was forbidden by etiquette to attend the ceremony—stood on his balcony in the rain without a hat or coat, tears rolling down his face. "They are the only tribute I can offer her," he said to his servant.[13]

When her friend Voltaire heard of her passing, he wrote, "I am greatly afflicted by the death of Madame de Pompadour; I weep when I think of it. It is very absurd that an old scribbler like myself should be still alive, and that a beautiful woman should have been cut off at forty in the midst of the most brilliant career in the world. Perhaps if she had tasted the repose which I enjoy, she would be living now."[14]

A few days after the funeral the queen said, "Finally there is no more talk here of her who is no longer than if she had never existed. Such is the way of the world; it is very hard to love it."[15]

THE BUSINESS OF LIFE

Not all royal mistresses suffered tragic endings. Most of them aged, were ousted, and went about the business of daily life, pockets stuffed with the wages of sin.

Early in the reign of George I of England, three ancient royal mistresses of dead kings ran into each other at the English court. The duchesses of Portsmouth, Dorchester, and Orkney, mistresses of Charles II, James II, and William III, respectively, had beaten the odds and lived into a healthy old age. Like a trio of barnacled old scows bobbing in the harbor, the elderly dames looked at each other. Suddenly the plucky duchess of Orkney crowed, "Who would have thought that we three old whores would meet here?"[16]

After the exile of her lover, James II, Catherine Sedley, duchess of Dorchester, was given a pension by William III. She would afterward say that "both the kings were civil to her, but both the queens used her badly."[17] James had granted her a large pension from lands, but after his exile the House of Commons threatened her with the loss of it. Spirited Catherine went before the bar of the house to present her case herself and won it.

When Catherine was forty, a Scottish baronet, Sir David Colyear, made an honest woman of her. Sir David was an officer in William III's army and highly respected, so much so that many wondered at his choice of a bride. Despite her age Catherine provided her husband with two healthy sons. Her earthy humor is best revealed in her advice to her sons with Colyear: "If anybody call either of you the son of a whore you must bear it, for you are so," she counseled, "but if they call you bastards, fight till you die; for you are an honest man's sons."[18]

Elizabeth Villiers, the duchess of Orkney, never flaunted her position at court as mistress of William III. But in 1694, when Queen Mary died of smallpox at the age of thirty-two, she left

William a letter containing a stinging rebuke for his affair with Elizabeth. Admonishments from the dead are the most tormenting of all. And so William, after endowing Elizabeth with ninety thousand acres in Ireland and an annual income of five thousand pounds, dismissed her.

When Elizabeth was cast aside, she was nearing forty and had never married. Despite her advanced age and lack of physical attractions—she was described as squinting "like a dragon"—she soon found a respectable husband, George Hamilton, a younger son of the duke of Hamilton.[19] King William promptly created him earl of Orkney, and his wife automatically became a countess. Never one to mince words, Elizabeth had told her husband soon after meeting him that she had been "on very good terms with a certain person, but that she did not wish to hear any reproaches or insinuations on that score."[20]

The marriage was not only happy but fruitful. Elizabeth, who had never had any children during her tenure with William, bore her husband three children in her forties. She outlived her royal lover by thirty years. One witness described her at the coronation of George II in 1727: "She exposed behind a mixture of fat and wrinkles, and before a considerable pair of bubbies [breasts] a good deal withered, a great belly that preceded her, add to this the inimitable roll of her eyes and her gray hair which by good fortune stood directly upright, and 'tis impossible to imagine a more delightful spectacle."[21]

Another of James II's mistresses, Arabella Churchill of the ugly face and lovely limbs, married Colonel Charles Godfrey after her liaison with James ended. Having borne James two girls and two boys, she gave her husband two daughters. They lived happily together for forty years.

Napoleon's discarded mistress Maria Walewska also found happiness in marriage, albeit briefly. After Napoleon's downfall in 1815, she devoted herself to their son Alexander and to regaining the estate left him by the emperor. After the death of her first husband, whom she had divorced, Maria was pursued by the dashing General Philippe Antoine d'Ornano, who had fallen deeply in love with her. She finally relented, marrying him in

1816. Nine months later she gave birth to a boy. But the pregnancy had taken a serious toll on her weak kidneys. She spent her last weeks dictating her memoirs—making herself out to be a Polish patriot rather than a lascivious mistress—and died in December 1817 at the age of thirty-one.

On his desert exile of St. Helena, no one had the heart to tell Napoleon about her death. He thought she had stopped writing because she was happily married. When he died three years later, he was still wearing the ring she had given him, encasing a strand of her blonde hair, with the inscription, "When you cease to love me, remember, I love you still."[22]

Upon parting from Lady Castlemaine after a liaison of twelve years, Charles II said, "All that I ask of you for your own sake is live so for the future as to make the least noise you can, and I care not who you love."[23] She could not help whom she loved, but she did make a great deal of noise. After countless messy love affairs, at the age of sixty-five she was finally unburdened of her long-suffering husband. Within weeks, the merry widow wed handsome Robert Fielding, a fifty-four-year-old who had married two fortunes and had the good luck to have both brides die.

Fielding had been on the lookout for a third fortune when he happened to find two wealthy widows: Anne Deleau, worth about sixty thousand pounds a year, and Lady Castlemaine, whose vast income was well known throughout the kingdom. Fielding decided he need not limit himself to one—he would marry both women and take their fortunes.

But instead of marrying Mistress Deleau, Fielding married an imposter named Mary Wadsworth, a friend of the heiress's hairdresser, who pretended to be the wealthy relict, whom Fielding had never seen. At the third meeting, the couple was married by a priest and consummated the marriage. The "heiress," however, said she needed to return home until she had broken the news to her father. She visited Fielding several times, each time having sex and collecting generous gifts from him.

In the meantime, Fielding also married Lady Castlemaine—though unknown to her, this marriage was bigamous and illegal. Fielding soon discovered that his legal wife was not Mistress Deleau at all, but a penniless adventurer. He beat both her and the hairdresser accomplice black and blue. Meanwhile, he immediately began pocketing Lady Castlemaine's pensions from Charles II. He began to sell off her valuable furniture and when she protested, he locked her in a room and refused to feed her until she agreed. When Lady Castlemaine told her sons, Fielding broke open her cabinet and took four hundred pounds, then beat her severely until she broke free to the open window and cried, "Murder!" Fielding then shot a blunderbuss into the street. Lady Castlemaine's sons got a warrant for Fielding, who was taken to Newgate Prison and convicted of bigamy. But Fielding must have worked his magic on Queen Anne as well, for she pardoned him. After two years, Lady Castlemaine's marriage was declared null.

The experience with Fielding had finally ended Lady Castlemaine's lifelong cacophony. Shortly thereafter she left London to live with her grandson. In 1709, at the age of sixty-nine, she developed dropsy, which swelled her once incomparable body into a revolting mass of flesh. Three months later she was dead.

THE COMFORTS OF RELIGION

"When women cease to be handsome, they study to be good," said Benjamin Franklin, and he could have been talking about most royal mistresses. Many experienced religious epiphanies—rarely while still holding the title of maîtresse-en-titre, more often after their disgrace and rustication. Most women sinned at leisure, as long as they were buoyed by youth and vitality, and repented in haste, when the hand of age or illness fell heavy upon them. Many a woman hoped to win points in heaven after a sinful life, as Sir Horace Walpole put it, by "bestowing the dregs of her beauty upon Jesus Christ."[24]

In 1678, when Charles II's mistress Louise de Kéroualle felt herself dying, she "preached to the King, crucifix in hand, to detach him from women."[25] But her piety lasted just as long as her illness. Just a few days after her deathbed supplication to the king, hearing that Charles was attending the theater with her rival Hortense Mancini, Louise painted her face and dragged herself to the king's box, where, fangs bared, she hastily reclaimed her position. She did not find God again for another forty years.

We must not assume that royal mistresses neglected church duties while in office, or that religion did not call to them during their adulterous lives. Most attended daily religious services, and many were involved in charitable projects for the poor. In the 1670s Primi Visconti described two of Louis XIV's mistresses in church, "rosary or prayer book in hand, eyes raised heavenward, as ecstatical as a pair of saints!"[26]

One of these ecstatical saints, Louise de La Vallière, fled the sparkling court of Versailles for the sanctity of a convent at the age of twenty-nine. Louise, who for years had played lady's maid dressing her replacement Madame de Montespan, told Louis that "after devoting her youth to him, all the rest of her life was not too long to devote to her salvation."[27]

Before Louise left court, Madame de Maintenon, herself extremely devout, asked Louise if she had considered the bodily discomforts that awaited her among the Carmelites, the strictest convent of the day: clothing that itched and rubbed, long fasts, backbreaking work, extreme heat and cold. Nuns were forbidden to speak and were forced to sleep in hard beds shaped like coffins. "When I shall be suffering at the convent," she replied, "I shall only have to remember what they made me suffer here, and all the pain will seem light to me."[28] She gestured across the room to Madame de Montespan, giggling and whispering in the king's ear.

The day Louise bade farewell to her friends at court, she threw herself at the feet of Queen Marie-Thérèse to beg forgiveness. "My crimes were public," the penitent explained; "my repentance must be public, too."[29] The queen, who had detested her for many years, must have wished the respectful Louise could regain her former place and oust the nasty Montespan. But Louise, leaving her two surviving children to be raised at Versailles, set off in her ducal carriage to the convent, leaving the world behind her.

"She has drunk the cup of humiliation to the dregs," reported Madame de Sévigné.[30] During the ceremony to become a novice, Louise had her lovely ash-blonde hair sheared off, though Madame de Sévigné noted gleefully that "she spared the two fine curls on her forehead!"[31] Perhaps more embarrassing to Louise's slender vanity was the loss of her specially made heels, one slightly higher than the other to make up for a short leg. Wearing the flat sandals prescribed in the convent would force Louise to walk with a pronounced limp.

A year later the convent was packed with courtiers gathered to watch the unique spectacle of a royal mistress taking her final vows to become a nun, accepting her black veil from none other than the queen, who kissed and blessed her afterward. Invitations to the ceremony were hard to come by, and there was a great deal of jostling, pushing, and shoving to watch the show. One witness wrote, "She never looked more beautiful or more content. She should be happy if only because she no longer has to lace up Madame de Montespan's stays."[32]

The king, who felt flattered by Louise's years of reproachful glances and silent suffering as he flaunted her successor, had wanted to keep her at court, a reminder of how irresistible he was. He was peeved that she preferred God to her king. For years courtiers, eager to see the novelty of royal mistress turned nun, visited Louise in the convent. After saying a prayer to ward off temptation, she who had given up the world was forced to meet members of it in the convent parlor. But not the king. He never saw her again.

Perhaps the devout queen wished at times to follow Louise into the quiet sanctity of a convent, to leave the vicious Montespan and backbiting courtiers. But queens, unlike mistresses, left court only in coffins. For years, Marie-Thérèse had enjoyed spending brief sojourns at the Carmelite convent for spiritual consolation and repose. One day after Louise had taken her vows, the queen looked out her convent window and saw a little nun in a coarse habit limping across the courtyard, bearing an enormous bundle of laundry. This, then, was her husband's mistress whom she had treated so cruelly in her jealousy. Shorn of her pearls and silks and the king's love, the sweet, hopeful girl had come to this. The queen wept.

The world revolved quickly at Versailles. Actors and actresses boasting the most glorious parts were forgotten almost the moment they left the stage; there were throngs of new characters pushing to take their places on the crowded boards. Louise de La Vallière had never quite fit the resplendent part assigned her. She had far more character and conscience than the script required. The scenery about her was too lavish, the costumes too ornate, the music shrill, the plots hollow. Her retirement into a convent was the court's hottest topic, and then bored courtiers looked elsewhere for fresh gossip. "After all," yawned Anne-Marie de Montpensier, the king's cousin, "she is not the first converted sinner."[33]

Madame de Montespan, while happy to incarcerate her former rival in a convent, was not without her own kind of piety. She was known to fast during Lent, even to weighing her bread. When one visitor expressed surprise at this, Louis XIV's mistress replied, "Because I am guilty of one sin, must I commit them all?"[34]

The duc de Saint-Simon wrote, "Even in her sinful life she had never lost her faith; she would often leave the King suddenly to go and pray in her own room, and nothing would induce her to break a day of abstinence, nor did she ever neglect the demands of Lent. She gave freely to charity, respected good church-goers, and never said anything approaching scepticism or impiety. But," he added acidly, "she was imperious, haughty, and most sarcastic, and she had the defects of a woman who had climbed to her position through her own beauty."[35]

In 1691 fifty-one-year-old Madame de Montespan was instructed by the king to leave court, but she did not go meekly into a quiet retirement. Shrieking, raging, storming, she had one last audience with Louis. Madame de Noyer wrote, "She let herself go in a fury, reproaching him for his ingratitude in the face of the sacrifices she had made for him. The King endured this tantrum because she was a woman, and because it was the last he would have to put up with from her."[36]

Madame de Montespan was an extremely wealthy woman, boasting castles, manors, and a fashionable house in Paris. But the beating heart of French society was with the king, usually at his favorite palace of Versailles. Gone for her were the colorful festivities, the need for jewels and satin gowns, the power and honor, the obeisance of the whole world.

Though she was refused permission to attend her children's Versailles weddings, she was allowed to visit them periodically at court. Madame de Caylus wrote that she "wandered like a lost soul, doomed to return again and again to the scene of a former life in expiation of former sins."[37] During these few visits to Versailles, her haughty arrogance and imperious temper were deflated. Unsure of herself, hoping to be accepted, invited, the formerly imperious royal mistress became a ghost of the marble halls, wandering about ignored where for decades she had reigned. During her brief court visits, she caught glimpses of the king, though always in the company of many others.

Madame de Montespan purchased a château in the forest of Fontainebleau, where the king periodically went hunting. When she heard the royal trumpets blow, she went outside and strained for a glimpse of him galloping in the distance. The restless exile bought another château, Oiron, in her native land of Poitou, turning it into a shrine to the king, portraits and statues of him adorning every room. Portraits of Louis on a white horse, tapestries representing his conquests, a silver bust of Louis with solid gold hair. Her bedchamber alone boasted four images of her former lover.

Madame de Montespan even fitted up a special room designated the King's Chamber, as if expecting the monarch to visit. It had an impressive canopied bed capped with a crown, hung with black velvet embroidered with gold and silver, set behind the traditional low gilded railing used by royalty. There was indeed some speculation at court that, particularly after Madame de Montespan's husband died in 1701, Louis would recall her, possibly even marry her. Some hoped that Madame de Maintenon would obligingly clear the way by dying, and then, with Madame de Montespan back at court, they could all have fun again. But Louis never visited his King's Chamber at Oiron. And Madame de Maintenon would outlive the king by three years.

Gradually, Madame de Montespan accepted that she would never be invited to live at court again. Her last years saw a religious transformation—perhaps all the more heartfelt to expiate her youthful dealings in black magic to win the king. She built a hospital where a hundred aged men and women would be cared for at her expense. Whereas she had always been generous to the poor, she now sewed clothes for them with her own hands every day and gave them most of her possessions. The woman who had feasted herself to fatness at Versailles now fasted routinely. She would often leave her last little pleasure—card games with visitors—to go to her oratory to pray.

In a gesture reminiscent of Louise de La Vallière more than thirty years earlier, she took to mortifying the flesh with rough shirts and sheets. The duc de Saint-Simon wrote, "She always wore a belt and wrist- and ankle-bands of iron with spikes, which frequently chafed her skin into ugly sores."[38]

In the greatest irony, Madame de Montespan would periodically visit Louise de La Vallière in her convent. The royal mistress who had found repentance early and had willingly fled the glories of the court was truly happy. The other royal mistress, however, found repentance only when she had been forced from her earthly position biting and kicking. Aging and disgraced, there was no other place for her to go except an altar. She wanted to learn how Louise could accept the loss of earthly position and joyously replace it with the love of God. Forgiving the cruel treachery of the past, Louise gladly counseled her former friend in the mysteries of divine grace. But unlike Louise, whose penance and good works were done behind cloister walls, Madame de Montespan publicized her piety with as much ostentatious fanfare as she had formerly trumpeted her sins.

While Madame de Montespan's religious epiphany had blunted the qualities of lechery, greed, and gluttony, her pride remained more pointed than ever. The duc de Saint-Simon reported that in her retirement she was as haughty as she had been while reigning over Versailles, still grasping the trappings of royalty she had insisted upon during her glory days. She received visitors sitting in an armchair while they were forced to stand. A few select members of the royal family were brought chairs, but even then she would not rise to welcome them or accompany them to the door. Many of them stopped coming. But court women were eager for their daughters to introduce themselves to the former mistress, to look on the face that had enchanted a king and defined an era.

Terrified of dying alone, Madame de Montespan hired women to read and play cards in her room as she slept at night. She kept her bed curtains open and numerous candles lighting the chamber. Perhaps she felt Death silently padding through her castle, looking for her.

When he found her, she was ready for him. No more fear. On her deathbed, according to the duc de Saint-Simon, "she summoned her entire domestic staff, down to the humblest, and made public confession of her publicly sinned sins, asked pardon for the long and open scandal of her life. The terror of death which had so long obsessed her was suddenly dissipated. . . . She gave thanks to God that He had permitted her to die far removed from her children, the fruits of her adultery."[39]

Madame de Montespan's body—the one which had delighted a king, propelled her to riches and power, and been daily massaged with oils—now received ghoulish insults. An apprentice surgeon botched the autopsy. Only the lowliest servants said prayers over the corpse, the rest having disappeared. Her body was dumped outside her door while various priests argued about possession of it. The parish church won the argument; the coffin was placed there and seemingly forgotten for some two months. Finally, a funeral procession "remarkable for its shameful parsimony" set out for Poitiers, where her remains were placed in her family crypt, under a black marble stone.[40]

Meanwhile, according to custom, her entrails were placed in an urn to be buried separately. A porter was hired to take the urn to a convent, but, smelling something rotten, he peered inside the poorly sealed vessel. The man was so revolted by what he saw that he threw the contents into the gutter, where a herd of pigs stumbling by promptly ate them. When this story was told at Versailles to great guffaws of laughter, one noblewoman remarked, "Her entrails? Really? Did she ever have any?"[41]

Madame de Montespan's bastard son the duc du Maine "could not conceal his joy" at his mother's death. Her only legitimate child, the duc d'Antin, rejoiced, "Here I am at last—thawed out!"—perhaps alluding to basking in the Sun King's rays without his mother's shadow blocking them.[42]

Surprisingly, Madame de Maintenon, who had been quite cold to Madame de Montespan in her final years, was so upset to learn of her death that she locked herself in her toilet. Nor was anyone less astonished at the king's utter indifference to the death of his longtime lover who had borne him seven children. When the king's beloved granddaughter-in-law found the nerve to ask him why he did not grieve, he replied coldly "that when he parted from Madame de Montespan he never expected to see her again and so far as he was concerned she had been dead from that day."[43]

The most surprising penitent of all was the impetuous Lola Montez—whorish, selfish, deceitful Lola who had broken old King Ludwig's heart and lost him his kingdom. After her 1848 banishment from Bavaria and his abdication, Ludwig prayed that she would one day realize the error of her ways and sincerely repent.

He was not disappointed, though it took Lola several years to comply. Lola had a unique talent for reinventing herself. After her exile from Bavaria she moved to the United States, where crowds rushed to see the former royal mistress dance. In her thirties, when the physical demands of dancing became more difficult, she launched an acting career. She starred in a successful play about herself called *Lola Montez in Bavaria,* in which she was portrayed as a virtuous proponent of constitutional freedom, a political adviser to the king, and—in the ultimate irony—a great friend of his wife, Queen Therese, who had heartily detested her.

Ever the romantic, Lola remarried twice, though neither

marriage was legal, since her first husband was still alive. In 1853 Lola settled down in the California mining town of Grass Valley and seemed well suited for the Wild West. She raised a bear in her backyard, invested in a mine, and was known to tour the mine shafts chomping on a cigar. During her two-year stay in Grass Valley, she had only one major fracas, hunting down a journalist in a saloon and horsewhipping him for bandying her name about unkindly in his newspaper. Otherwise Lola was known for her charitable works and, surprisingly, Bible study.

In 1857, at the age of 37, Lola began to lecture in numerous American cities. In her most popular lecture, "Beautiful Women," she described the attributes of Europe's most celebrated beauties, many of whom she had never seen but claimed as good friends. Lola amused her American audiences with lectures on European habits and character, and then went to Europe to lecture on American habits and character. In many cities the lecturer was decried in the press for her immorality, which resulted in even greater attendance. Lectures earned Lola substantial fees and simultaneously whitewashed her reputation. Her audience was surprised at the straitlaced piety of this former fallen woman.

In June 1860, Lola suffered a paralyzing stroke. She was not expected to live, and many European newspapers reported the death of the famous dancer. With characteristic determination, Lola fought hard to regain her health. Looked after by old friends, by December she could walk and talk again. But during an airing in an open carriage Lola caught pneumonia, and she died on January 17, 1861, at the age of forty. She was buried in Greenwood Cemetery in Brooklyn, New York. A European paper ran the headline "Lola Montez Is Dead—Really Dead This Time."[44]

Despite her success as a lecturer, Lola left only $1,247 because she had already given much of her earnings to charity. In her will, Lola left $300 to the Magdalen Society for reformed prostitutes.

After Lola's death, a friend wrote seventy-four-year-old Ludwig in Munich that Lola "often spoke to me of your Majesty and of your kindness and benevolence, which she deeply felt—

and wished me to tell you she had changed her life and companions. . . . She wished me to let you know she retained a sincere regard for your great kindness to the end of her life. She died a true penitent, relying on her Savior for pardon and acceptance, triumphing only in His merit."[45]

The former king replied, "With great satisfaction I was hearing the repentance of L.M. of her former behavior. . . . It is a great consolation to hear her dying as a Christian."[46]

In his last years, Ludwig's increasing deafness isolated him from society. He lived to see many of his children die, including his son and successor, Maximilian II. He saw Bavaria's defeat against the Prussians in 1866. He saw his insane teenage grandson Ludwig II generate his own political rumblings.

In retirement, Ludwig wrote a poem about his love affair with Lola Montez:

> *Through you I lost the crown*
> *But I do not rage against you for that*
> *For you were born to be my misfortune,*
> *You were such a blinding, scorching light!*
> *Be happy! So my soul calls after you,*
> *Into the ever-receding distance;*
> *Now at last choose the path of salvation;*
> *Vice brings only ruin and shame.*
> *The best friend you ever had,*
> *You thrust faithlessly away,*
> *The gates of happiness were closed against you,*
> *You simply followed your lascivious longings.*
> *For life we remain divided,*
> *And never again will meet face to face,*
> *Leave me my heart's so painfully won peace,*
> *Without it life is such a burden.*[47]

THE LOSS OF BEAUTY

The destructive hands of time often deal more kindly with women wrenched mud-ugly into this world than with those who slipped effortlessly from the womb with preternatural beauty. There is less contrast between the glories of youth and the ravages of age.

The sister-in-law of Louis XIV, the hefty German princess Elizabeth Charlotte, often quipped that as she had never been beautiful even when young, she had no vanished beauty to bewail with the passing years. Thrilled to see age leveling the playing field, Elizabeth Charlotte wrote, "I see that those whom I used to see when they were so beautiful are now as ugly as I am. Madame de La Vallière no one in the world would know any more, and Madame de Montespan's skin looks like paper when children do tricks with it, seeing who can fold it into the smallest piece, for her whole face is closely covered with tiny little wrinkles, quite amazing. Her lovely hair is white as snow and her face is red, so her beauty is quite gone."[48]

Charles II's mistress, the peerless Hortense Mancini of sparkling black eyes and raven curls, was another mistress whose beauty faded rapidly. After the king's death, Hortense plied herself with alcohol, ravaging her looks and her health. Feeling unwell, she retired to a country house in the hopes that the air would improve her health. It didn't. She died in 1699 at the age of fifty-three. Having successfully avoided her insane husband for thirty-three years, Hortense fell into his hands again after death.

The duc de Mazarin had always been insanely jealous of Hortense's inclinations for other men, so much so that he had personally lopped off all the private parts of his collection of ancient Roman statues. His insanity knew no bounds. One day he announced to his shocked servants that he was a tulip; he planted his feet in the ground and ordered them to water him, which they did. It was this gentleman, then, who bought his wife's corpse from her creditors. He took it to France and carted it around with him from place to place. The jealous duke finally knew where she was and had her in his complete control for the first time since she had escaped from the convent in which he had imprisoned her thirty-three years earlier. He eventually laid her to rest in the tomb, happy in the knowledge that she would never be unfaithful to him again.

The lovely Harriet Howard, mistress of Napoleon III, aged shockingly after her relationship with the emperor ended in 1853. Harriet had fulfilled her part of their separation agreement by going to England and marrying, but she returned unexpectedly eleven years later. She had changed greatly in the intervening years. At forty-one, her once exquisite figure had become so obese she had to have the door of her carriage widened to climb through. She rode in her fashionable carriage with the extra-wide doors up and down the Bois de Boulogne and the Champs-Elysées as if she were once again the emperor's mistress. One evening she attended the opera and fixed upon Napoleon with her opera glass, much to the discomfiture of both the emperor and the empress.

Harriet's sudden appearance caused a great deal of eager gossip. Many thought her reemergence in very poor taste, an effort to humiliate the emperor. Others wondered why the former beauty would show herself fat and ugly, rather than allowing people to remember her as she had been. But the fact was that Harriet knew she was dying of cancer and wanted just a few moments to relive those glory days before she sank into the darkness forever. She died soon after her Paris visit. In her will Harriet left a large bequest to found in England a home for girls who had been seduced away from their families.

Another mistress of Napoleon III did not withstand the ravages of time and illness as stoically as Harriet Howard. Virginie di Castiglione lost her sanity when she lost her looks—mainly because she had never cultivated anything besides her beauty. She had pursued no hobbies, disdained friendship, and sneered at religion. When Virginie was twenty, her youth and beauty insolent in their intensity, her spurned husband had predicted that her kindest friend, the mirror, would one day become her most bitter foe.

With the sizable fortune she had earned from love affairs with rich and powerful men after she had been dismissed by the emperor, Virginie took an apartment in Paris on the venerable Place Vendome. She continued her political machinations, meeting diplomats, writing urgent letters to statesmen, and giving herself far more credit for international influence than she in fact possessed.

But her husband's prediction came true with deadly accuracy. Virginie's most relentless enemy was not Austrian emperor Franz Josef, as she thought, but all-conquering time itself. When the son she had borne at sixteen became a gangly teenager, Virginie was afraid he would be living proof of her advancing years; she forced him to dress as a groom and ride with her servants on the back of her coach.

After the fall of the French Empire in 1870, Virginie tried in vain to influence the new government, which remained willfully ignorant of Virginie and her supposed political wisdom. Shortly after this, Virginie broke a tooth. She dropped a heavy rolling pin on her toe, part of which had to be amputated. Her once perfect beauty was now clearly flawed. She began to hate the world and everybody in it.

Virginie had slowly been growing more eccentric over the years. When she turned forty she painted her walls and ceilings black, closed the shutters, and turned all the mirrors toward the wall. Without a host of admirers she stopped taking care of herself. She received very few old friends—all of them men, as she detested her own sex—who were forced to drink tea in the dark with her. Sometimes she would bring out tattered silk and musty velvet ball gowns from her heyday and reminisce about the vital role she had played in European politics. "I created Italy!" she would cry. "I saved the Pope!"[49]

As her eccentricities grew, her beauty continued to deteriorate. Her rich chestnut hair turned white. Unsupported by a corset, her magnificent bosom dropped. She lived mostly in the company of her dogs, spending hours each day writing rambling letters to her few friends. "The more I see of men," she grumbled in one, "the more I love dogs."[50] Only after midnight, when no one was about who would recognize her, did she walk her dogs. A nocturnal phantom swaying in long black robes and thick black veils, this former royal mistress must have petrified late-night visitors to the Place Vendome.

As her madness seized control, Virginie refused to allow the servants in to clean and sat alone in her black rooms, filled with rats and trash, contemplating her lost beauty and the vanished days of splendor. Virginie was sixty-two when her servants, after seven days of trying to gain access to her room, forced their way in and found her decomposing body being gnawed by rats.

Her will stipulated that two of her dead dogs, which had been stuffed, should be adorned with jeweled collars and keep a vigil at her coffin during her wake. Before the coffin was closed, the two dogs were to be put inside and serve as cushions for her feet. She wanted to enter eternity in the gown that she had worn when she first slept with the emperor, the gray batiste edged with fine lace, adorned with her famous nine-string black and white pearl necklace and two bracelets.

But Virginie's wishes were not carried out. Her jewels were sold to pay her debts at a well-attended auction, fetching some two million francs. No one knows what happened to the stuffed dogs. Only one curious visitor attended her funeral.

Unlike Virginie, Edward VII's mistress Daisy Warwick didn't mind the loss of her beauty, but she was shocked to find her predecessor in the royal bed, Lillie Langtry, still waging the fruitless fight. During World War I, there was a curious meeting of these two aging mistresses of a dead king—Lillie in her sixties, Daisy in her mid-fifties. "Whatever happens, I do not intend to grow old!" Lillie protested. "Why shouldn't beauty vanquish time?"[51]

"I forgot what I answered," Daisy reported, "for I was busy analyzing what she had said. I stole a glance at her, and certainly Time's ravages, although perceptible to the discerning eye of one who had known her at the zenith of her beauty, were disguised with consummate artistry, while her figure was still lovely. But it came to me then that there was tragedy in the life of this woman whose beauty had once been world-famous, for she had found no time in the intervals of pursuing pleasure to secure contentment for the evening of her day. Now that she saw the evening approach, Lillie Langtry could only protest that it was not evening at all, but just the prolongation of a day that was, in truth, already dead."[52]

Lillie was lonely in her last years, puttering around her garden, playing with her little dogs. The young nobleman she had married ignored her but pocketed her money, and all the lusty kings and regal queens of her youth were sleeping a marbled sleep. After Lillie's death in 1929 at age seventy-five, a publisher who had known her wrote, "She always appeared to be a lingering leaf on an autumn tree which hangs on and will not die nor perish beneath the blast of Winter, because it has once belonged to a never-to-be-forgotten Summer. She could not let go. She fought in order not to let go."[53]

Daisy Warwick, on the other hand, laid down her boxing gloves. Gone was the slender hourglass figure which had so entranced the Prince of Wales in the 1880s. By the 1930s she was too fat to get out of a chair by herself. She collected a large menagerie of birds, donkeys, monkeys, cats, and dogs, and would stagger about her gardens trailing a feather boa, feeding them. One visitor was shocked to see the famous royal mistress in such a condition. But Lady Warwick stated, truthfully, "I am a very happy woman."[54]

TWELVE

MONARCHS, MISTRESSES, AND MARRIAGE

I would not be a Queen for all the world.

—WILLIAM SHAKESPEARE

❄

IF THE FIRST RECORDED CASE IN WESTERN HISTORY OF A monarch marrying his mistress is that of King David and Bathsheba, the ensuing tragedy of sackcloth and ashes set the tone for millennia to come. The marriages of kings and their mistresses were almost always tinged with grief or bludgeoned with catastrophe.

The world of past centuries was not round but pyramid-shaped, and the higher up one found oneself, the more tightly one was bound by religion and etiquette. Sitting at the apex, the king was so tightly constrained that he had little room to maneuver. Any monarch attempting to break through the conventions was soon engulfed in an international roar of derision.

Worse than raising taxes, worse than waging a senseless war, far worse than these was the marriage of a monarch to his mistress. The bride and groom were not the only ones kneeling in front of the altar. The nation's prestige was on its knees, utterly vanquished. Subjects found themselves gripped by foreboding, if not outright panic. As the monarch was the personification of a people and a nation, his disdain for ancient rules and traditions would taint them all.

Many a mistress turned royal wife soon found that the unceasing vigilance required to retain her former position could not be tossed aside at the altar. The mistress-wife was constantly challenged to validate her position, even as she had been while mistress. She was usually more detested than she had been as mistress, because she had clearly overstepped prescribed social bounds. Sniffing a wounded animal, vicious courtiers circled her with the hopes of a bloody kill.

In 1354 Prince Pedro of Portugal married his mistress of fourteen years, Inez de Castro, after his wife Princess Constanza died. Pedro's father, King Alfonso IV, was furious and feared that Pedro's four illegitimate children with Inez could take away the crown from those born with Constanza. The king sent assassins to stab Inez to death while her royal lover was away on a hunting trip. They fell upon her as she sat by a fountain in her garden and ripped her to shreds.

Royal mistresses who married their monarchs *and* were crowned invariably met with thinly veiled disgust. So many people protested Henry VIII's 1533 marriage to Anne Boleyn and her coronation that the king passed a law making it treasonable to write or act against the marriage, and forced all adult males to swear to uphold it. Those who refused to swear were executed. Anne, who was pregnant at the wedding, produced not the longed-for male heir, but a mere girl. After two more miscarriages, in 1536 she was tried on trumped-up charges of adultery and lost her head on the chopping block. English courtiers and subjects were not sad to see her go.

In 1568 the unstable Eric XIV of Sweden married his mistress Karin Mansdotter, whom he crowned queen. Eric's half brother Johan claimed this act was proof of the king's insanity. He locked

Eric up and in 1577 poisoned him, grabbing the crown for himself. Queen Karin was exiled to an estate in the country.

In 1578 Archduke Francesco of Tuscany married his mistress of twelve years, Bianca Cappello, and had the nerve to crown her in the cathedral. Upon hearing the news, the duke of Mantua, who had only a short time previously asked for the hand of Francesco's daughter Eleonora in marriage, rescinded his offer. He wrote angrily, "Now hath the character of the new Grand Duchess under whose care the Princesses live in Florence so increased by objection that it cannot be overcome."[1]

Despised by the Tuscan people and her husband's family, Bianca knew that life without the protection of Francesco would be worthless. When both lay ill of a fever in 1587, the archduke expired first. "And now must I die with my lord," she moaned, and, as if willing herself to, breathed her last.[2] Francesco's brother Ferdinando, the new archduke, had detested Bianca. Unable to revenge himself on Bianca while she was alive, within the bounds of propriety he dishonored her in death. As Pharaoh had done with the disgraced Moses, Ferdinando had her name effaced from every portrait and monument. He had her coat of arms removed from all public buildings and replaced with Johanna of Austria's. When asked if Bianca should wear the ducal coronet in her coffin, Ferdinando replied that she had already worn it far too long. While Francesco was given an elaborate state funeral, Bianca was placed in a plain coffin and dumped at night in an unmarked grave.

It was slightly more palatable to the nation at large when mistresses were content to remain morganatic—uncrowned—wives. At least the king's subjects would not have to bow down on bended knee to one they considered little more than a prostitute.

In 1612 the widowed Christian IV of Denmark was so besotted with his seventeen-year-old mistress, Kirsten Munk, that he married her. In his wisdom he did not crown her, bestowing upon her instead the title of countess. In sixteen years spoiled, nasty Kirsten brought into the world twelve children, whom she brutally beat, starved, and forced to wear rags. She never loved the monarch who idolized her, and began an affair with a handsome young German count who served in the cavalry. During the funeral of her one-year-old daughter with the king, Kirsten excused herself and had sex with the count in a garden.

The king always seemed to find himself out of clean shirts because his wife had given them to her lover. Kirsten danced when her husband was ill and even tried to poison him, instructing him to eat what turned out to be her acne medicine. One evening, when the king found two maids sleeping in front of her locked door, he had a workman inscribe the date on a stone in the courtyard and never touched Kirsten again. He refused to acknowledge the daughter she bore ten months later. Their turbulent marriage ended in 1628 when she was exiled to her estates, where she nevertheless continued to foment trouble.

In 1880, as his wife's body lay cooling in the grave, Czar Alexander II of Russia married his mistress of fifteen years, Katia Dolguruky, despite urgent pleas from friends and family to wait the required year of mourning. Having survived six assassination attempts, the czar wanted to make an honest woman of his mistress, a pretty but stupid brunette, and legitimize their three children before he was murdered. Horribly embarrassed, the imperial family pretended that the morganatic marriage had not taken place, even as rumors grew that the czar intended to crown Katia empress.

When the czar was indeed killed by a bomb eight months after the wedding, one courtier remarked that the czar's martyrdom may have saved him from committing further foolishness with Katia—crowning her at the expense of his country. Not knowing what to do with the inconvenient widow, Russian society heaved a collective sigh of relief when she went into self-imposed exile in France.

In 1900 King Alexander II of Serbia (1876–1903) announced that he would marry his mistress of several years, the nervous, dumpy Draga Mashin, and crown her queen in the Belgrade cathedral. The entire nation was horrified at Alexander's choice of bride, a poor commoner with a dubious moral background and considered too old to bear children. Additionally, poverty-stricken Serbia was emerging from a century of bloody violence and in dire need of the enhanced status that an alliance with a European royal family would bring. Upon hearing the news of the king's marriage, his cabinet resigned.

For three years the hated royal couple evaded assassination attempts, rarely going out of the palace, for they knew that Death lurked just outside the gates. In 1903 Death grew tired of waiting and invaded the palace. A band of revolutionaries broke in and tore the king and queen limb from limb, then held a Mass celebrating their liberation from a tyrant and the whore he had made queen.

We find an almost biblical morality lesson in cases where the monarch made an unseemly marriage. Divine wrath was swift and sure. It was as if the Almighty did not approve of the king transforming fornication into the sanctified sex of marriage. For a worse sin than fornication was ignorance of one's proper place in the scheme of things. When a mere pawn became queen in the chessboard of life, the game was forfeit.

The twentieth-century world was no longer pyramid-shaped but completely flattened by the rolling pin of equality, except for princes, who still found themselves tightly constrained when it came to marriage. Indeed, the biggest royal scandal of the 1900s occurred when a king insisted on marrying his mistress.

EDWARD AND WALLIS

On December 11, 1936, Edward VIII (1894–1972) told the world, "I have found it impossible to carry the heavy burden of responsibility and to discharge my duties as King as I would wish to do without the help and support of the woman I love."[3]

Like a triumphant cat bringing home the carcass of a vanquished chipmunk to his horrified owner, Edward dumped the sacred gift of his abdication in his mistress's lap. Wallis Warfield Simpson, the ultimate social climber, had been angling for years to become queen of England, a position that would finally even the score for the embarrassing poverty of her childhood in Baltimore. But now with the world staring hard at her, she was trapped into accepting the booby prize. As she listened to the king's radio address, tears rolled down her face, and we can assume they were not tears of joy.

Wallis was hardly queen material. An American, she had divorced her first husband, a dashing naval aviator, for his alcoholic brutality. When she met Prince Edward in 1931, she was happily married to handsome ship broker Ernest Simpson who had brought her to London. She nevertheless entered into an affair with the prince; five years later Edward's father, George V, died, and Edward was suddenly king. Shortly thereafter, Wallis filed for her second divorce, this time to become queen of England.

Wallis was completely mesmerized by the trappings of royalty. She wrote of Edward, "His slightest wish seemed always to be translated instantly into the most impressive kind of reality. Trains were held; yachts materialized; the best suites in the finest hotels were flung open; airplanes stood waiting. . . . He was the open sesame to a new and glittering world that excited me as nothing in my life had ever done before."[4]

While Wallis's fascination with the king was understandable, no one could comprehend his violent passion for a woman whose face resembled the metal part of a garden shovel and her body the wooden handle. Her nose was lumpy, her mouth large and ugly, her hands short and stubby. Some speculated that Wallis had conquered Edward with bizarre Asian sexual techniques she had learned in China after having separated from her first husband, who was stationed there. Others claimed the two were brought together by an avid aversion to sex—that Edward was hopelessly impotent and Wallis icily frigid. The theory of Wallis's frigidity melted in 2003 when the British government released secret files revealing that in 1935 Wallis, while married to Ernest Simpson and dangling the Prince of Wales, was having a torrid affair with Guy Trundle, a handsome car salesman. It is interesting to speculate whether the prince, while offering Wallis a glittering life, delivered a lackluster performance in bed.

Whatever their sexual relationship, certainly Wallis had a strong psychological hold over the prince. Whereas other women had melted into butter at his feet, Wallis completely dominated Edward, who became gushingly subservient. And, like many a royal mistress before her, Wallis offered scintillating charm and delightful wit.

But why did Edward insist on *marrying* the woman? Why didn't he simply keep her as his mistress? Perhaps Edward, stubborn, selfish, and intellectually limited almost to the point of imbecility, could not imagine himself on the throne without her seated on a throne beside him, smoothing things over, telling him what to do. Or maybe he never wanted to be king at all and used Wallis as a convenient and romantic excuse to liberate himself from a monarch's responsibilities.

Nothing in the British Constitution forbade the king from marrying a divorcée, a commoner, or an American. The Settlement Act of 1701—passed when a Catholic pretender was angling for the British throne—stated that the monarch could neither be a Catholic nor marry one. (Oddly, the act is still in effect today.) The Royal Marriages Act of 1772—pushed through by George III, who was furious that his brothers had secretly married for love rather than royal suitability—stated that heirs to the throne must obtain the monarch's consent to a marriage unless the heir was over twenty-five. Neither of these acts would have prevented Edward from marrying Wallis.

He would have found himself in an uncomfortable position with the Church of England, however, which forbade a divorced person from remarrying as long as the former spouse was alive. Wallis had not one but two former spouses very much alive. As king, Edward was also supreme governor of the Church of England and was supposed to uphold its precepts. Perhaps worse, public opinion was against the marriage. Yet, if Edward had had the patience and public relations savvy to calm his clucking bishops and smooth the ruffled feathers of his subjects, he could certainly have married Wallis.

But ignoring sensible advice from friends and advisers, Edward made every disastrous political and public relations blunder possible, insisting on an immediate marriage so the two could be crowned together. It is likely that Wallis, rather than persuading the king to wait for public opposition to die down, was pushing for an early marriage. Wallis knew how extremely fickle and cowardly Edward had been with his earlier amours, deciding from one day to the next to dump a mistress and letting someone else give her the bad news.

As the crisis over the king's proposed marriage deepened, people picketed the palace with placards: "Down with the Whore!" "Wally—Give us back our King!" "Out with the American Garbage!"[5] Bricks and stones were hurled at her windows. Children sang, "Hark the herald angels sing, Mrs. Simpson stole our King!"[6]

Agreeing with the age-old adage that the bedded can't be wedded, a patron of a London pub reportedly said, "It just won't do. We can't have two other blokes going around saying they've slept with the Queen of England, can we?"[7]

The customs of earlier centuries—which could have quickly dispatched the problem—were no longer acceptable in 1936. The royal family could not order courtiers to stab Wallis to death, as poor Inez de Castro had been six hundred years earlier, though perhaps they would have liked to. Nor was Edward in a position to hang and burn all who spoke against his marriage, as his ancestor Henry VIII had done four hundred years earlier. And so the lovelorn king abdicated, concealing his ineptitude with a legend of chivalrous romance and honorable sacrifice.

Edward and Wallis were married in France on June 3, 1937, a little more than a month after her second divorce was final. As part of his wedding gift to his bride, Edward gave Wallis a diamond coronet, a poor substitute for a crown. Edward's brother, now King George VI, gave them the honorary titles of duke and duchess of Windsor. But the royal family would snub Wallis until the end of her days, never receiving her into the family and never allowing her to be called a Royal Highness. It is likely that the bitterness of the royal family toward Wallis was intensified by their knowledge of her philandering with the car salesman. But the duke insisted that until his wife was received and allowed the title, he would stay clear of Great Britain.

Though the marriage caused a constitutional crisis for the British monarchy, Edward's abdication saved Britain from having a supporter of Nazi Germany on the throne during World War II. Edward, a fan of all things German and fluent in the language, was frequently seen to give a limp Nazi salute on the streets of London throughout the 1930s. When Hitler heard of the abdication he groaned, "I've lost a friend to my cause!"[8]

In 1937 the newly minted duke and duchess of Windsor visited the Führer for fourteen days, greeting the crowds with "Heil Hitler!" and scandalizing George VI and the British people. There is indeed some documentation that indicates Hitler was planning, once he conquered Britain, to install Edward and Wallis as puppet king and queen, dancing to Nazi commands.

After a stint as governor of the Bahamas during World War II—where Edward had been placed to keep him as far away as possible from his Nazi friends—the duke and duchess set off on a lifetime of meaningless wandering: shopping in Paris, fashion shows in New York, August in the south of France, winters in Palm Beach. Wallis's famed charm congealed behind a hard mask of disappointment, and the duke became more doddering than ever, playing the bagpipes drunk in the middle of the night, or speaking only German for hours at a party where no one could understand him. The desiccated pair seemed glued to each other at the hip, each holding a drink in one hand and a cigarette in the other. Like cracked and peeling portraits of their former selves, they became yellowed by tobacco, dried up by alcohol.

In Ernest Simpson, Wallis had given up a highly intelligent, hardworking husband and replaced him with a thickheaded man with nothing to do, a millstone of a mate she could only divorce to shrieks of laughter echoing across the world. At one party when the duke had left the room, his wife informed her guests, "No one will ever know how hard I work to try to make the little man feel busy!"[9] At social events she would often remind him, "Don't forget, darling, you're not king anymore!"[10]

In 1972 the duke died in Paris. The duchess soon slipped into senility, drank even more heavily to calm the phantoms of the past, and was down to eighty-five pounds by 1977. And yet she lived until 1986, stubbornly clinging to life, even as her body shriveled and her mind wandered. As she lay there, immobile, was she haunted by visions of crowns and scepters? Of thrones and coronation robes and the glory that might have been?

CHARLES AND CAMILLA

Nearly seventy years after Edward VIII's decision to marry his mistress, the same weighty question hangs over the head of a controversial prince.

As a girl, Camilla Shand, the great-granddaughter of Edward VII's last mistress, Alice Keppel, loved to hear Granny Alice stories and always laughed at her famous statement, "My job is to curtsy first . . . and then jump into bed!"[11] Little did Camilla know that she would have her own chance to curtsy and jump.

She met Prince Charles in 1970, as a pouring rain lashed the Windsor polo fields. Wearing a pair of muddy Wellington boots, twenty-three-year-old Camilla marched up to the twenty-two-year-old prince and introduced herself. "My great-grandmother was your great-great-grandfather's mistress," she said. "How about it?"[12]

Camilla, indeed, possessed many of the qualities that had made her great-grandmother a successful royal mistress. Though neither was classically beautiful, both had a colorful personality, dry wit, kindness, and intelligence that attracted more than high cheekbones or full lips. Both were fiercely loyal to their royal lovers, reassuring, calm, capable, and—rare in a world of scepters and crowns—unpretentious. Both were described by their contemporaries as exuding a raw sex appeal that cannot be captured in photographs.

Charles was immediately intrigued. Camilla was already an experienced woman of the world with the reputation of being a sizzling sex partner; the prince was comparatively inexperienced. The two of them dated for nearly three years, Charles wanting desperately to marry her. But the royal family was not amused—though from a proper English family, Camilla was no virgin. Nor was Camilla herself very interested in living in the fishbowl of Buckingham Palace. While Charles was in the Royal Navy,

Camilla married her old flame Andrew Parker-Bowles. Hearing the news, the prince locked himself in his cabin for hours and emerged red-eyed.

They remained friends, however, and became lovers once again in 1980 as Camilla's marriage gracefully deteriorated. Camilla, always on the lookout for a potential royal bride, pushed Charles into the arms of Diana, Lady Spencer. Camilla felt Diana was young and pliable enough to mold herself to Charles and palace life. She was from a noble family and boasted that most vital prerequisite of a princess bride: an unpenetrated hymen. Charles, deeply in love with Camilla, had serious doubts; his wooing of Diana was halfhearted and lackluster. He had been raised, however, to do his duty for his country and so allowed himself to be pushed down the path to the altar.

According to the prince's valet at the time, Stephen Barry, just before his engagement to Diana was announced Charles said, "I'm making an awful bloody mistake."[13] Days before the wedding, Barry said, "He told myself and Lord Romsey that Camilla was the only woman he had ever loved. He told us: I could never feel the same way about Diana as I do about Camilla."[14] In the eighteenth-century tradition, family friend Lord Romsey assured Charles that in time his feelings would change and he would grow to love Diana.

Diana, though only nineteen, quickly picked up on Charles's love for Camilla and began to detest her. Though Camilla was invited to the wedding, Diana struck her name from the guest list for the wedding breakfast and the reception. A few days before the wedding, Diana found a wrapped gift from Charles to Camilla on the desk of his assistant. She opened it and found a bracelet. Diana felt it was highly inappropriate for Charles to give an old girlfriend such a gift days before his wedding. She almost canceled the wedding of the century.

Diana certainly would have canceled had she known that the night before the wedding, while she was keeping a virginal vigil, her prince was rolling in bed with Camilla. He intended to be faithful to his wife, but wanted to get in one last night with his mistress as a single man.

Charles was caught between the pincers of Baroque traditions and modern values. His marriage for dynastic purposes to a woman he did not love—no matter how beautiful—was just as much a sacrifice as Louis XIV's to the dwarflike infanta of Spain. Diana, on the other hand, was living in the late twentieth century—not the seventeenth—fully believing Charles was marrying her for love. She had not been raised at a court where royal mistresses were an accepted convention that unloved royal wives were expected to endure with dignity. Worst of all, she had hoped that Charles was the solution to her life of aimless uncertainty and bruising loneliness.

On her honeymoon cruise Diana found photos of Camilla in her husband's calendar book and flew into a rage. "Why don't you just face up to the truth and tell me it's her you love and not me?" she cried, stricken with the awful knowledge.[15] Suffering from bulimia, Diana raced to the toilet to vomit.

After the birth of Prince Harry in 1984 and three years of marital fidelity, Charles, frazzled by Diana's violent temper tantrums, ran back into the arms of Camilla. Diana—convulsed at the realization that her husband had never loved her—sought comfort in affairs of her own, but never found a long-lasting relationship. Her venom-spitting hatred of Camilla as the individual responsible for all her sufferings never faded with time. Perhaps Diana, looking in the mirror at her glamorous beauty, knew it couldn't be Camilla's looks that had seduced Charles away from the marriage bed; worse than that, it was something that Diana lacked *inside* that Camilla *had,* and the bitter knowledge rubbed salt in her aching wound.

But Charles would endure far worse than his wife's tantrums. On January 13, 1993, the British press reported a cell phone conversation between Charles and Camilla. The sexually explicit conversation made clear that Camilla had been his mistress for some time. The "Camillagate" tape was played over and over on television and radio around the world. The public was outraged; public opinion of the royal family dropped to an all-time low.

It didn't help that Charles had expressed the desire to be reincarnated as Camilla's Tampax. Foreign press called him the

Tampax Prince, and British women began calling tampons "Charlies." Humiliated and reviled, Charles seriously thought of relinquishing his position as heir to the throne and leaving the country.

The prince's blackest moment came when Camilla's elderly father, Major Shand, demanded a meeting with his daughter's seducer, whom he harangued for ninety minutes. "My daughter's life has been ruined, her children are the subject of ridicule and contempt," the major roared. "You have brought disgrace on my whole family."[16]

It was a far cry from the father of Madame de Montespan, who, upon hearing that his daughter had become Louis XIV's mistress in 1667, cried, "Praise be to God! Here is a stroke of great good fortune for our house!"[17]

What had happened in the intervening three centuries? A great deal. For one thing, the financial rewards of a royal mistress today are severely limited, nor does she have an accepted position at court. Before the French Revolution, Diana would have found herself and Camilla, having been created a duchess, stuffed into a carriage with Charles between them. Camilla would have officially welcomed foreign ambassadors, while an unruly Diana may well have been locked in a tower. Camilla would have far outstripped Diana in jewels and gowns, in the number of rooms she possessed in their joint palace, in her power and influence.

Second, the modern royal mistress has no political power whatsoever—as her prince has none himself and therefore nothing to share. The Camillas of the world no longer stride down palace corridors to attend council meetings, make laws, and appoint generals, ministers, and ambassadors. Nor do they have influence over literature and the arts. Their position is much the same as that of a nineteenth-century mistress, kept discreetly in the background, the illicit sex acceptable as long as no one finds out about it.

Third, the modern royal mistress and her prince have a new enemy. More intently following the trail of royal indiscretions than the most jealous wife, the press does battle with telephoto lenses and secret recording devices, capturing the most intimate moments, then waving their war trophies about for all the world to see. History offers us not a single recorded cell phone conversation between Louis XIV and Madame de Montespan in which His Most Christian Majesty wishes he were a tampon, or photos of Nell Gwynn sunbathing topless in her walled garden near Whitehall Palace. It is most certainly our loss.

No wonder the reactions of Major Shand and Madame de Montespan's father were so different. But if Camilla suffers the nuisances of the modern royal mistress, she has dispensed with a different set of inconveniences that beset her predecessors. She is not expected to hunt boar in the rain and suffer interminable carriage rides with no chamber pot in sight. She has not caught smallpox in the palace or syphilis from Prince Charles, nor has she died birthing a royal bastard. Though if she had a choice between the intrusions of the press and the horrors of former centuries, Camilla might prefer to take her chances with smallpox.

After his bruising confrontation with Major Shand, Charles seemed to be giving up Camilla to appease public opinion and regain his honor. But he soon found, once again, that he simply couldn't do without her. Camilla swept back like an inevitable returning tide, only to ebb out to sea once more after Diana's tragic death in a car accident in 1997. However, Charles and Diana's eldest son, Prince William, soon invited Camilla to tea. William and his brother Harry asked her to accompany them and their father on a Mediterranean cruise in 1999.

Recently Charles has said that his relationship with her is nonnegotiable. Periodically, they attend public events together, during which it is quite noticeable that her appearance has been professionally resculpted. Hairdressers have tamed her frizzy horse's-mane hair. Makeup artists have taught her the most flattering secrets of their trade. Couturiers have suggested sleek dresses, which she adorns with tasteful jewelry. The remodeling work has turned Camilla from frumpy to elegant.

Camilla and Charles's relationship has now lasted an astounding thirty-four years—longer than that of Emperor Franz Josef of Austria and Katharina Schratt. Camilla, like Katharina, is winning points through her sheer endurance. We might all envy such a long-lasting relationship still sizzling with sexual passion. Her position is greatly aided by the acceptance of the young princes, who love their father deeply and want him to be happy. Even Queen Elizabeth II is warming to her.

In 2002 the Church of England, wrenching itself uncomfortably into the mid twentieth century, agreed to permit divorcées with a living ex-spouse to remarry in the church. This means that now Charles and Camilla can marry with the blessing of the church—something that Edward VIII and Wallis could not have done. If Charles and Camilla did marry, when he becomes king she would automatically become queen, barring a special act of Parliament making the marriage morganatic. If public opinion supports the couple, the British cabinet would be unlikely to object to the marriage.

However, a 2002 survey in Britain found that 52 percent of the people would not wish for a Queen Camilla. Softening the blow a bit, some 57 percent felt it would be acceptable for Charles and Camilla to live together once he becomes king. This couple certainly shows more wisdom in waiting for public opinion to change than Edward VIII and Wallis Warfield Simpson did in their catastrophic rush to the altar.

It is possible that Camilla will remain the prince's unofficial consort for many years. If Camilla does marry Charles, she will certainly fare better than her predecessors. Chances are she will not get her head cut off, like Anne Boleyn. Nor is she likely to be torn to pieces, like Queen Draga of Serbia, though at the height of the Camillagate scandal a battalion of women pelted her with rolls at the supermarket. She will certainly, however, be hanged, drawn, and quartered in the press.

THE NEW TREND IN ROYAL MARRIAGES

The reasons for a prince to marry a virgin princess no longer exist. The ancient tradition of keeping royal blood "pure" by marrying into like families resulted in the spread of insanity and hemophilia throughout European royalty. Not only is royal blood *not* superior to that of commoners, it may very well be genetically inferior because of centuries of inbreeding. If we could but look at this sanctified substance under a microscope, we might well be shocked at how many components are *missing*.

Modern princesses don't trail in their wake treaties that open up trade or prevent war. Nor do they bring dowries to fill the royal treasury. Nor has virginity remained a highly prized commodity. Today most educated, well-bred, healthy women in their twenties are *not* virgins.

Having personally witnessed with horror the unmitigated disaster of Charles's marriage to a virgin noblewoman, modern princes are now insisting on marrying nonvirgin commoners of their choice and are willing to fight for that right. In 2001 twenty-eight-year-old Crown Prince Haakon of Norway married his live-in girlfriend Mette-Marit Tjessem Hoiby, a tall blonde with a strong jaw and healthy good looks. Also twenty-eight, Mette-Marit was not only a commoner, but a very "common commoner" according to a public opinion poll. She was a former waitress and strawberry picker who had never completed her education. Worse, she had a four-year-old illegitimate son whose father was in jail on drug charges.

Prince Haakon pushed hard for the wedding and threatened to renounce his rights to the throne of his father, King Harald. Many compared it to the constitutional crisis of Wallis Warfield Simpson and Edward VIII. Holding very modern values, however, most Norwegians had nothing against the marriage; a poll found that 70 percent wanted the prince's fiancée for their queen. And so the tainted Mette-Marit was forgiven her trespasses; she promised she would never again be led into temptation; and her kingdom was come.

Prince Charles attended the wedding; it is said he returned home with a lighter heart and a spring in his step.

In 2002 thirty-three-year-old Crown Prince Willem of the Netherlands married twenty-nine-year-old Argentine Maxima Zorreguieta despite numerous protests. The problem was not Maxima's lack of virginity, which we can assume. Nor was anything deemed wrong with Maxima herself, who was well educated and worked as a banker on Wall Street.

But Maxima's father had been a member of Argentina's former junta, a regime that tortured and killed thirty thousand people. Some politicians said Willem should renounce his right to inherit the throne if he married a woman with such an inappropriate father. And Willem indicated he would be willing to do so if they tried to prevent his marriage. Despite the protests, Maxima won tremendous popular support among Dutch citizens. The couple was married in February 2002, but the bride's parents were requested to stay home in Argentina.

Charles was likely the last prince to immolate himself on the altar of Hymen as an exercise in duty to his country. Modern princes like Haakon and Willem will marry women they love. But many of us common folk who have married the partners of our choice are keenly aware of a painful fact—that the heady trip down the aisle often ends on a hard wooden bench in divorce court by way of a third party's soft, inviting bed. A marriage made for love, once strained by the contempt of familiarity, is no remedy for eventual adultery.

Public opinion, generous to princes who married ugly princesses out of duty and then took mistresses of their choosing, will not be as kind with the Haakons and Willems of the twenty-first century who fight hard to marry the women they love, and *then* take mistresses. And kings and princes, even those completely lacking in personal attractions, never lack female admirers. Swooning from the eroticism of royalty, in coming centuries women will continue, as Louis XIV said, to "lay siege to the heart of a Prince as to a citadel."[18]

CONCLUSION

Throughout history, women have been relegated to the kitchen and the nursery. A few have made it into the bedrooms, and throne rooms, of kings. We will never know the virtues and vices of most of these few, obscured as they are by the heavy shadows of time or only faintly illuminated by the guttering candle of semi-literacy. But we can focus our spotlight on others and scrutinize them quite closely at our leisure.

First, we close our eyes and inhale their heady perfume—water lily and orange blossom and rose water. We hear the crack of a fan and feel a fluttering movement of air. Opening our eyes, we see that the mistresses standing before us are not all what we would expect. Some indeed are young and sexy, their skin moist and supple, pampered and well oiled, boldly offering their sexuality. Some are motherly and comforting, while yet others are just plain ugly but exude an earthy sex appeal.

Looking more closely, we see that our spotlight shines unmercifully on many vices. We see greed, certainly: Alice Perrers prying rings from the stiffening fingers of the freshly deceased Edward III; Lady Castlemaine grabbing so much cash, silver, jewels, land, and pensions that Charles II had nothing left to pay his soldiers and sailors; Madame du Barry as dazzling as the sun, covering herself in gems and playing in gardens while French peasants starved. We see ruthless intrigue: the viperous Mailly-Nesle sisters vying to unseat one another; the treacherous Madame de Montespan dumping foul potions of toads' excrement and babies' intestines into the king's meat to keep his love.

We see the vaunting ambition of Bianca Cappello, Lola Montez, and Wallis Warfield Simpson, roiling entire nations and ruining their men to achieve personal goals. We see the collateral damage of heartbroken wives: Charles II's Catherine of Braganza, blood streaming from her nose, fainting upon meeting Lady Castlemaine, the woman she knows her husband truly loves; Louis XV's dowdy Queen Marie sighing over the younger, prettier, wittier Madame de Pompadour, flushed and triumphant from the king's embraces; and Princess Diana, crouched over a toilet at the thought that her husband loves not her, but Camilla.

Is it hopeless to hope for love on the battlefield of greed, ambition, and cruel adultery? Is the woman who lays her gift of lilies—or is it thorns?—at the base of an altar worshiping not love, but an idol, a graven image of fame and wealth and power?

Is the real goal of the royal mistress, as one eighteenth-century French courtier put it, to "find glory in a whoredom that is part of History"?[19]

But in the patchwork of light and dark and good and evil that is human nature, our spotlight illuminates virtues as well. In it we see Agnes Sorel, sitting before a hearth doing needlework, gently persuading a cowardly Charles VII to drive the English from French soil; the courageous Gabrielle d'Estrées, who faced cannonballs on the battlefield to stay by the side of Henri IV, ably ending a bloody civil war with clever diplomatic persistence; Madame de Pompadour, mentor of artists and writers, eagerly turning in her silver, furniture, and priceless diamonds to build hospitals and pay the soldiers of Louis XV.

We see Wilhelmine Rietz, willing to face imprisonment and possibly death rather than leave Frederick William II to die without her by his side. We behold loyalty in the face of betrayal in Maria Walewska, long ago dismissed by Napoleon while pregnant with his child, trudging up a steep hill on Elba to visit in exile a man whose princess bride and fawning courtiers have forgotten him.

We see Katharina Schratt, stout and matronly, tiny glasses perched on the bridge of her nose, sitting on a concrete garden bench reading dispatches to eighty-year-old Emperor Franz Josef, whose eyes have failed. And Camilla Parker-Bowles, offering calm advice and loving support to a man torn between duty and inclination.

Those who tread the earth wearing crowns—and we the crownless—all worship at altars of greed, ambition, and desire. But sometimes flowers sprout in the blood-soaked battlefield or the fire-ravaged forest, and a glorious tree grows from an unlikely crack in a crumbling wall. Afraid to see the truth of what we have been worshiping, we cast down our eyes. Yet if we look up, we might find that our altar has no idols, or that the idols we put there have fallen and we behold something else shining in their place. In searching the darkness, we have found light.

NOTES

INTRODUCTION

1. D'Orliac, p. 171.
2. Delpech, p. 23.
3. Andrews, p. 161.
4. Bray, pp. 467–468.
5. Pöllnitz, pp. 251–252.
6. Hume, p. 208.
7. Trench, p. 182.
8. Hervey, vol. I, p. 42.
9. Trench, p. 172.
10. *Memoirs*, p. 183.
11. Hardy, p. 42.

CHAPTER ONE: SEX WITH THE KING

1. Sutherland, p. 137.
2. Erickson, p. 300.
3. Ibid.
4. Weir, p. 397.
5. Ibid., p. 403.
6. Ibid., p. 405.
7. Ibid., p. 406.
8. Mossiker, *Sévigné*, p. 284.

9. Crankshaw, p. 263.

10. Ibid., p. 264.

11. Williams, *Rival Sultanas*, p. 131.

12. Leslie, p. 100.

13. Ibid., p. 101.

14. Parissien, p. 77.

15. Ibid., p. 224.

16. Pevitt, p. 16.

17. Forster, p. xviii.

18. Cawthorne, p. 67.

19. Kent, p. 44.

20. Ibid., p. 45.

21. Smythe, p. 129.

22. Mitford, pp. 78–79.

23. Haslip, *Madame du Barry*, p. 24.

24. Ibid., p. 25.

25. Ibid., p. 99.

26. Hilton, p. 243.

27. Tarsaidze, p. 138.

28. Ibid., p. 171.

29. Ibid., p. 175.

30. Ibid., p. 173.

31. Bierman, p. 241.

32. Ibid.

33. Ibid.

34. Seymour, p. 234.

35. Ibid., p. 241.

36. Ibid., p. 235.

37. Aronson, p. 44.

38. Ibid., p. 339.

39. Ziegler, p. 276.

40. Hardy, p. 40.

41. Somerset, p. 136.

42. Andrews, p. 153.

43. Wilson, p. 122.

44. Cawthorne, p. 67.

45. Andrews, p. 229.

46. Ibid., p. 230.
47. Seymour, p. 209.

CHAPTER TWO: BEYOND THE BED— THE ART OF PLEASING A KING

1. Ziegler, p. 151.
2. Mitford, p. 27.
3. Smythe, p. 155.
4. Ibid., p. 147.
5. Lever, p. 182.
6. Ibid.
7. Smythe, p. 210.
8. *Memoirs*, p. 230.
9. Haslip, *Madame du Barry*, p. 50.
10. Ibid., p. 90.
11. Lewis, p. 193.
12. Smythe, p. 210.
13. Haslip, *Emperor and Actress*, p. 186.
14. Ibid., p. 43.
15. Ibid., p. 186.
16. Dunlop, p. 118.
17. Ziegler, p. 162.
18. Mossiker, *Sévigné*, p. 224.
19. Cronin, p. 181.
20. Andrews, p. 174.
21. Ibid., p. 91.
22. Pöllnitz, p. 266.
23. Ibid.
24. Mossiker, *Affair of the Poisons*, pp. 123–124.
25. Ibid.
26. Cronin, p. 182.
27. Bierman, p. 171.
28. Ibid.
29. Ibid.
30. Ibid.

31. Ibid., p. 173.

32. Ibid., p. 174.

33. Trench, p. 4.

34. Ibid., pp. 52–53.

35. Hardy, p. 68.

36. Ibid., p. 69.

37. Ibid., p. 45.

38. Ibid., p. 46.

39. Ibid., p. 48.

40. Cronin, p. 295.

41. Pevitt, p. 52.

42. Hardy, p. 68.

CHAPTER THREE: RIVALS FOR A KING'S LOVE—
THE MISTRESS AND THE QUEEN

1. Trench, p. 127.

2. Cronin, p. 183.

3. D'Orliac, p. 57.

4. Ibid., p. 56.

5. Andrews, p. 55.

6. Ibid., p. 54.

7. Ibid.

8. Coote, p. 120.

9. Andrews, p. 63.

10. Ibid., p. 64.

11. Ibid., p. 65.

12. Wilson, p. 106.

13. Shellabarger, p. 57.

14. Hardy, pp. 86–87.

15. Hervey, vol. I, p. 42.

16. Ibid., p. 43.

17. Hardy, p. 80.

18. Somerset, p. 217.

19. Trench, p. 157.

20. Somerset, p. 219.

21. Trench, pp. 172–173.

22. Ibid., p. 199.

23. Ziegler, p. 153.

24. Mossiker, *Affair of the Poisons,* p. 33.

25. Ibid., p. 63.

26. Ibid., p. 77.

27. Ibid.

28. Cronin, p. 181.

29. Mossiker, *Affair of the Poisons,* p. 77.

30. Ibid., p. 81.

31. Ibid., p. 103.

32. Cronin, p. 177.

33. Bernier, p. 84.

34. Smythe, p. 89.

35. Ibid., p. 91.

36. Ibid., p. 92.

37. Ibid., p. 101.

38. *Memoirs,* p. 160.

39. Ibid., p. 166.

40. Ibid., p. 170.

41. Ibid.

42. Ibid., p. 171.

43. Williams, *Last Loves of Henri of Navarre,* p. 135.

44. Haggard, p. 393.

45. Mahoney, p. 361.

46. Haggard, p. 392.

47. Mahoney, pp. 362–363.

48. Ibid., p. 367.

49. Ibid., p. 368.

50. Ibid., p. 371.

51. Williams, *Last Loves of Henri of Navarre,* p. 74.

52. Mahoney, p. 376.

53. Ibid., p. 377.

54. Ibid., p. 376.

55. Williams, *Last Loves of Henri of Navarre,* pp. 82–83.

56. Mahoney, p. 383.

57. Ibid., p. 390.

1. Bierman, pp. 169–170.
2. Mossiker, *Affair of the Poisons*, p. 118n.
3. Sutherland, p. 36.
4. Ibid., p. 62.
5. Ibid., p. 63.
6. Ibid., p. 66.
7. Ibid., p. 67.
8. Ibid., p. 69.
9. Kent, p. 243.
10. Ibid.
11. Sutherland, p. 75.
12. Ibid., p. 142.
13. Smythe, p. 253.
14. Ibid., p. 254.
15. Pöllnitz, p. 157.
16. Ibid., p. 158.
17. Ibid.
18. Given-Wilson and Curteis, p. 128.
19. Lewis, p. 125.
20. Mahoney, p. 414.
21. Ibid., p. 416.
22. Ibid.
23. Mossiker, *Affair of the Poisons*, p. 68.
24. Cronin, p. 177.
25. Mossiker, *Affair of the Poisons*, p. 71.
26. Ibid., p. 118.
27. Ibid., p. 93.
28. Ibid., p. 315.
29. Ibid., p. 316.
30. Ibid.

1. Mossiker, *Sévigné,* p. 55.
2. Ibid., p. 225.
3. Ibid., p. 235.
4. Dunlop, p. 221.
5. Ziegler, p. 34.
6. Shellabarger, p. 73.
7. Mossiker, *Affair of the Poisons,* p. 49.
8. Ibid., p. 30.
9. Cronin, p. 176.
10. Ziegler, p. 124.
11. Mossiker, *Affair of the Poisons,* p. 82.
12. Ibid.
13. Ziegler, p. 104.
14. Mossiker, *Affair of the Poisons,* p. 114.
15. Ibid., p. 119.
16. Ibid., p. 125.
17. Cronin, p. 233.
18. Ibid., p. 235.
19. Mossiker, *Affair of the Poisons,* p. 126.
20. Ibid., p. 208.
21. Ibid., p. 228.
22. Ibid., pp. 233–234.
23. Ibid., pp. 235–236.
24. Bernier, p. 87.
25. Kent, p. 194.
26. Hausset, p. 69.
27. Smythe, p. 210.
28. Lever, p. 237.
29. Ibid.
30. Algrant, p. 234.
31. MacDonogh, p. 32.
32. Ibid.
33. Smythe, p. 264.
34. Ibid., p. 271.

35. Pöllnitz, p. 221.

36. Ibid., p. 225.

37. Ibid.

38. Ibid., p. 249.

39. Ibid., pp. 249–250.

40. Ibid., p. 251.

41. Ibid., pp. 252–253.

42. Wilson, p. 99.

43. Ibid., p. 182.

44. Ibid., p. 179.

45. Kent, p. 109.

46. Wilson, p. 137.

47. Ibid., p. 143.

48. Ibid.

49. Ibid., p. 198.

50. Wilson, p. 190.

51. Carlton, p. 72.

52. Delpech, p. 106.

53. Williams, *Rival Sultanas,* p. 213.

54. Wilson, pp. 197–198.

55. Hardy, p. 35.

56. Williams, *Rival Sultanas,* p. 213.

CHAPTER SIX: LOVING PROFITABLY—
THE WAGES OF SIN

1. Bierman, p. 188.

2. Andrews, p. 48.

3. Ibid., p. 126.

4. Ibid., p. 127.

5. Ibid., p. 176.

6. Hardy, p. 33.

7. Cronin, p. 179.

8. Andrews, p. 181.

9. Bierman, p. 127.

10. Williams, *Rival Sultanas,* p. 148.

11. Andrews, p. 253.

12. Haslip, *Emperor and Actress,* p. 247.

13. Ibid.

14. Aronson, p. 363.

15. Ibid., pp. 176–177.

16. Mossiker, *Affair of the Poisons,* p. 95.

17. Andrews, p. 189.

18. Ibid., pp. 190–191.

19. Jerrold, p. 311.

20. Ibid., p. 46.

21. Ibid., p. 163.

22. Ibid., p. 218.

23. Ibid., p. 417.

CHAPTER SEVEN: POLITICAL POWER
BETWEEN THE SHEETS

1. De Gramont, p. 112.

2. Lewis, p. 101.

3. Ibid., p. 136.

4. Ibid., p. 146.

5. Ibid., pp. 219–220.

6. Ibid., p. 221.

7. Mossiker, *Affair of the Poisons,* p. 99.

8. Williams, *Rival Sultanas,* pp. 116–117.

9. Ibid., p. 119.

10. Ibid., p. 120.

11. Ibid., p. 122.

12. Ibid., p. 127.

13. Kent, p. 103.

14. Smythe, p. 176.

15. Kent, p. 182.

16. Algrant, p. 145.

17. Rappoport, p. 128.

18. Smythe, p. 320.

19. Smith, p. 128.

20. Ibid.

21. Ibid.

22. Ibid., p. 146.

23. Ibid.

24. Somerset, p. 216.

25. Hervey, vol. 1, p. 40.

26. Trench, p. 191.

27. Ibid., p. 202.

28. Hardy, p. 91.

29. Trench, p. 274.

30. Ibid., p. 236.

CHAPTER EIGHT: RED WHORES OF BABYLON—
PUBLIC OPINION AND THE MISTRESS

1. Trench, p. 183.

2. Ziegler, p. 124.

3. Mossiker, *Affair of the Poisons,* p. 312.

4. Algrant, p. 46.

5. Bernier, p. 133.

6. Mitford, p. 231.

7. Algrant, p. 290.

8. Haslip, *Madame du Barry,* p. 79.

9. Ibid., p. 92.

10. Ibid., p. 127.

11. Coote, p. 119.

12. Andrews, p. 136.

13. Ibid., p. 128.

14. Hardy, p. 22.

15. Ibid., p. 34.

16. Wilson, p. 120.

17. Ibid.

18. Ibid., p. 239.

19. Ibid.

20. Carlton, p. 2.

21. Seymour, p. 198.

22. Aronson, p. 337.

CHAPTER NINE: THE FRUITS OF SIN—ROYAL BASTARDS

1. Hilton, p. 252.

2. Carlton, p. 6.

3. Williams, *Last Loves of Henri of Navarre,* p. 91.

4. Marvick, pp. 52–53.

5. Ibid., p. 82.

6. Williams, *Last Loves of Henri of Navarre,* p. 93.

7. Lewis, p. 138.

8. Farquhar, p. 20.

9. Wilson, p. 155.

10. Williams, *Rival Sultanas,* p. 211.

11. Mossiker, *Affair of the Poisons,* p. 293.

CHAPTER TEN: DEATH OF THE KING

1. Ziegler, p. 378.

2. D'Orliac, p. 138.

3. Smythe, p. 301.

4. Ibid., p. 303.

5. Ibid., p. 306.

6. Carlton, p. 147.

7. Kent, p. 78.

8. Ibid., p. 81.

9. Williams, *Rival Sultanas,* p. 338.

10. Ibid.

11. Hardy, p. 39.

12. Williams, *Rival Sultanas,* p. 340.

13. Haslip, *Madame du Barry,* p. 102.

14. Ibid., p. 105.

15. Ibid., p. 201.

16. Rappoport, p. 140.

17. Stanhope, p. 333.

18. Haslip, *Emperor and Actress*, p. 272.

19. Aronson, p. 345.

20. Ibid.

21. Ibid., p. 346.

22. Ibid., p. 375.

CHAPTER ELEVEN: THE END OF
A BRILLIANT CAREER AND BEYOND

1. Wheatley, p. 654.

2. Andrews, p. 197.

3. Lewis, p. 267.

4. Mahoney, p. 353.

5. Mossiker, *Sévigné*, p. 302.

6. Mossiker, *Affair of the Poisons*, p. 260.

7. Smythe, p. 15.

8. Kent, p. 225.

9. Smythe, p. 346.

10. Ibid., pp. 346–347.

11. Ibid., p. 347.

12. Ibid.

13. Ibid., p. 348.

14. Ibid., p. 350.

15. Ibid., p. 351.

16. Trench, p. 37.

17. Hardy, p. 51.

18. Ibid., p. 52.

19. Ibid., p. 57.

20. Ibid., p. 62.

21. Ibid.

22. Kent, p. 309.

23. Andrews, p. 249.

24. Shellabarger, p. 179.

25. Williams, *Rival Sultanas*, p. 231.

26. Mossiker, *Affair of the Poisons*, p. 125.
27. Mossiker, *Sévigné*, p. 80.
28. Ferval, p. 275.
29. Cronin, p. 178.
30. Mossiker, *Sévigné*, p. 182.
31. Ibid.
32. Mossiker, *Affair of the Poisons*, p. 92.
33. Cronin, p. 179.
34. Mossiker, *Affair of the Poisons*, p. 108.
35. Flower, p. 122.
36. Mossiker, *Affair of the Poisons*, p. 306.
37. Ibid., p. 308.
38. Flower, p. 123.
39. Mossiker, *Affair of the Poisons*, p. 325.
40. Ibid.
41. Hilton, p. 305.
42. Mossiker, *Affair of the Poisons*, p. 326.
43. Flower, p. 124.
44. Seymour, p. 395.
45. Ibid., p. 396.
46. Ibid., p. 397.
47. Ibid., p. 275.
48. Hilton, p. 292.
49. Kelen, p. 117.
50. Ibid.
51. Aronson, p. 362.
52. Ibid.
53. Ibid., p. 363.
54. Ibid., p. 371.

CHAPTER TWELVE: MONARCHS,
MISTRESSES, AND MARRIAGE

1. Steegman, p. 213.
2. Ibid., p. 282.
3. Birmingham, p. 158.

4.   Ibid., p. 50.

5.   Ibid., p. 134.

6.   Ibid., p. 154.

7.   Ibid., p. 104n.

8.   Ibid., p. 182.

9.   Ibid., p. 194.

10. Ibid.

11. Graham, p. 3.

12. Ibid., p. 4.

13. Ibid., p. 63.

14. Ibid., pp. 66–67.

15. Ibid., p. 74.

16. Ibid., p. 184.

17. Mossiker, *Affair of the Poisons,* p. 67.

18. Ibid., p. 119.

19. Lever, p. 11.

BIBLIOGRAPHY

Algrant, Christine Pevitt. *Madame de Pompadour, Mistress of France*. New York: Grove Press, 2002.

Andrews, Allen. *The Royal Whore: Barbara Villiers, Countess of Castlemaine*. Philadephia: Chilton Book Company, 1970.

Aronson, Theo. *The King in Love: Edward VII's Mistresses*. London: Corgi Books, 1989.

Bernier, Olivier. *Louis the Beloved: The Life of Louis XV*. New York: Doubleday, 1984.

Bierman, John. *Napoleon III and His Carnival Empire*. New York: St. Martin's Press, 1988.

Birmingham, Stephen. *The Story of Wallis Warfield Windsor*. London: Book Club Associates, 1981.

Bray, William, ed. *The Diary of John Evelyn, Esquire, FRS, from 1641 to 1705–06 with Memoir*. London: Frederick Warne, 1818.

Carlton, Charles. *Royal Mistresses*. London: Routledge, 1990.

Cawthorne, Nigel. *Sex Lives of the Kings and Queens of England*. London: Prion, 1994.

Coote, Stephen. *Samuel Pepys, a Life*. New York: St. Martin's Press, 2000.

Crankshaw, Edward. *Maria Theresa*. New York: Viking Press, 1970.

Cronin, Vincent. *Louis XIV*. London: Collins, 1964.

De Gramont, Sanch. *Epitaph for Kings*. New York: G. P. Putnam's Sons, 1967.

Delpech, Jeanine. *The Life and Times of the Duchess of Portsmouth*. New York: Roy Publishers, 1953.

D'Orliac, Jehanne. *The Lady of Beauty: Agnes Sorel, First Royal Favorite of France.* Philadelphia: J. B. Lippincott, 1931.

Dunlop, Ian. *Louis XIV.* New York: St. Martin's Press, 1999.

Erickson, Carolly. *Great Harry.* New York: St. Martin's Press, Griffin, 1980.

Farquhar, Michael. *Royal Scandals.* New York: Penguin Books, 2001.

Ferval, Claude. *The Martyr of Love: The Life of Louise de La Vallière.* London: Stanley Paul, 1914.

Flower, Desmond, ed. *The Memoirs of Louis de Rouvroy, Duc de Saint-Simon, Covering the Years 1691–1723.* New York: Heritage Press, 1959.

Forster, Elborg. *A Woman's Life in the Court of the Sun King: Letters of Lisellote von der Pfalz, Elisabeth Charlotte, Duchesse d'Orléans, 1652–1722.* Baltimore: Johns Hopkins University Press, 1997.

Given-Wilson, Chris, and Alice Curteis. *The Royal Bastards of Medieval England.* London: Routledge and Kegan Paul, 1984.

Graham, Caroline. *Camilla, the King's Mistress: A Royal Scandal.* New York: HarperPaperbacks, 1995.

Haggard, A. C. P. *The Amours of Henri de Navarre and of Marguerite de Valois.* New York: Brentano's, 1910.

Hardy, Alan. *The Kings' Mistresses.* London: Evans Brothers, 1980.

Haslip, Joan. *The Emperor and the Actress: The Story of Emperor Franz Josef and Katharina Schratt.* London: Weidenfeld and Nicolson, 1982.

——. *Madame du Barry: The Wages of Beauty.* New York: Grove Weidenfeld, 1991.

Hausset, Madame du. *The Private Memoirs of Madame du Hausset, Lady's Maid to Madame de Pompadour.* New York: Elam Bliss, 1927.

Hervey, Lord John. *Some Materials towards Memoirs of the Reign of King George II.* 3 vol. London, 1931.

Hilton, Lisa. *Athénaïs, the Real Queen of France.* New York: Little, Brown, 2002.

Hume, Martin. *The Court of Philip IV: Spain in Decadence.* New York: G. P. Putnam's Sons, 1907.

Jerrold, Clare. *The Story of Dorothy Jordan.* New York: Brentano's, 1914.

Kelen, Betty. *The Mistresses: Domestic Scandals of 19th-Century Monarchs.* New York: Random House, 1966.

Kent, Her Royal Highness Princess Michael of. *Cupid and the King: Five Royal Paramours.* London: HarperCollins Publishers, 1991.

Leslie, Anita. *Mrs. Fitzherbert*. New York: Charles Scribner's Sons, 1960.

Lever, Evelyne. *Madame de Pompadour: A Life*. New York: Farrar, Straus, and Giroux, 2002.

Lewis, Paul. *Lady of France: A Biography of Gabrielle d'Estrées, Mistress of Henry the Great*. New York: Funk and Wagnalls, 1963.

MacDonogh, Katharine. *Reigning Cats and Dogs: A History of Pets at Court since the Renaissance*. London: Fourth Estate, 1999.

Mahoney, Irene. *Royal Cousin: The Life of Henri IV of France*. New York: Doubleday, 1970.

Marvick, Elizabeth Work. *Louis XIII: The Making of a King*. New Haven, Conn.: Yale University Press, 1986.

Memoirs of the Courts of Europe: Memoirs of Marguerite de Valois, Queen of France, Wife of Henri IV; of Madame de Pompadour, of the Court of Louis XV, and of Catherine de Medici, Wife of Henri II. New York: Collier and Son, 1910.

Mitford, Nancy. *Madame de Pompadour*. New York: Pyramid Books, 1966.

Mossiker, Frances. *The Affair of the Poisons: Louis XIV, Madame de Montespan, and one of History's Great Unsolved Mysteries*. New York: Alfred A. Knopf, 1959.

———. *Madame de Sévigné: A Life and Letters*. New York: Alfred A. Knopf, 1983.

Parissien, Steven. *George IV*. New York: St. Martin's Press, 2001.

Pevitt, Christine. *Philippe, Duc D'Orléans*. New York: Atlantic Monthly Press, 1997.

Pöllnitz, Count Karl Ludwig von. *The Amorous Adventures of Augustus of Saxony*. London: George Allen and Unwin, 1926. Translated from the original French, *La Saxe Galante*, of 1734.

Rappoport, Angelo S. *Royal Lovers and Mistresses: The Romance of Crowned and Uncrowned Kings and Queens of Europe*. London: private printing for the Navarre Society Limited, 1924.

Seymour, Bruce. *Lola Montez, a Life*. New Haven, Conn.: Yale University Press, 1996.

Shellabarger, Samuel. *Lord Chesterfield and His World*. Boston: Little, Brown, 1951.

Smith, Alison J. *A View of the Spree*. New York: John Day, 1962.

Smythe, David Mynders. *Madame de Pompadour: Mistress of France*. New York: Wilfred Funk, 1953.

Somerset, Anne. *Ladies-in-Waiting from the Tudors to the Present Day*. London: Weidenfeld and Nicolson, 1984.

Stanhope, Gilbert. *A Mystic on the Prussian Throne: Frederick-William II*. London: Mills and Boon, 1912.

Steegman, Mary G. *Bianca Cappello*. Baltimore: Norman Remington, 1913.

Sutherland, Christine. *Marie Walewska, Napoleon's Great Love*. London: Robin Clark, 1979.

Tarsaidze, Alexandre. *Katia, Wife before God*. New York: Macmillan, 1970.

Trench, Charles Chevenix. *George II*. London: History Book Club, 1973.

Weir, Alison. *The Six Wives of Henry VIII*. New York: Grove Weidenfeld, 1991.

Wheatley, Henry, ed. *The Diary of Samuel Pepys*. New York: Random House, 1893.

Williams, H. Noel. *The Last Loves of Henri of Navarre*. New York: Dingwall-Rock, 1925.

———. *Rival Sultanas: Nell Gwyn, Louise de Kéroualle, and Hortense Mancini*. New York: Dodd, Mead, 1915.

Wilson, John Harold. *Nell Gwynn, Royal Mistress*. New York: Pellagrini and Cudahy, 1952.

Ziegler, Gilette. *At the Court of Versailles: Eyewitness Reports from the Reign of Louis XIV*. New York: E. P. Dutton, 1966.

INDEX

Saint-Simon, duc de, 5, 35, 68, 84, 100, 109, 224, 226–27

Santi, serving woman of Archduchess Johanna, 191, 192

Scarron, Françoise, 110

Schratt, Katharina, 44–45, 83, 143–44, 207–8, 250, 255

Schulenberg, Ermengarda Melusina von, 51, 141, 149

Sedley, Catherine, 52, 218

Serguidi, secretary of state of Tuscany, 156

Settlement Act of 1701, 243

Seven Years' War, 9, 146, 164, 174

Sévigné, Madame de, 4, 16, 46, 104–5, 109, 214, 223

Sèvres porcelain factory, 146

Shakespeare, William, 237

Shand, Camilla, 246–51

Shand, Major, 249, 250

Shore, Jane, 177, 197

Simpson, Ernest, 242, 245

Simpson, Wallis Warfield, 11, 210, 241–46, 251, 252, 254

smallpox
Josepha with, 16
Louis XV with, 23, 202
Mary II with, 218
mistresses nursing monarchs with, 196
scars from, 41
Schulenberg with, 51

Sobieski, John, king of Poland, 140

Sophia Dorothea, queen of Prussia, 55

Sorel, Agnes, 2–3, 57, 137, 139, 197, 255

Soubise, prince de, 83–84, 166

Soubise, princesse de, 83, 109

Spencer, Lady, 247
see also Diana, Princess of Wales

St. Albans, duke of, 188–89

Staatliche Museum, 3

Stainville, comte de, 119, 120

Stanhope, Philip Dormer, 51

Stuart, Frances, 62

Suffolk, duchess of, 141
see also Schulenberg, Ermengarda Melusina von

Sully, duc de, 74–75, 76, 79, 96

taboret, 140, 141

Taisey-Châtenoy, marquise de, 25

Talleyrand, Charles Maurice de, 85

Teschen, princess of, 140

Therese, queen of Bavaria, 142, 228

Tournehem, Le Normant de, 88–89

Trundle, Guy, 242, 243

Tuscany, archduchess of, 156

Uriah the Hittite, 83

Ursins, Jean Juvenal des, 57

Vaillant, Marshal, 131

Valerie, Archduchess, 208

Valois, Marguerite de, 5, 72–74

Vatel, François, 105

Ventimille, Madame de, 115, 215
see also Mailly, Pauline-Félicité de